AmericanHeritage®

★MY
BRUSH WITH
HISTORY★

AmericanHeritage®

★MY BRUSH WITH HISTORY★

By 95 Americans Who Were There

As Selected by
the Editors of *American Heritage* Magazine

BLACK DOG
& LEVENTHAL
PUBLISHERS
NEW YORK

Published by
Black Dog & Leventhal Publishers, Inc.
151 West 19th Street, New York, NY 10011

Distributed by
Workman Publishing Company
708 Broadway, New York, NY 10003

Designed by Liz Trovato

Manufactured in the United States

ISBN: 1-57912-204-3

h g f e d c b a

Library of Congress Cataloging-in-Publication Data

My brush with history / by 50 Americans who were there; from the editors of American heritage magazine ; general editor, Michael Driscoll.
p. cm.   At head of title: American heritage.
ISBN 1-57912-204-3
1. United States—History—20th century—Anecdotes. 2. United States—Biography—Anecdotes. I. Title: American heritage my brush with history. II. Driscoll, Michael, 1973- III. American heritage.

E742 .M9 2001

973.91'092'2—dc21
2001037670

TABLE OF CONTENTS

FOREWORD

What is clearly *American Heritage*'s most popular regular feature began as an attempt to mark a not especially resonant anniversary, the magazine's thirty-fifth. We had received an unsolicited manuscript from a writer named Stephen Shields, a fairly long memoir that pivoted on an arresting encounter with a man whose malignity was powerful enough to tarnish half the last century.

This set my predecessor, Byron Dobell, to thinking about how everyone has, at one time or another, bumped up against the larger historical forces of the era. We decided, for our anniversary issue, to write various historians, authors, and public figures, inviting them to remember a moment in their lives that might be called a "brush with history." All the responses were fascinating, some of them moving indeed. (The one from Garry Wills, which appears in this anthology, is a small masterpiece of wrenching concision.) We ran them, along with Mr. Shields's reminiscence and another unsolicited arrival, John R. McCormick's charming account of his encounter with the *Graf Zeppelin*, in the December 1989 issue.

The response was immediate, vigorous, and, apparently, eternal. Readers sent us their brushes, and in a matter of days we had dozens that we thought should be published. So we began to do so, in a column called, of course, "My Brush with History."

Ever since that first marshalling, I have been reading the brushes piecemeal; they are by their nature anecdotal, and I came over the years to assume that they were most satisfying in little servings of two or three. It is particularly gratifying, then, to discover what a strong book they make. The ones gathered here have been drawn from the whole twelve-year run of the feature, but arranged chronologically, and it turns out that they form a stimulating, lively, and of course highly personal history of the twentieth century. And for all the engaging informality of these reminiscences, there are valuable historical truths to be found here; take a look, for instance, at how much is encoded in John Clark Albert's three short paragraphs on Page 11.

The book also offers a clearer sense than more formal narratives can of the capriciousness of history. Who would have thought that the "bubble dancer" Sally Rand should make two equally appealing appearances years apart? Who thinks of the practicalities that must follow the sad grandeur of the death of a great public figure? The young assistant operations training officer for the U.S. Corps of Cadets at West Point certainly did, when he learned to his astonishment that he was to be in charge of Franklin Roosevelt's funeral. In here, you'll meet a young woman who got to be an old one because a chance office chore kept her from walking out right into the great Wall Street bombing of 1920. And you'll find out what it was like to be propositioned by Mae West.

For the editors of *American Heritage*, going through the "brush" submissions is about the most enjoyable part of the job. I think this book makes clear why. It also, on every page, ratifies one of the most valuable of all historical lessons: history is not just what happened to the 24th Michigan on the first day of Gettysburg or the sleepy sailors at Pearl Harbor; it is as much and as easily with us as the air we breathe, and it happens to all of us every hour, every minute, of our lives.

—Richard Snow
Editor, *American Heritage* Magazine

NOT QUITE OVER, OVER THERE

The November rain came steadily down—cold, persistent, promising snow—as it had for days. The last fallen leaves of autumn floated down the streets, carried along by the steady streams flowing toward the storm-sewer gratings. Some people thought the rain was caused by the firing of the guns in Europe, where the Great War had gone on for more than four years. Others said, no, there had been many other Novembers with rain like this, at the beginning of winter.

In northern France the armies—German and Austrian on one side; French and British, and lately American, on the other—had dug miles of trenches, facing each other across the torn and ravaged strips of

Jubilant Americans in Washington, D.C., show newspaper headlines announcing the surrender of Germany, ending World War I, November 8, 1918.

earth known as no-man's-land. From time to time men from one army or the other would climb on crude ladders from the trenches, going "over the top" to try to take the positions held by their opponents. They advanced through no man's land, in the face of rifle and machine-gun fire, artillery and mortar shells, and, if weather and wind were favorable, poisonous gases.

In America children ran up to each other, threateningly, shouting, "Are you for Kaiser Bill, or are you for Uncle Sam?" Grown people bought Liberty bonds and complained about the high cost of living. People ate "Liberty Cabbage," instead of sauerkraut, and children got "Liberty Measles," the German variety being out of fashion.

Out of the November rain a boy of twelve or so years crashed through the front door of one of the big houses, shouting, "School's out! The war's over!" In his hand he carried a newspaper, with great black headlines covering half the page.

His mother cried, "Let me see that!" She grabbed the paper, read the lead story, and ran to the telephone, to call neighbors and friends. Turning back to her son, she said, "Raymond, get the flag out of the hall closet and put it up on the front porch. Charles can help you." So Raymond and Charles took the flag, carefully unrolled it, and inserted the staff in a bracket on one of the pillars of the front porch. It hung limply in the rain.

Charles, who was five years old, went back in the house and put on his cap and his sweater and his coat and his mittens and his red rubber overshoes. From his room he got an old brass school bell, with a black wooden handle, which was loose. He took the bell out on the porch and sat down on the wooden steps leading down to the sidewalk. He was close to the flag, and the overhang of the porch protected him from the rain. He sat there for a long time, ringing the bell, with the flag overhead. People passing by waved to him, and he answered with an extra ring of his bell.

Later that day the news came that it was a false armistice after all. The Allied generals had decided that the fighting would go on until the eleventh hour of the eleventh day of the eleventh month, for the sake of symmetry and symbolism.

I grew up, and as a man, I did not remember the real armistice, two days after the false one; but I never forgot sitting on the steps, ringing my bell in the cold November rain.

—Duane Charles Sours, a retired finance officer, lives in Hemet, California.

Two Handshakes Away

My mother loved parades and early on imbued me with a love of same. An incident at one sticks in my mind. I believe it was in 1926 or 1927. I can't be sure as I was only a small boy then.

While standing on the curb in Newark, New Jersey, watching a Decoration Day parade pass by, I found myself near a group of seven or eight ancient Civil War veterans. I looked over their beards, their blue Grand Army of the Republic coats and broad-brimmed campaign hats, and I wished I could grow a beard like one of theirs. One old soldier called,

"Sonny, come over here," and "Sonny" obediently did. He said, "Shake my hand," and I did. "Now," he said, "you're only two handshakes from the Revolution." When he was about my age, six or seven, he had shaken hands with a veteran of that war.

I fully intend someday to pass on this membership in an exclusive club to another young hand. He'll be three shakes from the great event. We certainly are a young country.

—John Clark Alberts, Lt. Col., U.S. Air Force (Ret.), lives in North Barrington, Illinois.

A veteran of the Union Army shakes hands with a Confederate veteran at a celebration in Gettysburg, Pennsylvania, around 1913.

THE SECRET ROOM

The early 1930s were not good to my grandmother. About all she had left were her memories of her childhood at the old home place. In Grandmother's case the old home place was a farm outside of Glasgow, Kentucky. This was the center of her universe and now, in 1937, we were all going on vacation there for a visit.

People today accept a vacation as a God-given right, but in the Depression a vacation was a major event to be planned, discussed, and saved for. Those going were my grandmother, my mother, myself, and our boarder. Mother and Father had divorced, and the boarder had been with us for the past seven or eight years and was considered one of the family. He

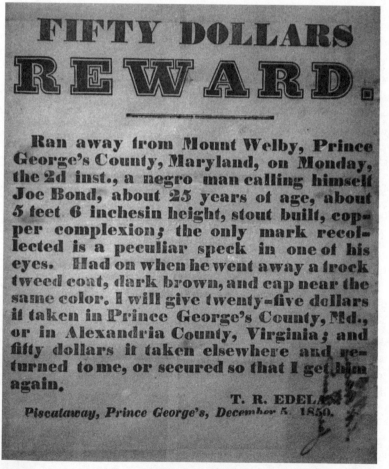

FIFTY DOLLARS REWARD.

Ran away from Mount Welby, Prince George's County, Maryland, on Monday, the 2d inst., a negro man calling himself Joe Bond, about 25 years of age, about 5 feet 6 inches in height, stout built, copper complexion; the only mark recollected is a peculiar speck in one of his eyes. Had on when he went away a frock tweed coat, dark brown, and cap near the same color. I will give twenty-five dollars if taken in Prince George's County, Md., or in Alexandria County, Virginia; and fifty dollars if taken elsewhere and returned to me, or secured so that I get him again.

T. R. EDELEN

Piscataway, Prince George's, December 5, 1850.

A handbill from 1850 shows what runaway slaves faced as they fled North to freedom.

would do most of the driving and pay for the gasoline.

As I counted off the days, Grandma made the wait even longer by telling me that when we reached Glasgow I would see a big secret. I'd ask, "What secret?" but she would only say that I would have to wait.

I'd like to say that the trip down to Glasgow from Louisville was all fun and excitement, but that would be far from the truth. Less than twenty miles out of Louisville, the family found out that I had car sickness. By the time we reached Glasgow I was a hot, sick, and irritable little boy who was making life miserable for all around him.

Then the second blow fell: I saw the old home place. I had expected it to look like a Georgia plantation with high columns and wide verandahs. But the house was none of this. Its current owners had not been able to spare a lot of money for upkeep, and to a city boy used to urban newness, it seemed shabby and rundown.

But there was a cold pitcher of lemonade and an electric fan in the living room. Grandma asked if I would like to see the bedroom. I didn't really want to see a bedroom, but I was pushed upstairs and into a chamber dominated by a large bed and little else. The headboard of the bed stood solid into the rear wall, and my grandmother told me I was to push against the top left of it. After one missed push, I made part of the headboard slide back into the wall.

The owner of the house came upstairs with a flashlight, and I looked into my first secret panel. I was told I could go in, but all I could see was cobwebs, and I decided I could see all I wanted from the bed. As I shone the light in, Grandma told me that this passage went around the chimney and was three feet wide by three and a half feet tall. The only way in or out was by way of the bed.

Grandma explained that after thinking hard on the subject, her granddaddy had decided that slavery was wrong. Being a man who acted on his beliefs, he had built this room and become part of the Underground Railroad, helping runaway slaves to freedom.

Then Grandma gave a warning. Although the Civil War (or rather the War Between the States) had been over for more than seventy years, feelings for the lost cause still ran high. If the purpose of the secret passage were known, we might no longer be socially accepted in Glasgow. I had to promise never to say a word about it.

That night and for a number of nights after, I dreamed of being Great-Great-Granddaddy's helper taking those slaves toward freedom. Mother and Grandma promised that we could come back again to see more of the farm's secrets; but it was not to be.

The 1930s kept us too poor for another vacation, and then came Pearl Harbor. The boarder was drafted and later came home to marry my mother. Grandma did not get back to Glasgow until the late 1940s. By then the owners had sold the property, and the house had been torn down for an industrial plant. Granddaddy's secret passage was gone forever.

I never knew my grandmother's grandaddy, or any of the blacks he helped to spirit North; but occasionally in dreams I still go back to Glasgow to help Great-Great-Granddaddy.

—William M. Dorr lived in West Paducah, Kentucky.

WILD WEST SHOW

I was born three months before the Wright brothers launched the first airplane at Kitty Hawk, and I stood transfixed with awe when Halley's comet stretched in eerie silence across the heavens above me. I heard Teddy Roosevelt make one of his Bull Moose speeches, and I watched Charles Lindbergh fly triumphantly over Philadelphia when he returned from his transoceanic flight. Having seen all but three years of the world's most fantastic century, somewhere down the line I should have encountered at least one historical event at closer range than those just mentioned. And indeed I did. One warm summer evening when I was just a youngster, Annie Oakley came to our town to compete in a trapshoot with the town's best marksmen. And because my father was president of the rod and gun club that had sponsored her visit, Miss Oakley came to our house for supper. Annie Oakley, of course, was nationally recognized as one of the world's greatest markswomen, proficient with either rifle or shotgun. For reasons of her own she had stopped performing on the stage and in circuses, preferring to earn both her livelihood and easy money for gun clubs by traveling from town to town competing against their best.

It was late in the afternoon of the day of the match when Dad's rented spring wagon arrived with Annie and her staff. With Dad's help she dismounted, and I was close enough to make a hasty and critical appraisal of her. She was wearing one of the darkest, longest, and heaviest skirts I ever saw—much too heavy for such a hot day. She had on high-button shoes and a black cotton blouse with a flimsy yellow scarf tied around her neck. Over the blouse was a tanned elk jacket trimmed with Indian beads and fringes.

The sharp-shooting Annie Oakley.

Annie Oakley was not pretty! Her face was drawn and, despite her outdoor life, deathly pallid. She had clearly been ill. Her hair fell over her shoulders and was caught, hip-high, by a very large and ornate barrette. Modern movie buffs and theatergoers who saw her portrayed in Annie Get Your Gun and other productions would have been shocked to discover that she was neither blonde nor sexy. On the other hand, she exuded warmth, and I was immediately attracted to her.

Mother rushed out to greet her, and they hit it off at once. Two men had been in the wagon with Miss Oakley. The older one busied himself at the rear of the wagon, removing from its freight box a brass-bound, canvas-covered trunk. This man was obviously a loner. He wore a dirty sombrero that partially concealed a weather-beaten, tragic face. No conscientious merchant would ever sell this man a rope without a prescription.

The younger man seemed to be in his late teens. He was dressed in typical cowboy attire—a soiled wide-brimmed hat, a leather jacket, a double-breasted California madras shirt, and faded Levi's tucked into soft leather walking boots. He was deeply tanned and showed sparkling white teeth when he smiled at my sisters.

The sad one, called Swamp, refused to eat with us, so a plate was fixed for him and he ate on the lawn under the cherry tree. "Dougie-boy," as Miss Oakley referred to the younger man, took my place at the table, and I ate at the Burdick sewing machine with its head dropped and the lid closed.

Although the males wanted to talk guns and shooting, the meal became a medical clinic. "I have had enough gun talk to last a lifetime," said Annie, "and you fellows are not going to spoil my chance to talk to the first intelligent lady I've met on this tour." So we reluctantly ate a meal spiced with symptoms, pains, and cures, and never got a word in edgewise. My sisters sat silent with Dougie-boy between them, stealing occasional side-glances at him and blushing nervously when he caught them at it.

After this strange meal had gone on for some time, Annie consulted the tiny watch pinned to her blouse. "If we are to catch our train to Sunbury," she said, we've got to leave soon. I want to thank all of you for this wonderful meal. I have spent many, many years sleeping and eating in tents, boarding-houses, and hotels, and I have missed the joy of family life and the comfort of being surrounded by my loved ones." Her tone was soft and wistful. "You have entertained us royally," she said, "and while we can't match your hospitality, we'd like to return the favor as best we can. Will you please excuse Douglas? He will help Swamp with the props."

Dougie-boy left the room and after a few minutes we followed him into the yard. We found that Swamp had placed an easel halfway down the garden path. On it he had placed a sheet of tin, which was nailed to a wooden backing about twenty-four inches square. He and Douglas had opened the steamer trunk and removed and loaded some small-caliber rifles, which they cradled in their arms ready to hand to Annie when needed.

Miss Oakley walked to the edge of the shade and, smiling, turned to face the rather large gathering of neighbors, which had quietly formed as the news of her presence spread.

"Ladies and gentlemen," she said. "If I am not too unlucky, I will succeed in drawing you a picture of the typical American Indian chief as I have seen him on our Western reservations. I scare easily, so please don't make too much noise as I shoot."

Turning, she placed herself about thirty yards from the easel. She reached out for the guns, and as they were pressed into her hands, speedily pumped round after round into the target. On it, as if by magic, appeared the outline of an Indian chief in a full-feathered headdress.

The spectators, not certain whether to applaud, stood motionless as she turned to them again. "Thank you for your attention," she said. "I appreciate your kindness in not reminding me that my Indian friend has no eyeball. So, if you will bear with me, I'll try to remedy that at once."

Swamp passed her a hand mirror and a rifle, which I took to be a 30-30, and she turned her back to the target. With her thumb on the trigger, she placed the rifle on her shoulder. Then, looking into the mirror, she fired precisely into the place where the eye should be.

Because my father considered the tin Indian an artistic masterpiece, my sister Margaret called it the "Mona Annie." Marion, my other sister, called it "Chief Lead-in-the-Face." By whatever name it was known, it was the focus of many eyes. Admirers came daily to our back porch, where it was on display.

When the stream of visitors dwindled to a trickle, Dad came in one evening bearing the tin man in one hand and his tool kit in the other. Suspicious, my mother looked up from her sewing. "What are you going to do with that?" she asked.

"I thought I'd hang it in that vacant space by the parlor door," he said. Mother looked at him. Her reaction was quick, not stern, but it had that finality which brooks no appeal. "Over my dead body," she said.

To borrow my father's favorite piece of purple prose from Ned Buntline, the author of many popular Western dime novels, "Bang! Another redskin bit the dust!"

—Burton R. Laub was a dean of the Dickinson School of Law.

THE DINNER PAIL

In the years since I have had to use the services of a baby-sitter, inflation has hit this little business. I was amazed to find that the rate per hour has more than doubled. My grandchildren are baby-sitters, and they make a lot of money. Listening to one of their conversations, I discovered that accompanying fringe benefits are important to them and are carefully considered before they accept jobs: large color televisions, for instance, and families that leave out lots of snacks.

I couldn't resist a lecture on how tough things were when I was young and how lucky they were to be able to earn money so easily. I had a different way of earning money, and memory came flooding back as I described it.

I was born in Fall River, Massachusetts, a hilltop city overlooking Mount Hope Bay, an arm of Narragansett Bay. These deep-blue waterways were carved out by the same glacial activity that forged a chain of long, narrow lakes east of the hill, which funnel into the Quequechan River. With the force of the lakes behind it, the river descends rapidly with a fall of 130 feet in one-half mile before it joins the waters of the bay.

As early as 1700 gristmills and ironworks were standing along its banks, and when a few decades later the spinning jenny made such improvements in the weaving of cloth that what had been a cottage industry moved into mills, the swift Quequechan proved an ideal site for them. Eleven mills were strung along the banks of the lakes in 1872, and there were forty-three by 1876. By 1900 Fall River was largely given over to the weaving of cotton cloth.

The mills were enormous affairs, three stories

Turn-of-the-century dinner pail.

high, built of the granite that was abundant in the area. They were insatiable in their demand for workers. Sometimes whole families labored in them, and what long hours they worked! The starting whistle summoned them to the job at seven o'clock and, except for a toot at noon, didn't blow again until five-thirty, with no coffee breaks and only a half-hour for lunch. The short lunch break posed a problem in getting these hardworking people fed. It was before the days of the company cafeterias, and there wasn't time enough to go home. This is how my friends and I earned our spending money. We carried dinners to the mills, either for our parents and relatives or for families whose children were grown.

Fall River has been called the City of the Dinner Pail. Although I haven't seen a dinner pail in many years, I remember it well. It was made of galvanized tin, had three nesting compartments, and a bail handle. A hot drink in the bottom compartment kept meat and potatoes warm in the smaller compartment above. A still smaller compartment on top held dessert, and a tight-fitting lid covered the whole thing. Thus this ingenious pail carried a whole dinner. The meals were prepared at home and carried by us children to the mills. The school day was broken up into two sessions, with a two-hour break in between, so at eleven-thirty hundreds of schoolchildren poured out of my school, rushed home to pick up the dinners, then set off for the mills, hurrying to get there before the noon whistle blew. There was no lingering to talk with friends on the way, but coming back I could saunter along if it was warm. If it was cold, I wasted no time getting back to my own warm dinner. I remember walking through snow up to my hips and through drenching rainstorms that made it feel as though my journey was a long one. But it couldn't have been very far if I walked to the mill and back,

ate my own dinner, and got back to school by one-thirty.

So it was that I began my working life at the age of seven. We were very poor but weren't aware of it since all the families we knew were poor too. There was nothing unusual in women going to work as soon as the youngest child was in school. So when my younger sister started school, my mother went back to her old job as a weaver, and I was considered old enough to bring her lunch. After all, my grandmother, who had been born during the Industrial Revolution in England, had actually worked in a mill from dawn to dusk when she was just a year older than I. All I was asked to do was carry a pail. I felt capable of it and proud to be "carrying dinners" along with my friends.

The weavers worked in a downstairs room. To get to it, I opened a heavy door at the top of a flight of brass-bound stairs that led to another heavy door at the bottom. I was so short that the bottom of the pail bumped on the steps as I went down. The handle was not rigid, and the pail tipped perilously at each bump. The brass bindings were loose, and I was terrified that I would trip on the step and spill the dinner pail's contents. Each trip down was a nightmare as I made my way, step-by-step, until I reached the bottom and struggled to open the other heavy door. Only then could I relax my vise-like grip on the pail and breathe a little more easily as I crossed the spinning room: rows and rows of spindles where that marvelous spinning jenny quietly twisted the yarn into thread.

On the other side of this room was the door to the weaving room. I always hesitated before opening this door; the noise from the clattering looms, combined with the hot, oily smell, was a blow in the face, and I hated to go in. Hundreds of looms were lined up here, each working away with a life of its own. I would watch fascinated as the shuttle carrying the warp flew back and forth between the two rows of thread, while the heavy harness banged each row taut. It always looked as though the harness was trying to catch the shuttle in mid-flight, and I would wait nervously for the disaster to happen. But in spite of appearances, the looms were well under the control of the workers, who paced back and forth between the rows, changing bobbins and watching for imperfections in the woven cloth, each one tending from two to six looms. Spoken communication was impossible, but the workers became adept at carrying on long conversations in sign language. I couldn't understand all of it, but I watched with admiration as they talked. A woman told my mother of a telephone call she had had, and the motions of her hands described the conversation perfectly.

The end of my journey came as I delivered the pail to my mother, its contents intact. At twelve o'clock the looms stopped, and the weavers were free to enjoy their lunches in the deafening silence.

We were paid twenty-five cents a week for this work. It doesn't sound like a demanding job; the pain was in the doing of it every day. Many children carried two pails in each hand, and I remember one enterprising boy who used to load six or eight pails into a wagon. For a while I carried dinner to a supervisor who thought it beneath his dignity to be seen carrying a pail home at night. He paid me an extra ten cents a week to carry the pail home for him.

The job began to seem to be beneath my dignity, too, as I neared the end of grammar school. After struggling through a particularly heavy snowstorm, I told my employer not to expect me if we had another one. My days as a dinner carrier came to an inglorious end when I didn't appear after the next storm and was abruptly dismissed. I can't believe my own callousness in not thinking of the poor soul who missed his dinner!

Naturally, my grandchildren thought this was a pretty hard way to earn twenty-five cents. Looking back on it now, I can see benefits other than the money. The walk to the mills in all kinds of weather strengthened our legs, and the fresh air sharpened our appetites. It isn't the long walk that I remember most when I think of those days. Rather, it is the rattling of loose brass as I crept down the steps toward the pandemonium and my mother's smiling face.

—Alice Grinnell Killam lived in New Hampshire.

Crowds gather on Wall Street after the explosion that killed 30 and injured 400.

Seventy Years Before the Twin Towers

In the early fall of 1920 I was nineteen years old and one year out of high school, working in the engineering department of an import/export firm that dealt in steel. We were located at 49 Wall Street at the corner of William Street, exactly three buildings from J. P. Morgan & Co. at Wall and Broad. Unlike the nineties when any clerk who can type is euphemistically referred to as a secretary, in the twenties young graduates who took dictation and transcribed it were called stenographers. The president, vice president, and general manager had private secretaries of many years' experience who were very much older.

All the stenographers occupied a central, windowless room. The junior supervisors occupied one-windowed small offices, and the bosses were on a lower floor in many-windowed, spacious, mahogany-furnished offices.

On the stroke of noon, half of the stenographic pool began their one-hour lunch break, and on their return at one the remaining stenographers went out for an hour. I had selected the noon group. All through my life I have been an organized, methodical person at work and at home, and on September 16 I decided to relinquish a few minutes of my lunch break to complete a letter. When I finished it, and while it was still in my Underwood typewriter, I started to proofread it. Then an explosion propelled me from my chair, hitting my head so hard it stunned me.

All the typewriters bounced heavily, and the skeleton force of stenographers had bruises; several had broken ribs. The electric light bulbs fell into shards. While it isn't now, and was not then, pleasant working from nine to five in a windowless room, windowlessness was what saved us.

The bosses on the floor below all had offices with windows facing Wall Street, and they all had their desks up close to those windows so a modicum of sun could penetrate the canyon of office buildings. Most of the executives lunched after twelve-thirty, so they were all victims of broken glass and the sash-weights that had been packed into the wagon left by the never-to-be-apprehended Wall Street bomber.

I always went out to lunch promptly, and I used to walk down to Broad Street, passing the Morgan offices. Their entrance was cater-corner, so that the left side of the building was on Wall Street and the right side on Broad Street. When I reached Morgan I took a left turn and walked past their right side (directly opposite the New York Stock Exchange) until I arrived at the next block, Exchange Place, then I crossed over diagonally to Weber and Heilbroner, the haberdashers, and on to Schrafft's restaurant, where I enjoyed my daily lunch. Had it not been for that letter, I would have been in the very center of the explosion.

After the debris was cleared and business resumed, a plainclothes detective (always wearing his hat) was stationed as a lookout just inside the entrance to J. P. Morgan & Company. Many years later, after I had moved to another state, I was on vacation in New York and made a nostalgic visit to Wall Street. As I stood at the Morgan Building examining the deep gouges that remained from that fateful day, I noticed the detective, in his hat, just inside the door. I thanked God for having been a lookout for me.

—Ana B. Isaacs lived in Staunton, Virginia.

THE GREAT TRI-STATE TORNADO

On the afternoon of March 18, 1925, a warm day for mid-March, about sixty-five degrees, threatening clouds began to gather in southeastern Missouri, forming a vast dark, menacing super thunderstorm cell. From this blackness a funnel descended, touching down three miles north of the little Ozark town of Ellington. There it killed a farmer, the first of nearly seven hundred who would perish that day in America's most deadly tornado.

For the next three and a half hours, the tornado followed a remarkably straight northeastern course, never leaving the ground. Sucking up huge quantities of debris—dirt, houses, trees, barns—it ejected them as deadly missiles along its route. It cut a path of destruction one-half to one mile wide across three states, Missouri, Illinois, and Indiana. Before its wrath was spent, it had traveled 219 miles, the longest uninterrupted track on record.

My father had just opened a new automobile dealership in the southern Illinois town of Murphysboro. A former mining and farming community of twelve thousand people, Murphysboro had become a bustling manufacturing and railroad center. On that Wednesday at 2:34 p.m., most men were at their jobs and most women were at home. As the blackness approached, bells had just signaled the end of recess, summoning children back into their classrooms.

Striking with demonic fury from the southwest, the monster storm smashed its way through the city, killing 234 people and injuring 623, while laying waste to 152 blocks and destroying 1,200 buildings. Water mains burst, electric wires fell, and fires raged out of control. Tall brick school buildings collapsed on students gathered in the hallways. Twenty-five died. Some children crawled from under the debris and in shock wandered home to find no house and, in some cases, no neighborhood. Years later a friend told me that when she reached home, she found only an open field; in the middle of it was her decapitated grandmother, still sitting in her rocking chair.

Searching through old newspapers, I found a remarkable letter published in the St. Louis Post-Dispatch four days after the storm. It was written by May Williams, a religious mission worker from the St. Louis area, who was in Murphysboro assisting at a revival meeting held by the Reverend and Mrs. Parrot. Williams wrote her mother: "We left the Logan Hotel about 2:25 p.m. and a goodly crowd was awaiting us in the Moose Hall. Mrs. Parrott opened the service singing "More About Jesus." She had sung the first verse and chorus which we were repeating when it suddenly grew dark and there fell upon us what we thought was hail. Rocks began to break through. We were being showered with glass, stones, trash, bricks, and anything. I saw the concrete wall at the back of the hall collapse and come crumbling in. Then the roof started to give way. From outside as well as from within, we could hear terrible cries, yells, screams, and there was a great popping noise. The wind roared—I cannot describe it—and it tore great handfuls from the roof above us. You could see shapes hurtling over us in the air.

"Then the storm passed. We went out into the street. We walked the city for an hour or more, terror-struck by what we saw. People went about almost without clothes, with no shoes on, wrapped in rags or blankets. It was indescribable, the confusion. We picked our way among the tangles of wires, trees, poles, brick, and lumber to our rooms."

After nightfall, "...everything was on fire, it

seemed. There was no light except the flare of flames. There was no water. We were black from head to foot." (The skin of both living and dead who were exposed to the force of the wind was black from dirt and sand driven into it.)

"The fire came closer, and at last we were driven from the hotel and went over to the depot to wait for a relief train. Every place that stood was turned into a hospital. We visited the high school where the doctors were sewing up wounds, giving emergency treatment, and where other helpers were hauling out the dead. We saw numberless torn and bleeding bodies.

"They were dynamiting the city now in their effort to stop the flames, and the roar of the explosions added to the horror of the fires' glare. Everything was ghastly. We had to pick our way to the station by the light of the flames. Then the relief train came. Dead and injured were put on first. We followed."

One of the injured bound for St. Louis hospitals was my father, unconscious, suffering a massive head wound.

Continuing its deadly, unvarying course, the tornado killed 69 people in De Soto (33 were school-children) and another 31 in rural areas before reaching the largest city in its path, West Frankfort (population 18,500). There it destroyed one-fifth of the city, killing 148 and serously injuring 410, a toll second only to that in Murphysboro.

The last Illinois town in its path was Parrish (population 270). Arriving at 3:07 p.m., the tornado destroyed 90 percent of the town, killing 22 and injuring 60. There were many heroes during and after that great catastrophe, but none received more gratitude than the principal of the Parrish School, Delmar Perryman. Worried about the stormy weather, he refused to dismiss the 50 or 60 children at the usual time. His decision saved many lives; the school was one of only three buildings left standing.

A twister rips across the Tornado Belt in 1930.

Shortly before 4:00 p.m. the tornado crossed the Wabash River into Indiana and accelerated to an astounding seventy-three miles per hour. As if guided by some malevolent pilot, for the first time it changed course and headed directly for Princeton (population 9,850), its third-largest and final urban victim. Here it demolished 25 percent of the city, killing 45. Finally, at 4:30 p.m., the tri-state tornado lifted and dissipated, its great reservoir of energy spent.

The humanitarian response to the tragedy was immediate, thanks to railroad crews that relayed the news along their route and by telegraph. Medical teams rushed in from near and far, and neighboring fire departments dispatched equipment. Trains carried the wounded to hospitals as far away as Chicago and returned laden with emergency supplies and relief personnel. Throughout the night the medical teams struggled to operate under battlefield conditions, with candles, kerosene lamps, and lanterns providing the only illumination. Supplies of anesthetics, morphine, and antitetanus serum soon ran out. Fortunately, the feared typhoid epidemic did not develop; warnings had gone out to boil all drinking water. Meanwhile, trainloads of coffins arrived from St. Louis and Chicago, along with flowers to adorn them.

Why was the death toll so high? Most significant was the lack of any tornado forecast or warning system. The storm moved so fast that people had little time to seek shelter. Few witnesses reported seeing a funnel; they assumed what was approaching was just a thunderstorm.

An average tornado follows a path a few hundred yards wide and 16 miles long, causing damage across 3 square miles. The tri-state tornado covered 164 square miles. Its intensity, wide path, rapid movement, and long life suggest that it was located near the center of a deep low-pressure system and beneath the core of a strong polar jet stream; the jet kept the storm going by removing air from the top, making way for air to enter at ground level. Also, because of the jet, it maintained its rapid forward motion.

Reading old newspaper accounts, I was startled to see my father's name on a St. Louis Post-Dispatch death list. He was indeed comatose for many weeks and not expected to survive, but he completely recovered and lived to old age. I was a two-year-old when the colossus struck, and as it lifted our house, I went sailing through the air like Dorothy on her way to Oz. Miraculously, I suffered only a minor wound from a piece of glass between my eyes. Like my father, I survived the great tri-state tornado, and I grew up in that town where forever after events were labeled "before" or "after" the storm.

—Wallace Akin is professor emeritus of geography at Drake University.

I was a pupil in Miss Henley's sixth-grade class in the Gorham Elementary School when history touched me. Gorham is and was a village located on the Missouri Pacific Railroad about fifty miles northwest of Cairo, Illinois. A substantial share of its five hundred residents were employees of that railroad.

The place hasn't changed much since March 18, 1925—the day the most lethal tornado in recorded history came roaring across the Mississippi River from Missouri and devastated Gorham, the first town it hit in Illinois.

The school was a two-story brick building. A wide hall separated the grade school from the high school. We were into the afternoon schedule when, between two and three o'clock, the wind started blowing and Miss Henley asked me and some other boys to close the windows. As I looked out I saw the backboards tearing off the posts of an outdoor basketball court and the outside toilets tossing about. Most of the children ran out the door at the back of the room into a side hall where coats and hats were hung on a partition. The partition blew against the wall and became a partial shelter for some of them.

Along with some of the larger boys, I ran out the side door into the wide hall that separated us from the high school. I remember seeing the high school wall crumble, the plaster turning to dust, before I was knocked unconscious. When I came to, I was a patient in the Catholic hospital in Cairo.

The wife and daughter of Mr. Brown, the principal, were killed, yet he, realizing that he could do nothing for them, went with his injured students to the hospi-tal. The railroad donated a passenger train that was in the area to take the injured and their families there. There were hospitals closer by in Murphysboro and Carbondale, but those cities were in the tornado's path and had to take care of their own injured.

Eight or nine of my fellow pupils and upward of forty townspeople were killed. My skull and jawbone were fractured. Two of my classmates were dug out from the same area of debris. One, whose last name was Murray (I forget his first name) was dead, and the other, Lee Casey, was crippled for life.

—John M. Schofield lives in Sarasota, Florida, and manages his own small publishing company.

Indiana residents survey the damage done by the great tornado in March 1925.

On March 18, 1925, at 3:55 p.m., I was in the third-floor classroom of the Crossville, Illinois, Community High School. As I opened the front door for school that morning my mother called from the kitchen, "Wear your sweater." When I protested that it was too hot for a sweater, she called back, "This is March. Anything can happen on a March day. Wear your sweater."

By the time I got to school, the air was still heavy, and my sweater felt uncomfortable. In the afternoon Ol Reiling, the school custodian, burst into our class-room and, ignoring the teacher, said, "Boys, if you've never seen a tornado, you're going to see one now." In seconds we were crowded at the east windows, looking southward. The teacher was there, too. So was Ol.

That morning it would have meant nothing to me if someone had told me that a maritime polar air mass had rolled across the Sierras and the Rockies and invaded the Great Plains, or that a Bermuda high was fighting every foot of its advance with strong moisture-laden winds from the Gulf of Mexico. I would have been interested had I been told that along a line stretching from Texas to Canada cumulonimbus clouds were pushing their anvils fifty to sixty thousand feet above the surface of the earth. Along that line continual flashes of light-ning, the screaming of the wind, and the reverberat-ing explosions of thunder reminded people of the artillery duels of the Great War, which had ended nearly seven years earlier. No wonder the scientists of that day had labeled the line between contending air masses a front.

In Arkansas one of those clouds thrust a dark ten-tacle earthward, withdrew, touched again, and began a mad dance across Arkansas, Missouri, and southern Illinois, leapt the Wabash River, and gave one final vicious kick at Griffin, Indiana, almost demolishing that small community. In the path of that tornado 695 people lay dead, hundreds were maimed or crip-pled, and thousands were left homeless.

Ol Reiling muttered into my ear, "I'm afraid that Bramlet boy is going to find some damage when he gets home." The Bramlet home was about a mile away and was clearly visible from my vantage point. That is, part of the house was visible. A section of the roof was flying through the air. There was a dark mass surrounding the house. Had there been a fire? The blackness resembled the smoke from the stack of a locomotive laboring under a heavy load. It could-n't be a train; the Big Four tracks were a hundred yards to the west. All of a sudden it struck me. That black cloud was a tornado!

Then I saw the funnel!—no, the two funnels. As I watched, the tornado split into twin demons of darkness that danced for more than half a mile across the open fields, until they met and merged directly in front of a tall farmhouse less than four hundred yards away. The whirling cloud stopped, stared at the farm-house. The farmhouse stared back; then slowly, almost gracefully, it rose until its underpinnings were as high above the ground as the roof had been. Segments of the roof and weatherboarding fell to the ground while other segments joined the circling mass of debris. The tornado was now moving northeast along a road with which I am quite familiar.

Many times each summer my sister and I had trudged barefoot along that road, watching the gey-sers of dust squirt between our toes. We had been going to our grandparents' home, where I would sleep on a fat featherbed. In every house along that road there lived a relative. Yet now I felt no fear, no sadness, no feeling of any kind. It was as if part of my brain had been switched off. I had no realistic con-cept of the terrible tragedy I had witnessed. Every house was either partially or totally destroyed. Only the log-cabin sections of the two oldest houses escaped damage, and one of them had shifted on its foundation.

In the cellar of that house two of my cousins were sprouting potatoes for spring planting. Annoyed by the noise above, the eldest said, "I'm going up and find out what's making all that racket." When he reached the top of the ladder, the cabin shifted on its foundation and his head was severed from his body. The younger brother huddled in the darkness of the cellar, a white leghorn chicken roosting on his shoulder.

Down in the river bottoms, neighbors hunted frantically for a missing woman whose house had been completely destroyed. There was no sign of her body in the wreckage, but they felt certain she had been at home when the storm struck. Eventually one of them saw something white and glistening high up in a tree. As they grew closer, they realized it was the naked body of their neighbor, wedged into the fork of the sycamore.

For the next few days, students picked shingles, pieces of weatherboarding, strips of tin roofing, anything that could smother the tender plants of winter wheat, and carted it all away. We piled debris into two different piles—one from which wood might be salvaged, the other to be burned. We buried dead animals. The most gruesome sight I recall was the body of a Jersey cow that had been run through by a two-by-four.

There were the usual phenomena that accompany such storms—straws driven into oak trees, a pitchfork with the handle pointing skyward, impaled by a single tine on the top of a fence post. On one farm a wire fence had been ripped from its post and rolled into a crude ball in the center of which sat a live chicken, plucked as clean as if the wind had been preparing it for the pot.

The days of the cleanup were hard days, tiring days, but they were good days, and I feel certain that everybody who worked in the field matured considerably.

That was seventy years ago, but I can still close my eyes and see that farmhouse rising slowly into the air. For years a barren strip a half-mile wide marked the path of the tornado. Along the edge an occasional oak or elm or sycamore held out a bone-white stump of an amputated limb in mute testimony of the savagery of the tornado.

—Howard E. Rawlinson lived in Mt. Vernon, Illinois, and survived two later tornadoes.

Two Union infantrymen engage in mock saber combat.

THE BROKEN SABER

During my years of growing up in a county-seat town in central Illinois, the memory of Lincoln and the Civil War was still a near thing.

First, there was Decoration Day, when the graves of departed soldiers were decked with flowers and little flags. A few surviving veterans of the Grand Army of the Republic shuffled along in the march to the cemetery. I remember, too, when I was quite small, eyeing the green binding with gold lettering on the spine of my father's two-volume Personal Memoirs of U.S. Grant. The "U.S.," I surmised, was doubtless an honorific title bestowed upon the general by a grateful nation. Later an old gentleman lectured in the assembly hall of the Carrollton High School and told of being present in Ford's Theatre the night Lincoln was assassinated. In a dramatic closing of his recital, he held up a discolored handkerchief. He said it was stained by the blood of the martyred president. One does remember an experience like that.

But most vivid of all is the recollection of my grandmother Kemper holding a broken cavalry saber and telling me of her two brothers, Napoleon Bonaparte and Thomas Jefferson Kemper, one fatally wounded in a skirmish on the Rapidan River, the other shot as he carried his brother from the scene. Even after fifty years her grief was unassuaged. The memory of her pain still stirs me, and I think of the words and hear the tune of the state song of Illinois: Grant and Logan and our tears, Illinois, Illinois/Grant and Logan and our tears, Illinois.

The broken saber, with some six inches missing from the end of the blade, now hangs in my living room. I do not know whether it belonged to "Poly" or to "Tom."

—Gerald Carson was a contributing editor to *American Heritage*. An article by Carson appeared in the first issue of the magazine in 1954.

THE COMMANDER AND THE GRAVY BOAT

Near the end of the flapper era, most girls' finishing schools were islands in a sea of young people suddenly gone mad with freedom, and Highland Hall was no exception.

Miss Keats, our principal, was dignity personified. We all loved her but stood in great awe of her. Since an important part of our education was table manners, we had to take turns sitting at Miss Keats's table, where, among other things, we were taught the art of table conversation and etiquette.

Most of the rules were observed without protest, but one seemed completely unreasonable: A lady must never put gravy on her mashed potatoes. This act, we felt, could not possibly be interpreted as unkind, and gravy improved the taste tremendously. But Miss Keats was adamant; no gravy on mashed potatoes.

One evening Commander Richard E. Byrd was to give a lecture at the school. When there was an important guest, several girls were selected to entertain him while waiting for dinner to be announced, and this time Sally, Marnie, and I were chosen. I started out bravely: "Did you come by train, Commander Byrd?"

"I did indeed," he replied, "and while I was eating my lunch in the Harrisburg station, I became so interested in watching a mother and two small boys saying good-bye to a little dog that my mashed potatoes got cold. Is there anything worse than cold mashed potatoes?"

Sally blurted out, "Do you like gravy on your mashed potatoes?"

The commander looked startled but said that he did, and Sally proceeded to explain the situation at Highland Hall.

Our distinguished guest listened attentively, occasionally nodding his head in agreement. I felt embarrassed by this unorthodox turn in the conversation and stole a glance across the room at Miss Keats, who smiled at me sweetly, thinking that we were discussing penguins and the weather at the South Pole. My attention came back to Commander Byrd just in time to hear him say, "I understand perfectly, and I think I can help you. Leave everything to me."

The news traveled fast, and as we followed Miss Keats and the commander into the dining room, an air of hushed expectancy hung over us all.

Fruit cup, veal cutlets, lima beans, and mashed potatoes were served. Then the gravy was passed to Miss Keats, who ladled a little on her cutlet. The atmosphere was tense, the room so quiet I could hear a squirrel chattering outside the window.

As the gravy reached Commander Byrd, he hesitated ever so slightly, then nonchalantly poured it over his mashed potatoes. There was an audible gasp from the girls. Miss Keats asked for the gravy and quite calmly, but with a twinkle in her eye, poured some on her potatoes.

A very unladylike cheer went up. Commander Byrd laughed out loud, and from that day on, gravy and mashed potatoes were like pepper and salt at Highland Hall. We had learned two important lessons: A great man never loses his sense of humor, and a truly gracious lady can accept defeat so gracefully it appears to be victory.

—Lucy B. Nuttall lives in Hollidaysburg, Pennsylvania.

The Arctic explorer Richard Byrd.

Joe DiMaggio with Little League players in 1954.

THE SOUTHPAW

My family lived in San Francisco's Chinatown District during the late 1920s. I attended Francisco Junior High School, which drew its students from Chinatown and the predominantly Italian North Beach area. Like eighth graders then and now, we usually had time between classes to release the energy we had stored while listening to our teachers.

We had blackboards that were really black in those days, and when the teachers were away from the room, a favorite activity was throwing the erasers at them. One boy would draw a circle on the board and his friends would take turns seeing who could come the closest to hitting it.

One of my classmates excelled at this. He would throw his erasers from the back of the room. He threw the hardest, and was the most accurate. The signature mark of his throws was the cloud of chalk dust that arose when the eraser hit the board. I marveled at his accuracy and the strength of his arm. For whatever reason, his left-handedness also impressed me.

We attended Galileo High School together for one year before I transferred, and although we were never close friends, for some reason I always remembered the accuracy and strength of that left arm.

I continued school, got a job, married, and raised a family. My classmate went on to play baseball, where he earned the sobriquets "The Yankee Clipper" and "Joltin' Joe." I shall always remember him, however, simply as Joe DiMaggio.

—Ber-Je H. Luke lives in San Francisco, California.

President Coolidge, seated at his desk.

COOLIDGE SMILES

I still live on the farm where my father was born in 1898. When I was small, my grandmother lived with us in the summer and spent the winter with her oldest son's family in Baltimore. At Easter time in 1928 my mother and I took the train to Baltimore to visit before bringing Grandmother back with us to the upstate New York farm.

During that trip we all went to Washington to see the traditional Easter-egg roll at the White House. My cousin Bob was six and I was five, so we participated with hundreds of other children in the festivities on the White House lawn. Afterward the children and their parents were invited into the White House to meet President Coolidge. As a five-year-old, the only political name in my vocabulary was Al Smith, who was governor of New York and the lead-ing Democratic candidate for President. As we moved along in line to where President Coolidge stood shaking hands, I'm sure that Mother—a farm girl and a devoted Republican—was very excited. The excitement was lost on me, and as he took my hand, I looked up at her and asked, "When are we going to see Al Smith?" My mother was totally embarrassed, but President Coolidge broke into a wide grin.

My uncle told me afterward that I should never forget what I had accomplished: Even Will Rogers, the famous humorist, had commented that he couldn't make "Old Stone Face" smile.

—Richard McGuire is chair of the New York Farm Bureau Foundation of Agricultural Education, Inc.

THE BETTER SPEAKER

I hadn't the faintest idea I was having a brush with history one evening in the spring of 1929. I just knew that it was the end of a wearying, happy day.

The afternoon had seen me place well enough in several events to win my track letter. Now here I was being presented with a five-dollar gold piece as my reward for finishing second in Whittier High School's constitutional oratorical contest. My speech, "John Marshall and the Constitution," had just lost to one on the subject "Our Privileges Under the Constitution." I didn't begrudge the winner of the first-place ten-dollar piece. Richard M. Nixon had simply been the better speaker.

—Eldon A. Hunt, a retired school administrator, lives in Porterville, California.

Richard Nixon as a student in 1954.

OUT OF THE BLUE

In 1929 Germany announced that the mighty new dirigible Graf Zeppelin would fly around the world. This stirred a great deal of excitement in the United States, not only because such gigantic airships were thought to be the future of aviation but also because the newspaper publisher William Randolph Hearst had put up two hundred thousand dollars to finance part of the Zeppelin's flight and was promoting it aggressively.

Hearst had insisted that the journey begin not in Germany but in America, with the Statue of Liberty as the starting point. The Germans agreed, and on August 7, 1929, the Graf Zeppelin left Lakehurst, New Jersey, passed over the Statue of Liberty, and headed east—across the Atlantic and on to Poland, Russia, and Japan. Finally, on August 25, it was spotted just west of San Francisco approaching the Golden Gate.

By now the trip had become a major event. People all over the United States hoped to catch a glimpse of the great dirigible as it crossed the country to New York. The Hearst papers published an itinerary: The Graf Zeppelin would attempt to fly over as many towns and cities as possible.

There had not been so much excitement around the country since the news of Charles Lindbergh's landing in France. I was eight years old and already an avid reader. I followed all the accounts of the Graf Zeppelin and did my best to build a model out of small branches covered with newspaper.

For some time my father had wanted to own a radio. Now, inspired by the Zeppelin, he went out and bought one on credit. It didn't have a speaker. We listened to it, one at a time, through earphones, as stations in Chicago trumpeted news of the Zeppelin's progress. The nine inhabitants of our little farmhouse five miles from Tampico and fifteen miles south of Sterling, Illinois, had never before experienced such a high level of sustained excitement.

I listened to my father and Henie Schauff, our hired man, discuss the ship's dimensions. "It's nearly eight hundred feet long," my father said. "That's almost a sixth of a mile."

"Almost as long as the pasture is wide," said Henie.

"A hundred feet in diameter," Father said. "That's two windmills stacked on top of each other." It was hard to imagine that anything so large could get off the ground.

The phone rang. Only a few people in the neighborhood had a telephone, but since my father was chairman of the board of directors for our one-room school, he had reasoned that the expensive device was necessary.

The caller was Uncle John. He had just returned from Sterling, where he'd heard that at ten the next morning the Graf Zeppelin would fly directly over. The town was wild with excitement, and the word was spreading. Everyone from town, township and county for miles around would be heading to Sterling. It was harvest time in northern Illinois, time for wheat and oats to be cut and shocked, but no one dreamed of working on that red-letter day.

"We'll all get up at five, get the milking done, and head for town," my father said. "We want to get there at no later than nine. We can stand near the bridge along the riverbank and get a great view."

"I'll stay home," Grandma said. She was seventy-eight years old, and although she was healthy and spry, she no longer liked to leave home.

"You don't want to stay here alone," Aunt Kee said.

"I do," Grandma said.

"You'll miss all the excitement," my father said.

"I'll manage," she said.

"Someone will have to stay with you then," he said.

"I'll stay," I volunteered.

The words were a reflex. My grandmother and I were the best of pals. The family said that I was her favorite, and often, when the others went off to town, I stayed at home to keep her company. When we were alone, she would tell me stories of growing up on a prairie farm in the Midwest, of the great celebration at the end of the Civil War, of Indians—she thought they were Illini—looking in the windows of their house one winter night. And when she and I were home together, she always served the same main dish: bread and milk and afterward apple dumplings and strawberry pie.

But this time I really did want to go with the others. I had committed myself to stay before I had stopped to think. My heart sank.

"I don't want to see the Zeppelin anyway," I said. There was nothing in the world I wanted more to see.

And so we remained behind next morning while the whole neighborhood left for Sterling. Father and Mother, Aunt Kee and Henie, my older sister, Maxine, my younger brother, Howard, and baby Margie drove off in the Model T right after morning chores. A little later Grandma and I waved at the McGraths as they went by—and the Christensens, who lived just half a mile down the road. And last, always last, Homer Burns and his wife, arguing furiously, sped by on the dirt road at twenty miles an hour.

After the Burnses had driven by and there was no more activity to expect on the narrow road, Grandma went into the kitchen to prepare our double dessert.

I stayed in the yard for an hour or so, building sand castles and trying to forget about the Zeppelin. Time drifted slowly by. In addition to my disappointment, I was a little uneasy. Something wasn't quite right. Suddenly I realized why. We were alone, absolutely alone, and surrounded by a profound silence. That whole land, usually so full of sound and action, was empty and still. Even the animals were quiet. There was no wind, not the slightest breeze.

Into that remarkable silence there came from far away the smallest possible purring, strange and repetitive, gradually approaching, becoming louder—the unmistakable beating of powerful engines. I looked to the west and at first saw nothing. Then it was there, nosing down out of the clouds a half mile away, a gigantic, wondrous apparition moving slowly through the sky.

"Grandma!" I screamed.

She was out the kitchen door in an instant. I pointed to the sky. The great dirigible was very low, perhaps because the captain was trying to find some landmark.

There is a wonderful opening scene in the movie Star Wars. A great starship is passing very low and directly overhead so that one sees only the underside. That underside moves deliberately and interminably on and on and on until at last it is gone. The Graf Zeppelin, moving ever so slowly above us, was like that. We saw every crease and contour from nose to fins. It was so low that we could see, or imagined we could see, people waving at us from the slanted windows of its passenger gondola.

We stood entranced. Slowly, slowly the ship moved over us, beyond us, and at last was gone.

We looked at each other, my grandmother and I, then silently walked to the front porch and let ourselves down on the steps. And we gazed at each other in triumph.

The Graf Zeppelin arriving in Lakehurst, New Jersey, after its flight around the world in 1929.

Now we were suddenly aware that barnyard, pasture, and field were filled with alarm. The dogs were barking madly, the horses galloped in the pasture, cows mooed, pigs squealed, guineas screamed, chickens cackled, flocks of birds swept wildly by.

"They'll settle down soon," Grandma said.

I was speechless with excitement, but I was already constructing the triumphant tale I would tell anyone who would listen. Grandma rose, went into the kitchen, and came back with two glasses of milk and two chunks of strawberry pie. I could neither eat nor drink. Telling the world would be wonderful times ten.

My grandmother stirred a little beside me.

"John," she said. I looked up. Just for a second she was a young, smiling woman, filled with excitement and anticipation. Then she sighed and was Grandma again. "We have to keep it a secret. We mustn't tell the others what we saw."

I was astonished. "But why not tell?"

"Because they'll be disappointed enough that they missed it. We don't want to hurt them more."

"But, Grandma."

She shook her head. "It will be much more fun if we keep it a secret, just you and I. No one else will ever know. We'll just keep the Zeppelin to ourselves forever and a day. We'll never tell."

I loved her. "I'll never tell," I promised, and I never have until now.

—John R. McCormick is owner and president of the Communications Skills Company in Huntsville, Alabama. He is the author of *The Right Kind of War* and has written numerous articles for newspapers and magazines.

LINDY AND ME

When I was six, the great sensation
That thrilled the people of the nation
Was Lindbergh's flight across the ocean,
Achieved through that youth's cocky notion
That, all alone, he'd span the sea.
Before him, crews of two or three
Had failed to reach the sought-for goal.
He had the true lone eagle's soul.

The speed those old craft could attain
Meant thirty hours in the plane.
No automatic pilots then;
The flying must be done by men.
He did it with no radio.
To keep the fuel from running low,
An extra tank, with him behind;
No view ahead, he flew quite blind.

He took enormous risks in stride,
While soaring toward the other side.
(The moon shot, forty years since then,
Cost billions and a thousand men,
All experts in technology.
One can't compare the two, you see.)

For his return a planned parade
With ticker tape was being made.
In high silk hats were Mayor Walker,
The fashion plate and witty talker,
And Whalen with his white carnation,
Officials brimming with elation,
Awaiting with their nerves on edge
Arrival of the main cortege.

With highways not yet built by Moses,
The hero's fleet, bedecked with roses,
Rolled toward Jamaica Avenue,
Where crowds had gathered, all to view
Him pass. My family'd gone there too—
Without me since I had been bad.
"You'll stay at home!" pronounced my dad.

And so I lolled with thoughts unfertile,
Along the avenue named Myrtle.
And, as I stood there all alone,
Lindy came, as on a throne—
Aboard a limo led by cops,
He roared right past all traffic stops.
To speed his ride to the parade,
Officials had this detour made.
And, as he passed, my day was saved,
He glanced at me, then smiled and waved.
And when my folks came home, frustrated,
"I just met Lindy!" I related.

—Daniel Roth, M.D., a retired professor of pathology,
lives in Scarsdale, New York.

Col. Charles Lindbergh heads the parade through flag-draped and paper-strewn lower New York.

MYSTERY HOST

From 1929 to 1933 I danced with a traveling stage company known for Fanchon and Marco, well-known producers of the day. On June 9, 1931, we opened at the Capitol Theater in Chicago. That afternoon Felix, one of the chorus, burst into the dressing room to tell us we were invited to dinner and a big party at the Lexington Hotel. She said, "There'll be talent scouts there. Girls from all the big shows are invited!"

When I arrived at the Lexington with my dancing partner, Eve, we discovered an entire floor had been taken over for this party. The men wore tuxedos and most of the women were dressed in formals. Our "best" dresses were not ankle length.

Yet with all this formality something felt strange from the moment we stepped into a room where a band was playing. For one thing, no one seemed to know who our host was. The men appeared to know one another well and kept up a shouting dialogue that we didn't understand.

"Hey, Al, who's your bootlegger?"

This remark, called out to a short dark-haired man who was dancing, brought a roar of laughter. The room, blue with cigarette smoke, smelled of bootleg gin, and it didn't take long for us to decide it was not our kind of party. We managed to escape as the caterers came up the elevator, wheeling tables of everything from caviar to caramel custards.

That was when we made the mistake. We decided to spend our "taxi fare" for dinner at Lindy's and then walk back to the hotel. We'd started across a wide, deserted bridge to the North Side when we heard a lot of noise beneath. Exchanging fear in a glance, we went to the edge and looked over. A bon-fire burned at the river bank, and the smell of frying bacon drifted up. Light from the fire revealed ragged men lying on bedrolls.

A man shouted, "Dames!"

We started to run.

"Say you – wait!" someone shouted.

Words were lost in the wind, but the sound of running feet was all too clear. It was difficult to run in spike heels, and I began to panic as the footsteps behind us grew louder.

Then came another shout, so close I heard the words "Stop in the name of the law!" A policeman lunged and caught each of us by an arm. I looked up into a bewildered Irish face and burst into tears of relief.

He studied our faces for a moment. "Hey where are you kids from? I thought I was rounding up a couple of prostitutes." He insisted on walking us to our hotel to the tune of a severe lecture. Hadn't we read about gang wars in Chicago? No one walked these streets at night.

The last remarks we exchanged that night were: "Wasn't it a weird party?" and "I wonder who the host was?"

The questions were answered a few days later when Felix showed us an item in the Chicago Tribune: "Al Capone entertained in the Lexington Hotel on Saturday night, taking over the entire 6th floor. Among his guests, including Chicago showmen with their wives, were local show girls…"

—Shyrle Hacker is a writer who lives in Walnut Creek, California.

The gangster Al Capone.

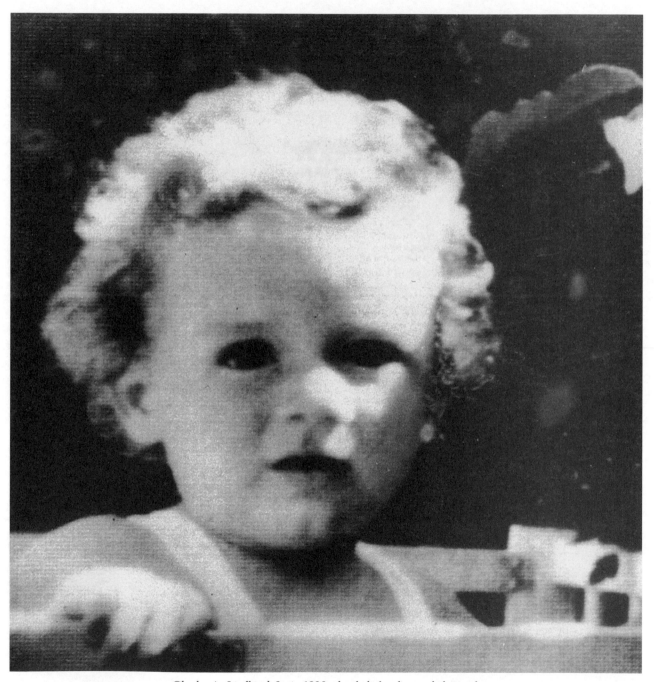

Charles A. Lindbergh Jr. in 1932, shortly before he was kidnapped.

ON THE SCENE AT
THE CRIME OF THE CENTURY

It was March 1, 1932, a balmy day in Princeton, New Jersey. I was seventeen, a high school student preparing to enter the university, where my father was a professor of military science and tactics.

The telephone rang, and it was an administrator at Princeton, informing my father that Col. Charles Lindbergh had just called to say that his infant son had been kidnapped. Lindbergh had said that his house in nearby Hopewell was full of police and many other people and had asked if the university could lend him ten or twelve cots to accommodate some of them. The administrator had turned to my father for help because he thought that the ROTC program might have some extra cots. This was indeed the case, and my father promised to send them over right away.

An earnest Corporal Boyd, a proficient truck driver but otherwise no competition for Albert Einstein (soon to be resident in Princeton), was directed to load all the available cots into a truck to be delivered to the Lindberghs. If the cots were to arrive in Hopewell that evening instead of Atlantic City or Philadelphia, a more astute presence was indicated. So I found myself in charge of Boyd and the truck and the cots.

Although Hopewell was only eight or ten miles from Princeton, I had never been there. After consulting a map, Boyd and I ventured out along a sparsely populated road into the black night. We arrived at our destination with only one wrong turn, which I assured Boyd was a planned shortcut. The sidewalks were already rolled up and the citizenry presumably snug in their beds, but we found a filling station open and got directions to the Lindbergh house, which was on top of a hill.

Coming around the last bend on the long, winding road, we emerged from the dark into a scene of utter confusion. Portable spotlights had been set up around the perimeter of the front yard, illuminating a swarm of men in various costumes: policemen of several descriptions, reporters with snap-brim fedoras and notebooks, and a considerable number of characters who seemed to have no purpose but to stand and gawk. Someone with an air of authority demanded to know what we wanted, and when we told him, he motioned to us to go into the house through the wide-open door.

We were greeted inside by Lindbergh himself. Although he looked haggard and distraught, he was the soul of courtesy, which I found remarkable under the circumstances. At his direction we began to carry the cots one by one up the stairs to the second floor. At the head of the stairs, in direct view from the landing, was the nursery, with toys spread around. What held me transfixed was the crib. A blanket was pulled back, and the depression made by a tiny body was clearly visible. The window was open, and the top of a ladder could be seen through it. Evidently the crime scene had been deliberately left untouched. I could hear Corporal Boyd catch his breath and mutter to himself, "Oh my God."

We passed on with our first cot and set it up in a large room that seemed to be some sort of recreation area. Mrs. Lindbergh came to the doorway to see what we were doing. She did not speak but managed a tight little smile. Like her husband, she looked distraught. She was obviously making a valiant effort at self-control.

Lindbergh asked me if I wanted him to sign a receipt for the cots. In the haste of getting our expedition under way, no one seemed to have thought of preparing one. I realized that in the peacetime Army receipts in triplicate were necessary for anything and everything, and unless I obtained one, there could be repercussions all the way to Washington. On the other hand, I didn't have the heart to force this grief-stricken father to wait while I wrote out something for him to sign. So I said that wouldn't be necessary, and we departed. I must confess it occurred to me that a receipt signed by Lindbergh at such a time could be a valued souvenir, albeit a somewhat gruesome one, but I quickly put this unworthy notion behind me and we headed back to Princeton.

The following day one of the New York newspapers carried a story about a "mysterious visit by a machine-gun truck which labored up the long hill to the Lindbergh house." The only mysterious thing about that was, What is a machine-gun truck?

—Thomas A. Parrott, a retired CIA official, lives in
Washington, D.C.

THE DAY I SAW THEM ALL

Like every American boy in the twenties and thirties, I revered Babe Ruth as the greatest name in baseball. What made him come alive for me was a genuine American League baseball that my father brought home after one of his trips to New York. Ruth had fouled it off, and Dad had jumped up and caught it one-handed, "just for you," he said. That was at Yankee Stadium, the "House that Ruth built."

Of course, I wanted to see Babe Ruth play too, but this wasn't easy. Dad and I were Cub fans. Ruth was an American Leaguer with the Yankees, so when they came to Chicago, they played the White Sox in Comiskey Park on the South Side.

In the fall of 1932 it became clear that Babe would be coming to Wrigley Field (the Cubs and Yankees had reached the World Series). It was beyond expectation that I would actually get to see those games; I hoped that perhaps I could sneak into the coach's office in the high school locker room and catch a few plays on his radio before the bell rang for afternoon classes.

One evening in September Dad came home in an unusually buoyant mood. I was doing a jigsaw puzzle at the family game table in the den. I watched him take off his suit coat and drape it deliberately over the back of his desk chair. As he unbuttoned his vest, he leaned forward and took a small envelope from his inside coat pocket.

Inside the envelope was a pair of tickets to the October 1 home opener of the World Series—the Cubs and the Yankees at Wrigley Field.

"Now you can see Babe Ruth," he said.

Our beloved Wrigley Field had been transformed for the Series, with red, white, and blue bunting draped everywhere. Temporary stands had been set up in the outfield to accommodate the huge crowd. Our seats were only six rows back from the playing field on the left-field side, between the end of the Cubs' dugout and third base.

"There's your man," Dad said, pointing to left field as we settled in. Sure enough, there he was warming up with his teammates, the Bambino, the Sultan of Swat, the Colossus of Clout, Babe Ruth, all six feet two inches and 215 pounds of him.

When the players left the field, the announcer introduced President Hoover, who was in the stands for the big game. The applause was scattered, and I was shocked to hear boos. (As a Boy Scout I thought you didn't do such a thing to a president.) When Gov. Franklin D. Roosevelt was introduced, there was much more applause and fewer boos. Both men were on the campaign trail for the presidential election coming up that November. If I had been politically conscious, I would have known right then that Mr. Hoover was in trouble, for it seemed most fans felt Hoover wasn't having nearly as good a year as Ruth.

Charlie Root took the mound for the Cubs. He was in trouble from the first pitch. With the first two Yankees on base on a walk and a throwing error by the shortstop Billy Jurges, Ruth lumbered up to the plate. He promptly did what he was famous for: lofted one of his patented homers out to the center-field seats.

The Cubs lifted our hearts with some good hitting, especially from Kiki Cuyler, but they never seemed to get real control of the game. The score was 4 to 4 when Ruth stepped into the box at the top of the fifth inning.

Babe Ruth is greeted at home plate by Lou Gehrig after hitting his famous called shot.

How lucky we were to be on the third-base side. As a left-handed batter, Ruth faced us, and we could see his every move and gesture. Root was very careful. After each strike the Babe raised his right arm, showing one finger for a strike, then two, to keep the stands posted on the duel between him and the pitcher. The crowd reacted wildly. When the count stood at 2 and 2, Ruth stepped back a bit and then pointed grandly to the outfield, making a big arc with his right hand.

Dad poked me in the ribs.

"Look at him point, son! Look at him point! He's calling a home run!"

The very air seemed to vibrate. I held my breath, digging my fingernails into my palms.

Ruth stepped back into the batter's box, ready for Root's next pitch. It came in knee-high, and the Babe connected solidly with his great swing. The crowd let out a volcanic, spontaneous gasp of awe. Everybody knew it was gone, gone, gone as it soared high and out over the center-field scoreboard for one of the longest homers ever hit out of Wrigley Field.

The Babe started his trip around the bases. When he rounded second and came toward us, we saw a triumphant smile on his face. Past third, he leaned over and pointed into the Cub dugout. I can only guess what he said to the Cub bench jockeys, although I probably wouldn't have known all the words then.

Root and Hartnett, the Cub battery, later denied that Ruth had called his shot or pointed. I guess that as great competitors they didn't want to give Ruth any more luster than he already had. Dad and I knew that Babe Ruth had pointed though. The Yankees went on to win, 7 to 5, and four of their runs were provided by Babe Ruth. That was the Sultan of Swat at his greatest.

As we were leaving the ballpark, a loud siren wailed just below us, and we rushed over to the ramp railing to see what was going on. Below was the big white touring car of the city greeter, and beside him on the back seat was Governor Roosevelt—gray felt hat and cigarette holder at the jaunty angle cartoonists loved to draw. For a brief moment my eyes locked with his as he looked up at the people lining the railing.

At that moment I realized I was seeing a new star about to enter a more serious arena. That day was a capsule of life. I passed from my boyhood interests to those of the greater game of politics on that bright autumn afternoon of October 1, 1932.

—Tom Fleming holds a master's degree in history from the University of Texas. He lives in Woodstock, Illinois.

THE MAN ON THE HORSE

The year was 1932; the country, like most of the world, was in the depths of the Depression. I was seven years old. My brush with history began one day when I heard my dad call my name as he burst through the back door. I thought, "What have I done now?" But when I saw his face, I knew he was not angry but very excited and even happy. My dad had not been happy in a long time.

We were living then in a big, run-down Victorian house near an old racetrack in Louisville, Kentucky. The track was no longer used for racing but was maintained for training, and its barns were kept for horses from Churchill Downs. My dad had lost his factory job a year before and had finally found a job doing odd jobs at the track. He would clean stalls or walk the horses after their morning workouts.

"Come quick," he yelled. "I want you to go with me up to the track." This was surely something special; he never allowed me near the barn area with its rough men and rough talk.

Dad walked so fast I had to run to keep up with him. As we neared one of the old barns, he turned toward me, smiled, and pushed me in front of him. I pushed the door open. The only light in the barn came from a long row of small, bare, dirty light bulbs high in the rafters.

I couldn't imagine what could be in there that had my dad so excited. As my eyes adjusted to the dim light, I saw at the far end of the runway between the two rows of stalls a big white horse with several men gathered around. One of the men was wearing a large cowboy hat. He turned toward me with a broad smile on his face. My heart stopped beating.

Could this really be happening to me? Would I next hear my mother's voice calling me to wake up for school? I actually prayed: "If this is a dream, please, God, let me finish it." The cowboy extended his hand to me, and I actually shook hands with Tom Mix, my all-time hero. He lifted me up and sat me on Tony. This had to be a dream.

When I returned to school on Monday, my excitement had abated only a little. When I told of my great adventure, I was crushed. The kids did not believe me. Some things are just too much to comprehend.

—Milton Shaw is a mechanical engineer living in Fairdale, Kentucky.

The legendary Tom Mix.

PRESIDENTIAL SPINACH

Naturally I was excited at the prospect at having lunch at the White House with the President of the United States. Very few eleven-year-olds get to do that. I told my friends at Pelham Day School in New York, and they wanted to hear all about it when I got back.

The President was Herbert Hoover, a long-time associate of my father. It was after the 1932 election but before the inauguration of his successor, Franklin D. Roosevelt, that I traveled to Washington, along with my father, Perrin Galpin, and my older sister, Penny. At the White House we were ushered in to see President and Mrs. Hoover. My father shook hands, my sister curtsied, and, flustered, so did I.

There were just the five of us for lunch in some private dining room, and the menu had been specially chosen for children: spinach with a poached egg on top. I don't remember what we talked about, but I suspect it was nothing important.

We returned to Pelham over the weekend, and on Monday I went back to school to tell my friends about my adventure. They were suitably impressed until one asked what we ate and I told them. With that, disaster. It seemed to them so unlikely that the White House would serve anything so lowly as spinach that they refused to believe that's what we had eaten, or in fact that we had eaten there at all. They ridiculed me. I was crushed. I went home near tears.

My parents shared my distress, and my father told the President about it. The result was prompt and the remedy complete. Mr. Hoover wrote me the letter opposite, enclosing with it a Washington's Birthday bicentennial button.

—Stephen K. Galpin is a retired Wall Street Journal reporter and General Electric executive living in Connecticut.

THE WHITE HOUSE
WASHINGTON

February 2, 1933.

Stephen Galpin,
975 Esplanade,
Pelham Manor, N. Y.

My dear Stephen:

    This is to certify that you lunched at the White House with me.   I have never been strong for spinach myself, and I had meant to tell you that you didn't have to eat it.

    In order to make sure that you remember that you were at the White House I am sending you herewith a button which you are entitled to wear as proof thereof.

        Yours faithfully,

        Herbert Hoover

The Chief Executive dispels the doubts of Stephen Galpin's classmates.

THE LOOKOUT

When the name John Dillinger is mentioned, most people think of a notorious bank robber. My memory is of an unshaven, shadowy man who stood behind a dirty screen door and motioned to my father.

Daddy was a feature writer for an Indianapolis newspaper in 1933. His articles were almost always controversial. When you read a Robert A. Butler byline, you knew the story would contain the unexpected, and a bias toward the underdog.

While other papers were running headlines about the many banks being robbed, all supposedly by Dillinger, Daddy was writing different stories. He tried to point out that the criminal couldn't be in two places at once, that the distance between two banks was too great for Dillinger to have robbed them both on the same day.

Apparently Dillinger took note of what my father had written, for he asked to meet with him. Dillinger's father lived in a farmhouse in Mooresville, Indiana, just seven miles from our home, and he invited my father to visit there. Most of our neighbors knew when Dillinger was in town, and I can remember Daddy shaking his head and saying, "I saw John just last night, and here he is, supposed to have robbed a bank clear up north. He must have a look-alike."

We went to the farmhouse, my father and I, a nine-year-old left in his care for the day. We drove into the lane, which was empty except for a nondescript dog. We walked up the steps, and Daddy motioned to a porch swing. I sat down, making sure my skirt was where it belonged, and started the creaky chains in motion. After a moment, an old man, Dillinger's father, joined me. I can recall little about him except that he smelled much like the barns I loved to visit.

We were lookouts, Daddy told me. We were to alert the shadowy figure I saw behind the screen if anyone drove close by. I could think of little to say to the old man, and my eyes continually strayed from the road to a swaybacked horse in the pasture. I was hoping to be invited to ride, and I know I must have hinted about it several times. That black horse was much more interesting to me than anything going on in the room behind me. But Dillinger's father didn't respond to my hints as we sat and watched the lane.

I don't remember how long we waited while Daddy talked to Dillinger. Once, when a car came up the road, driving slowly, I hopped down ready to do my job. The old man shook his head and said that they were neighbors, not out to get John, and that we'd best not interrupt what was going on inside.

When my father came out, he tipped his gray felt hat to old Mr. Dillinger and motioned for me to go to the car. I remember that he was very quiet on the way home, smoking his usual tipped cigarette in its amber-colored holder. I asked him why he would talk to a bad man instead of calling the police. Wasn't he scared?

"If I thought Dillinger was as dangerous as the police make him out to be, I would not have taken you with me," he replied. "The young man wants to surrender."

Dillinger was bad, but not nearly as bad as the police made him out to be, my father explained. Then he gave me one of those moral lessons that parents of the day were wont to offer. "When you are older, you'll realize that no one is all good or all bad. Sometimes people are accused of things they haven't done. It's up to newspapermen like me to try to point that out."

I could certainly understand what he was saying. My brother was always getting in trouble for things I did.

"If the police catch Dillinger," he said, "he'll probably be gunned down. John knows that. It's a simple way to close the files on many crimes."

Daddy was to meet Dillinger at a Chicago drugstore in a week's time and take him to the police. The outlaw had told him it was the only way he could be arrested without incident, that they wouldn't dare kill him as long as a well-known reporter was by his side.

The day arrived, and my father stood and waited outside the drugstore. He had left the motor running in his black La Salle coupe. When Dillinger arrived, they were to jump in the car and head straight for a police station where my father had friends.

Unfortunately, at the same time Dillinger showed up so did a police car. The officers just wanted some ice cream from the drugstore fountain, but Dillinger, thinking that he had been set up, ran away unseen.

One week later what he feared most happened. He was set up, this time by a woman, and he was gunned down just as he had anticipated he would be.

My father was sad about his failure to accomplish the surrender. He went to see John's father and came home a bit poorer after financing a new shirt and haircut for the old man. I've often wondered what would have happened if the police had come by the Mooresville farmhouse that day. Would it have mattered that a little girl, her legs too short to touch the floor, was sitting on a porch swing outside the outlaw's hiding place? Would it make a difference today if there were more old-time writers dedicated to reporting truths even if they are less sensational?

—Elizabeth Klungness was the editor and publisher of *Writer's News*, in Vista, California.

WANTED

JOHN HERBERT DILLINGER

On June 23, 1934, HOMER S. CUMMINGS, Attorney General of the United States, under the
authority vested in him by an Act of Congress approved June 6, 1934, offered a reward of

$10,000.00

for the capture of John Herbert Dillinger or a reward of

$5,000.00

for information leading to the arrest of John Herbert Dillinger.

DESCRIPTION

Age, 32 years; Height, 5 feet 7-1/8 inches;
Weight, 153 pounds; Build, medium; Hair,
medium chestnut; Eyes, gray; Complexion,
medium; Occupation, machinist; Marks and
scars, 1/2 inch scar back left hand, scar
middle upper lip, brown mole between eyebrows.

All claims to any of the aforesaid rewards and all questions and disputes that may
arise as among claimants to the foregoing rewards shall be passed upon by the Attorney
General and his decisions shall be final and conclusive. The right is reserved to di-
vide and allocate portions of any of said rewards as between several claimants. No
part of the aforesaid rewards shall be paid to any official or employee of the Department of Justice.

If you are in possession of any information concerning the whereabouts of John
Herbert Dillinger, communicate immediately by telephone or telegraph collect to the
nearest office of the Division of Investigation, United States Department of Justice,
the local addresses of which are set forth on the reverse side of this notice.

JOHN EDGAR HOOVER, DIRECTOR,
DIVISION OF INVESTIGATION,
UNITED STATES DEPARTMENT OF JUSTICE,
WASHINGTON, D. C.

June 25, 1934

John Herbert Dillinger, Public Enemy No. 1 in all police stations of the nation.

Adolf Hitler admires a woman in an undated photograph.

HIS TYPE

In 1933-34 I was a junior at Smith College taking a year to study German literature and medieval art at the University of Munich. I lived with the Count and Countess von Armansperg and their son and daughter.

The count had been a page in the kaiser's court and was now one of Hitler's generals. Like so many other Germans, he hoped that the new chancellor would lead their country out of its financial mess.

Both the count and countess were thoughtful, well educated, and charming people, but thoroughly German. Every now and then they would have Hitler, Goering, Roehm, and all the rest of them over for tea. I was often invited to attend.

As a nineteen-year-old blonde, blue-eyed, very naive young girl, I was just the type Hitler liked. He had, I must admit, a great deal of teatime charisma. Of course, everyone courted the chancellor's attention.

One afternoon I caught his eye, and he invited me to have dinner with him at his home the following Saturday night. I took one look at the little fellow with the funny mustache, thought of the handsome intern I was going with, and promptly answered, "Thank you for asking me, but I already have a date."

The count and countess nearly fainted. One didn't turn down an invitation from the chancellor of Germany!

But that was that: my brush with history. How grateful I am it was just a "brush."

—Mary A. Saalfield lives in Hudson, Ohio, and was the first woman president of the Akron Art Museum Board of Trustees.

Franklin Roosevelt (seated far right) and other administration officials visit a Civilian Conservation Corps Camp.

WILDERNESS SEDER

In 1934 I was in my early twenties and was unemployed. When President Roosevelt offered the youth of America one temporary way out, I jumped at the opportunity to join the Civilian Conservation Corps, which had been designed to take young men like me off the streets and send them into the forests.

Before I knew it, I found myself in Montana, along with three hundred other city boys who were coming into close contact with nature for the first time. The towering blue-gray ranges of Glacier National Park were majestic, and the cedars, pines, and sycamores rose so high that they made my apartment house back home seem small.

In the middle of April, spring and Passover came together. There were only twenty-six Jewish men in our company, and most of us thought of the Seders back home. We talked it over and decided to have our own ceremony out there in the wilderness. I was chosen to be part of a three-man delegation that went to see our commanding officer, Capt. Daniel M. Wilson.

He was a West Point graduate and looked just as you would have imagined: tall, erect, with cool blue eyes and a crew cut. Even in the forests of Montana his uniform was always immaculate. He listened to us and said, "Of course. You can have the use of the recreation hall for one night."

The following day I put up a little notice in Timber, the wall newspaper that I edited. It read: "Passover Seder, Thursday, April 18 at 7:30 p.m. in the Recreation Hall. All are welcome."

When we entered the hall that evening, we were amazed. Twenty-six paper plates had been set around the table. Folded napkins lay alongside, with spoons, forks, and knives. Paper cups of wine stood already filled. Extra bottles of wine and napkins had been placed on another little table nearby. Somebody had arranged mountain flowers in a large coffee can in the center of the table. Plates of matzo, the bitter herbs, the parsley, and the eggs were covered with paper napkins. An electric heater of some kind had been set up at the other end, keeping the chicken and matzo balls warm. A delicious aroma reminded us of home.

Emilio Skitsko, our Polish cook, had done it all—how, I do not know.

We had no rabbi. But one of our men, Nathan Akiba from Brooklyn, seemed to know more than any of us. Naturally he was immediately dubbed Rabbi Akiba, and he was in command as we improvised our way along.

Nathan recited the Kiddush in excellent Hebrew. The four questions were asked by the youngest among us, Jim Lockwood, who had just turned nineteen. He was half-Jewish, and this was the first Seder he had ever attended.

At the proper intervals we drank the appropriate cups of wine. To our amazement, after the second cup, Captain Wilson appeared, accompanied by two of the men of our company, Frank Finneran and Jack Reidulski, a light-heavyweight boxer who had fought in Madison Square Garden. "Rabbi" Akiba nodded to them and beckoned them to join us at the table. They did. There was a scraping of chairs as we made room for them.

By the time we got to the third cup, another man from the company had appeared. He was Samuel Brownell, a quiet black man who listened far more than he talked and whose religious feelings ran deeper than any of us understood. So there we were—twenty-six Jews, one West Point officer, and three young men of different faiths observing the Passover Seder in the Montana wilderness.

Today almost all of that little group is gone. Capt. Daniel M. Wilson was killed in the Battle of the Bulge in the Ardennes. Skitsko, our Passover cook, Columbo, Cohen, O'Reilly, Greenberg, Simon, and so many others of Company 269 C.C.C. were also lost in the Second World War—at Pearl Harbor, Normandy Beach, Tarawa, Saipan, Guadalcanal, Okinawa, and Cassino.

Only four of us are left. Frank Finneran, who became a Catholic priest, is blind now and lives in a Boston nursing home. Rev. Samuel Brownell, in his middle eighties, is still the active head of a Baptist church in Akron, Ohio. "Rabbi" Akiba lives in California with his daughters; I hear from him from time to time.

—David Swerdlow lived in New York City.

NO TIME FOR DRESSING ROOMS

Here is an event that took place while I lived in Jasper, Texas, in the 1930s and was employed by the H. N. Gibbs & Co. department store.

Late one Saturday night Mr. Singletary, our hardware manager and part owner of the business, and I, buyer and manager for the men's department, were alone in the store. As I was going to the door with Mr. Singletary to lock and go home, a young, good-looking lady appeared and asked if we had boots and riding pants. I told her we did and asked her to come in.

I measured her feet and showed her a pair of H. J. Justin's Lady Boots for thirty-five dollars. She asked to see the riding pants. I proceeded to measure her and showed her a pair of D. J. Riding Pants, also for thirty-five dollars, and asked her to step into the ladies' dressing room to try on the slacks. She looked me straight in the eye and replied, "Hell, I don't have the time to go to dressing rooms. I'm in a big hurry."

Standing about two feet out in front of me, she placed her right hand on my shoulder. With her left hand she reached down and pulled her dress above her waist (she was wearing a pretty pair of pink panties). She told me to put those pants on her. Then she sat down, and I put the boots on her. She paid me seventy dollars and was gone in less than five minutes.

The following week, about Tuesday or Wednesday, a go-between betrayed the outlaw pair Bonnie Parker and Clyde Barrow to the police near Shreveport, Louisiana. He told the officers what road the couple would be on. He was to be standing on this road at a certain place, which would serve as a signal to Bonnie and Clyde that their route was clear. When they came around the curve, he stepped out

Bonnie Parker, partner of Clyde Barrow.

on the road. They slowed to a stop, and the posse cut them down. One hundred and eighty-seven bullets hit the car. Bonnie Parker was wearing the boots and pants I had sold her.

Bonnie had been born and raised in Texas. She was one of Clyde's last women, and he had trained her as a crack marksman. They kept several guns always loaded, in the car, and many times before they had shot their way clear of posses and road-blocks.

As for that previous Saturday night, Mr. Singletary had waited for me to finish serving Bonnie. He saw her pulling up her dress while I slipped on the riding pants. He told all of Jasper, which was very embarrassing to me—but I was also really afraid some of Bonnie and Clyde's henchmen might think I had something to do with their meeting their deaths. But at the time I didn't even know whom I was waiting on.

Of course, they always did their shopping at hours when people were not around.

—W. A. Jarrell, as told to his grandson, Dana Martin, a financial planner who lives in Macedon, New York.

LONELY (FIRST) LADY

The Roosevelt townhouse was only three blocks from Hunter College's main building at Park Avenue at Sixty-eighth Street, and one day in 1940 Eleanor just walked in off the street. The door she opened was the entrance to Echo, the college magazine. I was one of the writers, and I happened to be in the office with two other girls on the staff. We were flabbergasted. She was completely alone, without a secretary, Secret Service agent, or companion of any kind. She was looking for someone to talk to, she said, and she had slipped into a side entrance to avoid meeting up with the crowds one always encountered in the main lobby.

We dropped everything and asked her to sit down on the couch. I sat next to her, and the other two leaned on a desk facing us. Mrs. Roosevelt explained that she was a neighbor of ours and was out for a walk, and she wondered if she could rest a while and chat with us if we were not too busy. Not too busy! We were overwhelmed and gave her our full attention.

She asked about our magazine, how often it came out (monthly) and what kinds of articles we published. With her soft, rather high-pitched voice and genuine interest in what we were doing, she soon put us at ease. What was amazing was how quickly we accepted as normal the fact that the First Lady of the land was sitting here in our little office with no fanfare or bodyguard.

Even more amazing was her request, on leaving, that she be allowed to visit us again when she had time. She said she enjoyed talking to young people but asked that we not publicize her visits, since she had time to get to know only our small group for the present.

Over the next year she dropped in once or twice a month. We became quite friendly. She called me Marian, and I called her Mrs. Roosevelt. The war in Europe was in its first year and hovered over us always, but we did not say much about it. We covered other topics, however. She took a special interest in my new cocker spaniel puppy named Rusty, not yet housebroken. I would come home at night and tell my mother what Mrs. Roosevelt recommended based on her experience with Fala. Mother regarded Mrs. R's visits nonchalantly. "Isn't that nice," she remarked, "her being interested in Rusty's problems. She's really a very nice lady."

My father, too, appeared to take the First Lady's visits in stride. His parents had been immigrants who came here expecting freedom and equality, and the fact that the president's wife was conversing with his teenage daughter struck him as entirely appropriate.

In later years I looked back on these events and wondered what was going on in Eleanor Roosevelt's life at the time. I learned that the townhouse she and the president owned had been a wedding present from Franklin's mother. Sara Delano Roosevelt lived on East Sixty-fifth Street and built them a twin house adjoining hers, with a connecting passage on an upper floor (a detail not revealed to the newlyweds until after the house was finished). Once they were married, Eleanor would sometimes be startled to see her mother-in-law appear in her house. After a time, though, the young couple seemed to accept these visits as part of their married life.

Often when Mrs. Roosevelt dropped by Hunter, we would plug in our phonograph, push back the chairs, and dance the lindy to the popular tunes of the day. I have a vivid picture of her sitting on the couch laughing and clapping her hands to the music.

First Lady Eleanor Roosevelt in a 1933 photograph.

Could she have been blamed for choosing the company of lively Hunter girls over an afternoon with her mother-in-law?

I was especially flattered one day when she praised an article I had written for the Echo, "The War in the Bronx," about how the Navy had taken over Hunter's Bronx campus to train young women to be officers in the Waves. I even fantasized that she might tell her husband about it.

One day one of us asked her if the president would ever pay a visit to Hunter. She said she would ask him. Soon after, it was announced in our assembly that President Roosevelt would visit our college in October. Excitement gripped us; most of us had never seen the president.

His appearance proved more moving than anyone anticipated, because we hadn't known how crippled he was. When we entered the hall, he was already seated on the stage, flanked by his son James in Marine-officer uniform on his right and several Secret Service agents on his left. Our college president, George Shuster, stood at the podium as we filed in.

The hall was hushed. Roosevelt was a large man, and his aura seemed to radiate to every inch of the room. When the hall was full, we all rose to sing "The Star-Spangled Banner." The president got to his feet with the help of James and his cane. The audience remained standing while Dr. Shuster made a short statement about how honored we were to welcome the President, who had taken time from his wartime burdens to address the young women of Hunter College.

We held our breaths as Roosevelt started to walk the eight steps to the podium. For a moment he did not move at all, as if his feet were fixed to the ground. Then, overcoming the inertia of his large frame, he dragged his right leg sideways and forward and rolled his body after it, leaning on James to keep from falling. Meanwhile, he started rolling his left leg forward to take a step on the other side. In this way, rolling from side to side, he moved ahead.

A lump rose in my throat at the sight of the effort our President had to make to walk just eight steps. I glanced around at the audience, and many people had tears in their eyes. It was now clear why Roosevelt so often had James at his side.

When he reached the podium, he stood by himself, holding on to the desk. We applauded him wildly, while he smiled the famous Roosevelt smile. I don't remember what he said, but the picture of him standing there will be with me forever.

The following year Eleanor Roosevelt spent more time traveling to far-off places, "being the eyes and legs of the President," as he put it. I graduated in 1943, feeling the richer for my contacts with her.

Mrs. Roosevelt must have remembered her days with Hunter's jiving girls because her townhouse was dedicated to the college in 1943. For nearly fifty years it was a student center, and from what I hear (Hunter's having gone coed), plenty of dancing went on there. She would have been pleased.

—Marian Schomer Greene was a freshman at Hunter College in 1940. She is now the features editor at *The Concordian*, a local newspaper in New Jersey.

SHANE'S FATHER

Growing up as a small boy on a farm in Ridgefield, Connecticut, was for me a lonely experience. A brother four years older had his own world, in which there was no room for small fry. Living more than five miles from the village and three miles from my nearest schoolmates, I was isolated—except for Shane, a younger boy on the neighboring farm. In retrospect, I realized that he was as lonesome as I and that I was encouraged to come to Brook Farm, as it was called, to provide companionship for him.

I often crossed the back fields to his house, and we would spend many exciting hours together. He lived in a wonder world, with a large house to be explored when his parents were absent, an apple orchard with challenging tree trunks to climb, dark woods which lurked with unknown dangers, a mysterious pond, a great, friendly Irish wolfhound named Finn large enough to ride, and a galaxy of wonderful toys and illustrated books and magazines.

We discovered wild strawberries at the pond's edge and learned about poison ivy the hard way, caught frogs and fish occasionally, and fought mock battles, taking turns being King Arthur or a favorite knight. I recall that one day when Shane's parents were gone, or so we thought, we crept up the stairs to investigate the forbidden second floor, only to encounter his father sitting up in bed in his room, writing. Shane said that he did that all the time. His father's glare was sufficient to make us hastily seek safety out of doors and far away. On another occasion, when investigating the attic, we discovered his grandfather's trunk, filled with wondrous costumes and crowns and fabulous jewelry, all of which looked very real. Later, to my disappointment, I learned he had been an actor.

My visits did not always end in pleasure, of course. Several years younger than I, my friend invariably had to have his own way. If not, his loud screaming would bring in his father, to me a fearsome figure. We were told he needed quiet and must never be disturbed under any circumstances. I remember seeing him on many occasions—tall and thin with black hair and mustache and forbidding expression—and I never saw him smile. He was certain to appear when my young friend and I made too much noise, either engaged in one of our mock battles too near the house or chasing Finn, or when our friendship was about to end in mayhem. His sudden, silent materialization promptly resolved all conflicts, and we magically disappeared to undertake another adventure.

One day, engaged in the dangerous pursuit of destroying wasp nests, we ventured into the upper regions of the garage. In making our escape, we tumbled into a huge loft, and into serious trouble. There was his father sitting in a chair while another man was making a clay portrait bust that looked just like him. The bust tottered precariously from our onslaught but was saved in the nick of time.

It was not until many years later that I understood why my young friend's father required so much quiet while writing in his room. My friend's father was Eugene G. O'Neill.

— Silvio A. Bedini is Historian Emeritus at the Smithsonian Institution.

Eugene O'Neill.

A DATE WITH A BOMBING

Five minutes to eight! It was going to be a wonderful day. I had a date with Ens. Jim Watters to spend the day lazily exploring Oahu, stopping to swim wherever we wanted. Jim wasn't coming for me until ten, so if I decided now what I was going to wear I could sleep an hour longer.

I had come to the islands from California right after school let out in June. My older sister, Jean, and her husband, Buzz (Ens. R. C. Lefever), were living in quarters on the Naval Air Station at Ford Island, and my parents had given me a trip to visit them after my first two years of college. I was slated to return to school in September, but when September rolled around I was having such a good time that I prevailed upon them to let me stay until Buzz's orders arrived in January.

What a ball I had! Twenty years old and the only single girl on an island filled with naval aviators and officers from the Pacific Fleet. Today would be a typical example of how the days had gone. What was I going to wear?

My mind didn't get as far as the closet door before I realized that something was wrong. There seemed to be an unusual amount of noise, and I heard the excited voices of my sister and her husband in the next room. Buzz had just returned from two weeks on Wake Island, and Jean was telling him that the explosions we heard were part of the local training exercise that had been going on all the past week. I heard Buzz shout, "The hell it is! It's the Japs!" From the bedroom window he could see his Squadron VP-22 hangar in flames across the landing field.

The explosions were continuing and seemed to be coming closer to the house, but still I didn't stir. My sister kept her clothes in my bedroom closet, and

I lay bug-eyed watching her pull out a slack suit and put it on—only to realize that she'd forgotten to put on a girdle. Off came the slacks, on went the girdle, and back on went the slacks. Today I can still see her in that outfit, beige slacks and a coordinated top with a moss-green cable-knit front.

It was my turn. I thumbed through the hangers and frantically wondered what one wore to a bombing. I have chuckled for years over my choice: a starched white eyelet-pique dress and red canvas sandals.

When the noise quieted down, my brother-in-law told us he would drive us to our designated bomb shelter. We sped down the road toward the new bachelor officers' quarters (BOQ), the only steel-reinforced building on the island. The BOQ housed three hundred naval officers, and it was to be our home for the next three nights and four days.

Memories of the next half hour rush into confusion. Buzz drove on to his flaming hangar, and I can't remember seeing him again for days. Jean and I, along with the women and children who lived on the "Mauka" (mountain) side of Ford Island, were herded into the windowless corridor of the first-floor bedroom wing.

There, bedlam prevailed. I can understand now the emotional noise made by worried and scared mothers and the commotion of frightened children, but at twenty I found the hysteria, praying, and singing nerve-racking. Soon Jean and I went to work for Capt. Dan Closser, the acting officer in charge of all the Marines on Ford Island. The Japanese right then were making their second strafing run on the island and we watched Dan, five-foot-few-inches of vigor, storm up the main stairway of the BOQ and haul down the eager armed men who were rushing up to the roof to shoot at the strafing planes. Their fire from the rooftop would have guided the Japanese pilots to a prime target on a return trip.

In short order, Dan had a veritable task force working in that BOQ. Perhaps it was an hour, I don't remember, before the survivors of the attack began to stream in from the ships, and during that hour all available supplies had to be organized. From somewhere came hundreds of military cots to fill the lounges and hallways of the first floor. We volunteers were sent through the 150 rooms of the officers living in the building to gather bedding and clothes.

Men were dispatched to the station laundry on the other side of the island to bring back all the clothes there. They would be handed out to the men swimming to the island from the ships in the harbor and later channeled back to their owners through the laundry markings. Behind the counter of the reception area of the BOQ we hurriedly stockpiled underwear, socks, shoes, shirts, uniforms, civilian clothes, blankets, and bedspreads. The entire supply of cigarettes and candy bars from the BOQ "Cigar Mess" (store) was there for us to give out along with the limited amount of bottled water.

And then they started coming—by the hundreds and in all stages of undress. As the ships exploded, their fuel oil spread over the water, and men who were not thrown into the harbor by the force of the explosions had no choice but to jump overboard and swim to shore. When they reached the island they were covered with oil.

Eyes—big white eyes—stared out of blackened faces. We were seeing the uninjured and the less severely injured, those who could swim to shore and still walk to the BOQ. The oil ignited as it spread over the harbor, and many sailors had to swim through a sea of flames. We heard that the lawn in front of Adm. Patrick Bellinger's house near battleship row was a mass of wounded and dying and that many of the men who climbed up the small bank from the water just lay down and died on the grass.

I kept frantically searching for faces I knew, but it was impossible to recognize anyone. Some time passed before a huge mass of oil pushed its way through to me and said, "Betty! Thank God, you're alive! You look like an angel!" It was Ens. Joe Lightburn from the battleship California, and I immediately felt better about wearing that white dress. If it affected him in that way, maybe I gave some kind of encouragement to others in that teeming, frightened crowd.

Captain Dan made sure that the wounded were settled into semicomfortable places to rest until medical aid arrived. Behind the counter we passed out candy bars and cigarettes as fast as we could and filled very small paper cups with water for the many who asked for it. The men kept streaming in, crowding up to the counter. Often we had to light their cigarettes for them—their hands shook too violently to hold the match. For some we also held the cup of water.

Many men came to the counter and urgently asked for paper and pen. Some of them had been standing watch at the time of the attack, and it was their duty on board ship to make proper entries in the log. Now, with no ship and no logbook, they still felt obliged to report. Others just wanted to get it all down on paper. Each man started with the time and the date, but some never got any farther. One man stood at the counter for more than an hour. When we finally persuaded him to leave and get some rest, we saw that he had never finished his first sentence, which began, "My ship the U.S.S. Arizona was...." All around us glassy, immobile eyes spelled s-h-o-c-k.

We gave out clothing like crazy. Our supply of

shoes was quickly depleted, and few pairs really fit the feet that went into them. The young men walking patrol that night would come to the counter and say: "Please, ma'am, my feet are so cold. Could you let me have a pair of shoes?" When we told them that there were none, they would ask for additional socks. Then we ran out of socks.

That afternoon I bumped into my beach date, Jim Watters. We passed on the stairway of the BOQ, which was strewn with broken glass from the bullet holes in the stairwell windows. Jim said, "Great date, wasn't it!"

All Sunday we had expected the Japanese to return. I was so convinced they'd be back that at odd times during the day I had rigged a bomb shelter out of a large steel-topped desk. It had a knee-hole area large enough for Jean and me and I kept piling various items on top of it that I thought might repel flying fragments. As night darkened the skies we heard the awful drone of airplane engines. One frightened finger pulled a trigger, inviting the outbreak of noisy, terrifying machine-gun fire. Instead of dashing for the security of the desk, I panicked and fled.

I ran from the counter through the swinging doors into the women and children's shelter corridor and dived under one of the canvas cots that had been set up in the hallway. In the dark I lay there, scared to death, when suddenly I thought of my sister in the blacked-out entry with the huge glass windows of the BOQ facade staring at her. I wondered what in the world I was doing under that cot, and I ran as fast as I could down the dark hallway and back to the foyer. If I had stayed under that cot, I would have spared myself the memory of joining the crowd on the steps of the BOQ and cheering wildly as our gunners opened fire on planes flying overhead. We cheered and cheered as we watched a ball of fire fall into the bay, and I will never forget the sound of a telephone

ringing and the agonized hush that followed the announcement that we were firing at our own planes.

Our work went on all night Sunday, Monday, and Tuesday. We took turns falling into a dirty-linen cart for a twenty-minute break now and then. Ten thousand men from destroyed ships had come ashore onto Ford Island that Sunday. Many had lost everything they possessed. They had to be fed, clothed, and tended to physically and mentally. There was no Red Cross to come to our aid, no stores to sell even the most necessary items.

During the day we all strove to be considerate and to boost morale among the men as much as possible. Jean and I always wore fresh flowers in our hair, picked from the hibiscus bushes outside the BOQ. Of course, our attempts to be helpful sometimes failed miserably. Our hero, Dan Closser, trying desperately to comfort a dying sailor, put the wrong end of a lighted cigarette into the man's mouth. The blackened lips whispered, "That's all right, sir. I'm so burned now I couldn't tell the difference." Tuesday noon I cheerfully ask Joe Lightburn what he had been doing that morning. "What have I been doing?" he repeated in a dull, awful voice. "I have spent the morning identifying three hundred and fifty of my dead buddies from the California."

At dawn on Tuesday I watched the big front door of the BOQ slowly open. Into the foyer walked two strained and exhausted men, still in their flight suits. I gave a good second look to be sure, and rushed into the arms of Ens. Joe Garrett, who later became my husband. He and Ens. Forrest Todd, with only pistols aboard their patrol planes for defense, had aborted their mail-delivery mission at Johnston Island and searched for thirty hours for the Japanese carrier planes reportedly on their way to bomb Midway and Johnston islands. Joe and Forrest, leery of bringing

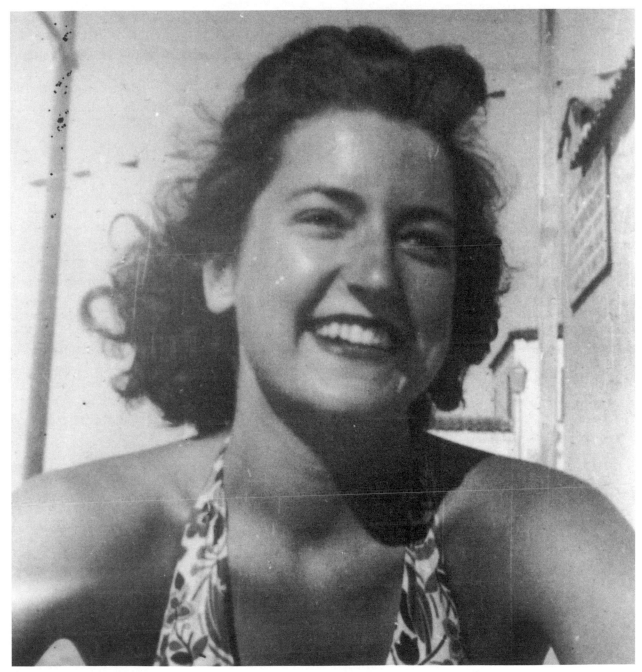

The author, photographed at about the time of her visit to Ford Island, Hawaii.

their seaplanes in to land in the debris-littered harbor, had radioed headquarters that the planes over Barbers Point at exactly six o'clock in the morning would be theirs and to hold the fire! My husband says that his navigation and timing that night were the most motivated of his career.

By Wednesday evening both Jean and I were feeling tired and unattractive in our Sunday clothes. Leaving me to tend the counter, Jean went back to the quarters to change. As soon as she left, I received a frantic message that we had a long-distance call at the quarters. I sped off to join her. It seemed an eternity since I had left Quarters 111B on Sunday, and it must have seemed even longer to our parents, who since the first news flash had been trying to get in touch with their daughters.

Once we were back in the quarters, the prospects of a hot shower and a bed were too tempting to resist. Knowing that we were no longer really needed, we sent word back to the BOQ that we were retiring from duty.

Although the Ford Island dependents had top priority for evacuation to the mainland, we delayed our departure from Hawaii until Buzz headed out for the South Pacific, and it wasn't until March that we boarded Pan American's converted China Clipper for San Francisco. When we landed very early one morning, we felt a lifetime away from Pearl Harbor. Consequently, we were surprised to be ushered into the combined Naval and Army Intelligence and FBI office at the airport. There Jean and I were very clearly informed that we were not to say anything about what had happened to the United States Fleet or Pearl Harbor on December 7. We were admonished so strongly that we obeyed. My father told us years later that he was hurt to the quick that we didn't even tell him what we had experienced.

One February, twenty-five years later, my husband and I took two of our children to Hawaii. We drove around Ford Island and found the Utah rusting hull side up out in front of Quarters 111B. We took the Navy barge trip around Pearl Harbor and listened to the lecture given by the guide. And then I told my children what I remembered of that day, when I was the age of my daughter, Ginger, accompanying me that spring.

—Betty Garrett lives in Ventura, California.

NOT RIGHT FOR THE PART

In April of 1942 I enlisted in Psychological Research Unit 3 at the Santa Ana Army Air Base. I had written the story for a historical film called Ten Gentlemen from West Point, and when it played at the post theater I became a local celebrity and was promoted from private to sergeant and assigned to the Public Relations Office.

I was sent to an old movie studio near Hollywood on orders of Gen. Henry ("Hap") Arnold, who had established the first Motion Picture Unit of the Army Air Corps to produce aviation training films and send combat camera units around the world. I presented my papers to the personnel officer, a handsome, friendly thirty-one-year-old lieutenant with horn-rimmed glasses and reddish brown hair, named Ronald Wilson Reagan.

In 1937 Reagan had enlisted in the U.S. Cavalry Reserve as second lieutenant. In April 1942 he was earning a thousand dollars a week as a movie star at Warner Brothers in Burbank when he was called to active duty at Fort Mason, San Francisco. Reagan expected to be shipped overseas, but when an eye examination showed him to be myopic, he was restricted to limited service in the continental United States.

After I saluted, he stared at me quizzically. "Haven't I seen you somewhere before, Sergeant?"

"Could be, Lieutenant," I replied. "I worked as a writer for seven months at Warner Brothers in 1939. We didn't meet because the only actors who ate at the writers' table in the greenroom were Errol Flynn and Humphrey Bogart." What I couldn't tell him was that the snobbish big-city writers, led by John Huston, regarded him as a small-town boy.

Reagan sent me to Capt. Robert Carson, head of production and a well-known novelist who had co-written the classic A Star Is Born. Carson studied my papers and sergeant's stripes. "So you've been in the Army for six months, like Ronnie Reagan?" I nodded. "And you completed your basic training and all that military crap?" I nodded again. "Well," he said, "we're lucky to get guys like you and Ronnie because the rest of us are really civilians pretending to be soldiers. We're fresh from studio lots, and the younger boys are right out of the mailroom at Warner Brothers.

"Writing assignments will be coming up soon. But in the meantime, there'll be odd jobs to keep you out of trouble."

One of these "odd jobs" was acting in a film. I had done radio and stage acting, but I'd never been on the screen, so it was with great anticipation that I reported to a hospital set. I was to play a pilot who had been shot down and badly burned.

The makeup people wrapped my face and head so that I looked like a mummy. The director ordered me to climb into a bed. He called out, "Lights, camera, action!" and my co-star entered. It was Ronald Reagan, resplendent in a pilot's uniform. He stood over me and asked me how I was. Since my lips were bandaged, all I could make were muffled sounds. Reagan patted me sympathetically on the head and walked out.

The director praised us for a great performance. Several weeks later a general put me in charge of overseeing the narration on a film. I walked onto a recording stage and found Reagan waiting to read the script. He stared at me in astonishment. "What the heck is this all about?"

"It means," I replied, "that I'm going to be your

Ronald Reagan in his Army uniform.

director." I was twenty-five years old at the time but looked closer to nineteen.

"Look, son," he began in a fatherly way, "I started out in this business as a radio announcer and then became a movie star. And you're going to tell me how to read lines?"

"That's what the general's order says," I countered.

A short heated discussion followed whether a general in the field had the jurisdiction to dictate to the film unit. I suggested that Reagan call Washington to settle the dispute.

"No," he said. "That won't work. We've got too many inspectors telling us how to make movies. Let's keep Washington off our backs and work it out between ourselves."

I later came to think the shrewd compromise was an early indication of Reagan's future as a politician. He recorded the narration in two ways—my way and his way. Then Bobby Carson decided which one he wanted to use.

That's the way we worked it out for the next two and a half years. On subsequent projects, while waiting for the sound men to get their equipment ready, Reagan and I discussed the war and politics. We both were loyal Democrats and admirers of Franklin Roosevelt. I told him I was working on Father Was President, a play in which Roosevelt was a minor character. The hero was Theodore Roosevelt.

After the war ended in August 1945, Paramount optioned the play for production at a local theater. When I told Reagan about this, he wished me luck.

"Who's going to be playing President Roosevelt?" he asked.

"Albert Dekker," I replied.

"Well, if it ever gets done as a movie, do you think there's a chance of my being loaned out by Warner Brothers to do the part?"

I shook my head. "Ronnie baby," I told him, "you're only thirty-five. You're too good looking and young to play the part."

He laughed. "Well, I could age. Gosh, it would be fun to play a President of the United States."

The rest, as they say, is history.

—Malvin Wald lives in Sherman Oaks, California.

"WHY DON'T YOU COME UP AND...?"

In November of 1944 I was a plebe—a freshman—at the Naval Academy. We sat at attention at mealtimes, spoke only when spoken to by an upper classman, and obeyed orders. All orders.

At lunch one day a youngster, a third classman, addressed me. I've forgotten his name; it wasn't Midshipman 3c. Jimmy Carter (who nailed me one day for not having my shoes properly shined), although it might have been Midshipman 3c. Stansfield Turner, who was in my company.

"Morris!"

"Sir."

"Whom have you asked to the Army-Navy game?"

"No one, sir."

"Ask Mae West."

"Aye, aye, sir?"

Miss West, I found, was appearing in a Broadway play, Catherine was Great (which she had written herself). I dutifully wrote her a polite note inviting her to the game.

To my surprise (and that of the youngster who put me up to it), an answer came within the week, with an inscribed photo. There was a Saturday matinee

Mae West, in her typical long black slinky gown with large feathered hat.

the day of the game, and she couldn't make it, but if I would be in New York for Christmas leave, there'd be tickets at the box office in my name, and I should please come backstage and say hello afterward.

Annapolis plebes did get Christmas leave (although West Point plebes didn't), and on a Friday afternoon I presented myself at the box office and was given two house seats. They were for the evening performance, which I attended with a casual date, a gorgeous, if somewhat slow, young lady named Raquel.

It was just as well Raquel wasn't swift on the uptake, as the curtain had barely gone up before I realized the play was, by 1944 standards, about as blue as Broadway would then sit still for, and not at all suitable fare for a seventeen-year-old, obviously sheltered maiden. The cast consisted of Miss West and forty-seven males, almost all of whom shared the same dramatic fate by the middle of the third act. The opening lines were an exchange between two courtiers in the deserted throne room:

"Where is Her Majesty?"

"She's out inspecting the Novgorod Regiment—man by man."

I began to prepare for a certain amount of flak from Raquel's parents when I got her home.

After the performance, we duly presented ourselves at the stage door. I sent my card in, and we were shortly ushered into Miss West's dressing room, a hot, cluttered chamber looking about what I thought dressing rooms looked like, except for the couch on which Raquel and I were invited to seat ourselves. I put my overcoat, my white scarf, my midshipman's cap, and my gloves on my knees.

Miss West was wearing a negligee (her costume during most of the play) and a wraparound, and the adjective that came to mind was grimy. She still had her make up on and it was running, and the collar of the wraparound was stained with layers of ancient make up.

She couldn't have been nicer. She poured modest shots out of an open bottle of Scotch into mismatched tumblers and shoved two toward me. I handed one to Raquel and suddenly realized she was in a state of mild shock. There was a lot of Miss West, and it was pretty overpowering, and it also was probably the first time in her life that Raquel had been offered a drink.

We made polite chitchat for a few minutes. Raquel announced she had enjoyed the play, and Miss West looked at her blankly, and what with one thing and another, it was ever the least bit awkward.

I finally arose; we all did. I thanked Miss West again, and we started for the door, with Raquel in the lead. She stepped down into the narrow passage, and just as I did, a gaggle of departing actors came along; I paused in the doorway and drew back, with Miss West just behind me.

As I was about to step out, a bare arm reached over my right shoulder, a hand cupped my chin and pulled my head firmly back against lips which whispered throatily into my burning left ear. "You should have come alone, sonny."

Galvanized, I shot forward without a word and rejoined Raquel.

After a late dinner at Sardi's we were halfway home by taxi when it suddenly occurred to me that my first reaction—that it wasn't really the sort of play I should have brought a girl like Raquel to—may very well not have been the correct interpretation.

I've been wondering about that these forty-eight years.

—Donald R. Morris, a historian, novelist, and journalist,
publishes a letter of news analysis and comment.

WHAT IKE REALLY SAID

The photograph has been printed and reprinted far and wide. It is found in schoolbooks, history books, and encyclopedias. It is on display at the Pentagon.

It is, of course, the photograph of Gen. Dwight D. Eisenhower taken the evening before D day, June 6, 1944, speaking to the men of the 101st Airborne Division. The caption always reads that he is urging his paratroopers "on to total victory." But to this day what really occurred and what was really said is still known only to the men with whom he was talking.

The troops had been moved into the marshaling area at Greenham Common airfield during the latter part of May and had been fully briefed with aerial

General Dwight D. Eisenhower, Supreme Commander of the Allied Expeditionary Forces, gives the order of the day.

photos and sandbox mock-ups on the coming invasion of Normandy. Restricted to the area after the sensitive information had been passed along, the men had little else to do other than check their equipment and go over the plans and their final objectives.

The "go" came on the evening of June 5, 1944, after an entire day's delay due to weather. Everyone was more than ready, in full battle gear. It was rumored that Ike was in the area, yet the men's reaction was surprisingly calm. Until it was added, "But you ought to see his driver—a woman!"

There was a wild dash down the temporary street between the tents to see the driver of Ike's car, Kay Summersby. As the men ran down the street, who should be heading up the same road but Ike and his group of officers and photographers? When the two groups converged, correct military courtesy prevailed, the parachutists standing at attention and Ike coming over to greet his men.

His words were not "total victory," as might be expected before one of the war's greatest battles, but rather, "What's your name, lieutenant?" and "Where are you from?"

"Strobel" and "Michigan, sir," were the replies.

Ike recalled in some detail the spectacular fishing he had enjoyed there. Then, quickly, he moved on, the photographers having captured the exchange on film.

The troopers' brief delay was over and they continued on to see Ike's car and its beautiful driver. Then, a few minutes later, the troopers boarded planes, and just hours later they were parachuting behind the beaches of Normandy.

In the following turmoil the incident was forgotten until early July, when the same lieutenant saw a grainy picture of Ike and his troops in the pony edition of Time magazine. There he saw himself, standing in front of Ike, with camouflaged face and the identifying number 23, his plane number, hung around his neck.

Over the years the photograph has found its way into countless publications about World War II, and almost always the caption has read "Ike urging his troops on to total victory." I have to smile along with the others who were there because we all know what was really said. You see, I was that Number 23.

—Wallace C. Strobel was a 1st lieutenant in Company E, 502d Parachute Infantry, 101st Airborne Division. He lives in Saginaw, Michigan.

SAVING THE LEANING TOWER

In the summer of 1944 I pointed my jeep in the direction of Pisa. The Germans were on the north side of the Arno River, the Americans on the south bank. My destination was a farmhouse that was the headquarters of an armored group—some tanks, artillery, and riflemen. A sign on the dirt road warned: SLOW—10 MILES AN HOUR. DUST RAISES SHELLS. In the distance I suddenly came around a bend and saw the Leaning Tower. I wanted to gun the engine, but dust would be a telltale of movement for an observer on the other side of the river. I felt exposed and naked, for I had heard that the Germans were using the Leaning Tower as an observation post (OP). As I got a little closer, I could see small figures moving between the columns of the tower on its highest floors. And I instinctively felt they could see me. Naturally my windshield was down and covered with a tarpaulin; otherwise, it could mirror the sun from a distance.

Finally I reached the farmhouse. The guys were standing around, with their maps and charts, looking at the tower and the other OPs where the Germans dominated the valley. They had lost a few friends to artillery and were not happy about the tower. The vino was passed around. As dusk approached, talk turned to retaliation: Let's shoot down their OP. What the hell, it's just another roadblock on the advance north. A small debate followed. The Germans had denied that they were inside the tower. But the forward scouts cold see them there. What should be done? All's fair….

They turned to me, an Army correspondent, for advice. I didn't say yes, or no; after all, I could leave by nightfall and they'd still have it eyeing them menacingly. Just then the colonel entered the farmhouse. "I know what you guys are thinking," he said, "but forget it."

The moment had passed; sanity was restored. The tower remained standing. A few days later I pulled up in front of it and saw orange-colored wire still hanging down: German signal-corps wire, proof that they had used it. I wrote my story; it was censored. So I bought a six-inch plastic replica of the tower, climbed the real one, and looked down at the valley below. It was a nice view.

— Herbert Mitgang, is a *New York Times* reporter and author, most recently, of *Once Upon a Time in New York*.

The Leaning Tower of Pisa.

FDR's Bedside Manner

In July of 1944 I was lying in a naval hospital bed in Honolulu, a very young Marine lieutenant shot full of holes in the Saipan campaign. I shared the room with an old friend I hadn't seen in months until we accidentally ended up together in the hospital, courtesy of the Japanese.

One bright morning an unusual flurry of activity began: cleaning personnel zipping about, corpsmen dashing down the corridor, nurses coming in to check if we had shaved and washed after breakfast. There even seemed to be an inordinate number of planes roaring by the hospital. Questions about what was going on were ignored, but finally a favorite nurse gave us the word: President Roosevelt was in Hawaii—for a conference with his Pacific commanders, as we learned later—and was visiting the hospital and would maybe visit a few rooms.

Later the corridor outside our room began to fill with men both in uniform and in civilian suits, and two of the latter came into our room and checked it out, even peering under the high hospital beds. At one point an older naval officer leaned against the doorjamb and chatted with us; it was not until he turned to leave that I saw the stars on his collar and recognized him as Admiral Nimitz. I kept watching the corridor, and suddenly the mob parted slightly, and I saw the president in his wheelchair. His chin drooped on his chest, and his face sagged in a mass of baggy wrinkles. He looked ghastly, almost unrecognizable as the exuberant, vibrant president I had often seen in news photos and on the newsreels.

A moment later the commanding officer of the hospital took one step into our room, announced formally, "Gentlemen, the President of the United States," and then stepped back out again. The president was wheeled into our room. I was stunned. You would have thought he was being wheeled onstage at Soldier Field, Chicago, before fifty thousand people. His head was thrown back, that famous broad, open Roosevelt smile on his face had wiped out the sagging wrinkles, and his right hand was raised high in cheery greeting. A complete transformation, and all for the benefit of two wounded Marines. He stayed for a few minutes and chatted, but I no longer remember what he said except that at one point he told a dull joke at which he laughed delightedly, and then he was gone.

For years afterward, when teaching American history at my university, I would tell this story to illustrate Roosevelt's astonishing appeal and his apparent personal concern for others. There were no reporters present, no photographers taking pictures, no public relations gimmick; all this had been for our benefit alone.

Once, years later, after I had told this to a class, a hand went up from an older student, a retired Army colonel. He said that he, too, had once met the president, and so I naturally asked him to tell us about it. He had been a duty officer at the War Department when the message had come in from General Eisenhower—to be delivered personally—informing the president that the D-day invasion was under way. The officer took off for the White House, which he found jammed with civilian and military brass waiting for this word. He insisted on delivering the message directly to the president, and this was agreed to. He also had the nerve to ask for the message back after the president had read it, and FDR smilingly agreed.

He told the story very well, and he had clearly topped mine, as I'm sure the class thought too. There was a long pause when he finished.

"Well," I said, "that's an impressive story, but there is one major difference between your experience and mine. You drove a few blocks across town to see the president. The president traveled six thousand miles to see me."

Cheers and laughter from the class, and my little brush with history remained secure for another time.

—G. D. Lillibridge is a professor emeritus of history at California State University at Chico.

President Roosevelt at his Hyde Park, New York, home in February, 1941.

Fiorella La Guardia, with Eleanor Roosevelt during a 1941 radio broadcast.

ALL'S FAIR

It was October 1944, and the pundits were busy analyzing Franklin Delano Roosevelt's bid for a fourth term. His opponent was Thomas E. Dewey, the former crime-busting district attorney of New York County and now governor of the state. FDR had lined up an impressive array of big names to support him in the state. My brush with history involves one of these.

I'm talking about Fiorello H. La Guardia, the mayor of New York City, the Little Flower. While ostensibly a reform Republican, he was strongly pro-Roosevelt. In fact, the President had just appointed him director of the U.S. Office of Civilian Defense.

I met Hizzoner on a number of occasions. My father was assistant manager of the New York Philharmonic and one of his duties was to oversee the summer concerts that took place in Lewisohn Stadium. La Guardia opened the Stadium Summer Series every year by conducting the Philharmonic in "The Star Spangled Banner." I had attended many of these opening concerts and had met La Guardia at the receptions that always followed. But now I was to meet him one on one—in a CBS radio studio.

Just out of school, I had managed to get a job as an assistant apprentice director in July of 1944. By September I was a full-fledged assistant director. Among other things, the assistant director was assigned to all the noncommercial programs such as Sunday-morning religious shows and political addresses. Such an address was to be given by Mayor La Guardia. The Democratic party had bought time on the entire CBS radio network and had asked the mayor of New York to address the nation on behalf of the President. He was to speak from 6:15 to 6:30 P.M.—live. There was no tape in those days.

La Guardia arrived at 5:30. I introduced myself and was gratified when he said he remembered me and asked about my father. Then I introduced him to our technician and to our organist, Abe Goldman. I explained that if his speech did not fill the fourteen minutes and thirty seconds required for a fifteen-minute program, the organist would fill the remaining time with music.

The mayor smiled enigmatically. He sat down at the table, took out his speech, and read it out loud. I timed it. It was thirteen minutes long and, with the opening and closing remarks by the announcer, would time out perfectly. I told the mayor that everything was fine, and I asked him if I could do anything for him. He said, "No, thanks." And then, reaching up to put his hand on my shoulder, he said, "But tell me again what happens if my speech runs short." I explained again that the organist would fill the time until the next program went on the air.

Imagine my total surprise during the broadcast when, following along with my copy of the speech, I noticed that the mayor had made huge deletions. I could not for the life of me figure out why. It had timed out perfectly. When he came to an end, we were very, very short. The announcer read his closing remarks, and I cued the organist to start playing. Abe must have played for three interminable minutes. I was probably going to catch hell for not having timed La Guardia's speech accurately.

His face was wreathed in smiles, La Guardia burst into the control room. I said, "Your Honor, what happened? The speech was perfect for time. Why did you make all those cuts? My boss is going to think I don't know how to use a stopwatch!"

"Not your fault at all, young man," squeaked the

mayor. "On the way over to the studio, I was looking at the radio listings in the evening paper and noticed that Dewey is scheduled to speak right after me, from six-thirty till quarter of seven. I figured if I finish early and the only thing going out on the air was organ music, people would either tune to another station or turn off the set entirely. I just wanted to do everything I could to reduce the size of Dewey's audience. I hope it worked. You just tell your boss that. Tell him all's fair in love, war—and politics."

— Bruno Zirato, a communications consultant, lives in Scottsdale, Arizona.

BRINGING THE PRESIDENT HOME

In the late afternoon of Thursday, April 12, 1945, my wife and I were relaxing on the front terrace of our West Point quarters. Such a mild, sunny day seldom came to the Hudson Valley so early in the spring. Suddenly from an open second-story window one of our young sons, who had been listening to the radio, called out, "Momma, Papa—Roosevelt is dead!" We sat in stunned silence.

At last my wife spoke. "You'll have to plan the president's funeral." As assistant operations training officer for the U.S. Corps of Cadets I was responsible for all cadet ceremonies and the preparation and coordination of military training programs.

I shook my head. "No, Washington will take care of everything. The Military Academy won't be involved."

The next evening my home telephone rang. It was Brig. Gen. George Honnen, commandant of cadets. "Mac," he said, "you're it. The War Department has just ordered us to plan and supervise President Roosevelt's funeral at Hyde Park, set for ten on Sunday morning. We'll go up there at seven-thirty tomorrow and look over the situation." My wife was right, as usual.

General Honnen and I arrived at the Roosevelt home in Hyde Park early Saturday morning and introduced ourselves to the superintendent of the estate, William Plog. At his invitation we briefly visited the inside of the house.

I shall never forget the sight of the dark blue Navy cape hanging in the closet of the president's upstairs bedroom, his Harvard pennant on the wall, his wheelchair, the ramps that replaced stairways. During his entire presidency, I had never seen him in a wheelchair.

Superintendent Plog led us outside and pointed to the exact spot in the rose garden that Mr. Roosevelt had selected for his gravesite some five years earlier. Then we walked through the wooded grounds, reconnoitering the roads and paths that allowed access to the burial site. A dense hemlock hedge, planted in the 1840s and some fifteen feet high, almost completely surrounded the garden. There was an opening on the west side through which a column of troops could pass, but the single opening to the south, facing the mansion, was much too narrow for the casket bearers. Mr. Plog promised to widen the archway by having his gardeners cut back several feet of tangled branches on both sides of the path.

Next we drove down toward the Hudson River along the winding lane that led to a spur track on the New York Central right-of-way, to determine the distance to the nearest point where the train could stop. Afterward we drove to the Hyde Park railroad station, clocking the mileage from the burial site.

Although these data would be useful, we still lacked much urgently needed information. How many mourners would attend the funeral? When and where would the casket leave the train? What other military units, besides the West Point cadets, would share in the final honors? Later in the day, when I saw workmen busily preparing the grave, my concern increased.

Nevertheless, some steps could be taken right away. Col. A. A. Heidner, our supply officer, hurried to West Point to arrange for the movement to Hyde Park of a battalion, to be chosen by lot from the Corps of Cadets, together with the brigade colors and the U.S. Military Academy Band. In addition, a black funeral caisson with seven horses, a black caparisoned horse, and a battery of field artillery would be brought up from West Point by bus and truck. All these were to reach the estate by 8:00 a.m. Sunday.

Later Saturday afternoon word came from Washington that two special trains carrying mourners would arrive at 9:00 a.m.; that our plans should provide for four battalions of Army, Navy, Marine, and Coast Guard personnel, who would be there at 7:00 a.m.; and that the Army Air Force would be represented by a formation flight over Hyde Park exactly five minutes before the service. A fleet of two hundred Army staff sedans would meet the dignitaries arriving on the special trains and bring them from the Hyde Park railroad station.

Before I could tackle the problem of how to deploy nearly two thousand people, I needed to know the route the funeral cortege would travel. Would it come south, along the highway from the

The Roosevelt family at the President's funeral at Hyde Park on April 15, 1945.

Hyde Park Station, or up the narrow gravel lane from the spur track inside the estate? The former route was several miles longer and would present more difficulties. Increasingly urgent telephone calls to Washington yielded little information. With President Truman and the suddenly widowed Mrs. Roosevelt aboard, the movement of the closely guarded funeral train was classified secret. "You had better make alternative plans," I was told. This at a time when I thought I'd be lucky to come up with one plan!

Recalling the military adage "There is no substitute for thorough ground reconnaissance," I headed back to the New York Central right-of-way about three-quarters of a mile from the house. There, alongside the spur track, I found a group of railroad workmen building a temporary platform of heavy timbers. They said it was to be used to enable a nine-hundred-pound copper-lined casket to be transferred to the motor hearse. I ran back up the hill to our temporary headquarters with this information. At last we knew exactly where to meet the funeral train and that we had to make only one plan after all.

Although service manuals prescribe the protocol for normal military funerals, these regulations did not seem appropriate on this most important occasion. Given the more personal nature of the traditional three rifle volleys, I recommended that the final salute be fired over the grave by a squad of cadets. (This would replace three salvos by distant cannon.) Only one artillery salute would be fired, the twenty-one-gun presidential salute. It would begin as the motor hearse carried the casket from the train to the meadow below the mansion. The Army Air Force formations would fly over while the cannon were firing.

We decided to use the cadet battalion as an escort of honor in the funeral procession. The cadets would form in the meadow, render honors when the casket was transferred to the caisson, then march in a slender column of threes up the narrow lane. The route would be lined on both sides with about one thousand soldiers, sailors, and marines standing shoulder to shoulder. On entering the rose garden, the cadet battalion would form in a compressed mass on the west side. Already posted around the other three sides of the garden, with their backs to the hedge, would be three hundred servicemen representing the other armed services. Barely sufficient standing room would then remain for individual mourners, journalists, and photographers.

My next task was to determine the specific military and musical honors to be rendered. After this had been worked out, I called the minister who was going to conduct the service and learned that he had never attended a military funeral. I asked him to come over to the garden. The dignified seventy-eight-year-old Reverend Dr. George W. Anthony, rector of St. James Episcopal Church in Hyde Park, where Mr. Roosevelt had served as the senior warden, arrived at dusk and quickly verified his part in the service.

Late that night Mike Reilly, chief of the White House Secret Service detail, arrived from Washington and approved our plans. By midnight we had written up and mimeographed detailed orders to issue to unit commanders as soon as they arrived on Sunday morning. Then I went home for a few hours' rest.

Four hours later, at 6:30 a.m., I was back at Hyde Park, shivering in the chill, damp wind. At first the quiet was broken only by the faint cawing of crows in the heavily wooded banks of the Hudson. Soon long convoys of trucks and buses began arriving, and the commands of the quickly briefed leaders could be heard as they formed their units and marched them to their designated positions.

Inside the garden, a florist was arranging truckloads of floral tributes; when occasional gusts blew down the wire standards, he hastily replaced the wreaths.

I had requested a state trooper to keep people from occupying the square of lawn reserved for the cadet battalion. As more and more dignitaries arrived, however, he kept retreating from his post. Finally I had to ask one gentleman to move backward about ten paces. Later the trooper came over and said, "Sir, do you know who that man was you moved? That was Mr. Morgenthau."

After I'd dislodged the secretary of the treasury, I stayed in the rose garden while fellow staff members monitored the formation of the troops outside. When the first cannon boomed, I knew that the motor hearse was moving the half-mile from the railroad. The sound of the guns soon blended with the roar of approaching P-47s, led by a B-25 Mitchell bomber.

Simultaneously the far-off notes of bugles sounding "Hail to the Chief" could be heard as the flag-covered casket was transferred to the horse-drawn funeral caisson. The slow, uphill march of the cortege to the final resting place began. As the procession drew nearer, the muffled drumbeats ended, and the band began to play Chopin's Funeral March.

Behind the black caisson, flanked by enlisted casket bearers chosen from all the services, a United States Military Academy private led the riderless, black-draped horse, the traditional symbol of a fallen commander.

With slow, measured steps, the procession moved along the narrow gravel roads encircling the rose garden. The cadet battalion entered from the west and massed in a solid phalanx of some four hundred men facing east toward the grave. The caisson halted at the garden's narrow gateway. The long journey begun at Warm Springs three days before had come to an end.

The commands "Present arms," "Parade, rest"; the bowed heads; the tear-stained faces: These I remember.

The tall, white-haired Dr. Anthony walked slowly to the graveside. The prayer ended, the minister lifted his right hand in benediction and intoned John Ellerton's hymn: "Now the laborer's task is o'er;/Now the battle day is past. . . ./Father, in thy gracious keeping/Leave we now thy servant sleeping." The casket was lowered into the freshly dug grave.

"Attention, escort, less firing party. Present arms.

"Firing party, fire three volleys.

"Ready, aim, fire!"

Three times eight rifles pointed skyward and cracked simultaneously.

The rifle volleys frightened Mr. Roosevelt's dog, Fala—held on a leash by Margaret Suckley, a cousin of the late president—and the little Scottish terrier barked repeatedly.

As the final volley echoed through the woods, muffled drums rolled once again, and the U.S.M.A. Band's cornet soloist sounded taps. FDR had come home.

After walking out of the garden, Mrs. Roosevelt talked with General Honnen. "General," she said, "I know that you were responsible for this beautiful service. But tell me, what officer arranged the many details? I would like to meet him." As the general graciously introduced me, she smiled, took my hand, and gave me a warm expression of appreciation.

The ceremony had proceeded as planned, despite the haste with which the arrangements had been made. When we departed, our mission complete, it was only eleven o'clock. In a single hour this spot that had been a peaceful, secluded garden for 134 years had become a national shrine.

—Col. A. J. McGehee, U. S. Army Ret.,
lived in Green Valley, Arizona.

BULL SESSION

None of us looked forward to going on duty and standing our watch. Four hours on and four hours off around the clock was not an easy routine. This was especially true if you were a radioman aboard the USS Missouri, flagship for the U.S. 3d Fleet deep in the Pacific Theater of Operations.

The year was 1945. As an eighteen-year-old eligible for the draft, I had enlisted in the Navy before graduation from high school in Davenport, Iowa. After boot camp and radio school, at Farragut, Idaho, I was assigned to the staff of Adm. William F. "Bull" Halsey aboard the Missouri, an Iowa-class battleship.

I felt honored to pull duty as a staff member with a four-star admiral. Halsey usually selected the New Jersey, another Iowa-class ship, but the Jersey had steamed stateside for some badly needed maintenance and repair. The Missouri got the call.

There were seven radio transmitting-and-receiving stations aboard the Missouri, and I usually spent my four hours handling routine communications among ships of the fleet. I had been onboard several weeks and had not even seen the admiral. Then I was transferred to the radio station just behind the ship's bridge. I would be copying coded messages from several military shore stations. When decoded, the transmissions would help our meteorologists map weather conditions over possible Japanese bombing targets. I quickly came to realize the importance of my work. The safety of our carrier pilots might well depend upon the accuracy and thoroughness of the radiomen on duty behind the bridge.

To obtain weather information I usually copied station NPG Honolulu or an Army station from Andrews Air Force Base on Guam. These were clear stations with little interference of any kind. But station KCT from Vladivostok, U.S.S.R., was different.

If our planes were to raid the Japanese islands or Hokkaido or Honsho, we needed the weather report from KCT. The Japanese, knowing this, constantly jammed the KCT frequency with music, loud laughter, foreign languages—anything and everything to drown out the signal. It required keen concentration to find our signal and stay on it while totally ignoring all the "trash."

One evening I was copying KCT with the usual Japanese garbage jamming my frequency. I had my eyes closed, and I was concentrating totally on that faint but distinctive signal: Dit dah dit. I automatically hit the R key on the typewriter (or mill, as the Navy called it). Dah dit dit dit, B. Dit dit dit, S.

Then a loud voice behind me asked, "Are they jamming our station?"

"Yes, sir," I replied, my concentration broken. I hit the space bar of the mill several times to indicate missed letters. I found the signal once again.

"Are you able to copy it?" The voice again. I hit the space bar several more times before finding my signal once more. "Will you be able to get enough for us?" And the space-bar routine again. But this time I blurted out, "Shut up!"

When the transmission was complete, I pulled the message from my machine. Wondering if the blank spaces would ruin our mapmaking effort, I turned in my seat—and looked up at the four stars on each lapel of a brown shirt. I had just met Admiral Halsey.

Oh my God, I thought. I was an insignificant radioman, third class, and I had told an admiral to shut up. At nineteen years my life would end. I would be fortunate to get a court-martial for insubordination along with a dishonorable discharge from the navy.

"Sir, are you the one I told to 'shut up'?"

This tough-looking admiral was standing there with arms folded and legs apart in a mild inverted Y, brown naval field cap pulled to his brow, jaw jutting menacingly with lips pressed firmly together. I could see now why they called him Bull Halsey.

"Yes, lad," he blared.

"I apologize, sir. I did not know it was you. I have no excuse, sir."

The admiral broke his stance and began to pace the floor. "Lad," he bellowed, "when I come into this radio shack and speak to you while you are on that radio, you do not tell me to shut up! do you understand?" His voice boomed like the nine 16-inch guns attached to the ship's three main turrets.

"Yes, sir, I understand." I was frozen at attention and, I am certain, tears were welling up in my eyes.

Then, stopping in front of me and looking me straight in the eye, he went on in a very calm and friendly voice. "If I or anyone else ever bothers you while you are on that radio, you do not tell them to shut up. What you tell them is get the hell out of here and that's an order. Do you understand, lad?"

I could only look at him and stammer, "Yes, sir."

We saluted. Admiral Halsey went on his way. I never met him again.

—Robert Roddewig, a retired history teacher, lives in Michigan.

Admiral William Halsey, skipper of the third fleet in the Pacific theater during World War II.

TRIUMPH AND TRAGEDY

It was the second of May, 1945, six days before the end of the war in Europe. We were members of Headquarters Battery, 608th Field Artillery Battalion, 71st Infantry Division—one of the spearheads of Patton's 3d Army, driving south through a conquered Germany toward Austria, the last unoccupied part of Hitler's Reich. Bridges over the Inn River, between Bavaria and Austria, had been wrecked by retreating German troops, but a large hydroelectric dam with a roadway on it was still intact, and that was our objective this beautiful spring morning.

There were four of us in the jeep. I was the driver, a twenty-one-year-old private first class. Beside me sat a first lieutenant, not much older than myself, and on the rear seat were a staff sergeant and a corporal, whose job was to operate the .50-caliber machine gun mounted between the seats. This was an unusually large weapon for a jeep at that time; some jeeps had .30-caliber machine guns, but most had none.

This formidable weapon had probably been given to us because, as members of a survey section, we were often by ourselves, away from the rest of the battalion, plotting new positions for the howitzers almost every day of that final, hectic offensive. Whatever the reason, we were glad to have it.

The jeep, not a roomy vehicle under any circumstances, was unbelievably crowded. In addition to four men and a machine gun, there was a large box of .50-caliber ammunition, a bulky radio, a five-gallon gas can, a five-gallon water can, rifles, grenades, maps, and sleeping bags. The sergeant and corporal sometimes had trouble finding a place to sit; for much of our thousand-mile odyssey across Western Europe, the sergeant perched precariously on the right rear wheel cover, clinging to the cylindrical machine-gun mount. Behind the jeep was the other vehicle of the section, a three-quarter-ton weapons carrier, a homely but rugged vehicle, practical and reliable. It carried the rest of the men in the section and the battalion's surveying instruments, equipment vital to an artillery unit. We in the jeep presented a more dashing appearance than our companions, partly because of that menacing gun, but they had the distinct advantage of being protected from the elements by a canvas top. We were a rather independent bunch, probably because our job kept us away from the main body of troops much of the time. We liked it that way.

The ten men of the survey section formed a cosmopolitan group. In the jeep alone the four of us were from four different parts of the country and from four different ethnic backgrounds. The lieutenant, from the Midwest, was Italian; the sergeant was a blond Scandinavian from the far West; the corporal was from somewhere in Appalachia; and I was from the Susquehanna Valley of central Pennsylvania, of British and German ancestry.

Among the others were a Southerner, a Californian, and someone from the upper Midwest. One of our members spoke fluent French, and another spoke fluent German, so it was fairly easy for us to deal with civilians, displaced persons, and prisoners of war. Our German-speaking member was Earnie, a Viennese Jew, a refugee from Nazi persecution. He was the driver of the three-quarter-ton, and like many European city dwellers, he was neither a good nor a courteous driver. After a number of minor scrapes and near misses, we began drawing silhouettes in chalk on the side of the truck of everything he had hit or come close to hitting: geese, horses, oxen, people, wagons, trucks, tanks, jeeps, and howitzers. Earnie wasn't insulted; he liked our joke.

Now, as we approached the border of the homeland he had left almost a decade before, I was aware of his mounting excitement. I knew he hoped we would go all the way to Vienna, at the eastern end of the country, but that seemed highly unlikely; I was almost sure the Russians were already there. Still, the remote possibility that we might somehow reach Vienna caused me to wonder, as we neared the Inn River, what it would be like for Earnie, or for any European Jew who had survived the war, to return to his old home and neighborhood and confront former Gentile friends and acquaintances—people who, while Germany was winning, never expected to see a Jew again.

We reached the Inn River dam around midmorning, and, following the directions of a military police (MP) officer, I drove onto its narrow top. Behind us stretched the battalion in convoy, a long line of trucks, 105-mm howitzers, and jeeps. In front of us there was no one. Because of the machine gun, the battalion commander often assigned us the dubious honor of being the lead vehicle. I had the uneasy feeling that we were leading not only the battalion but the whole division. I didn't realize it at the time, but except for reconnaissance troops and engineers, we were apparently leading the 3d Army into Austria.

On one side of us were millions of gallons of water, lapping a few feet from the jeep's wheels, and on the other side was a long drop to the river gorge below. As we started across, the lieutenant announced that our engineers had said that the dam was safe, that most of the dynamite planted in it by retreating Germans had been removed, and that wires leading to the remaining charges had been cut. Apparently he had picked up this disconcerting information at the morning briefing. His remark was supposed to be reassuring, but it had the opposite effect on me. I had a momentary vision of a gigantic explosion, of men, machines, and tons of water plunging to the gorge below. I wanted fervently to get off this monstrous pile of concrete.

But then I looked at the tree-lined opposite bank, and in a moment more pleasant thoughts occupied my mind. In a political sense that bank was part of Germany, but in reality it was in another country. I had very romantic notions about Austria; I had always thought of it as a very beautiful, idyllic place, and its name brought to my mind other pleasing names: Strauss, Mozart, Hedy Lamarr, the Danube, the Alps, Vienna, Salzburg, the Tirol.

In a few minutes we were safely across the Inn River. And here a strange, surprising, and very pleasant reception awaited us. There was no town, only woods, but hundreds of people, mostly women and girls, had lined both sides of the road, waving, smiling, cheering, and throwing flowers in our path. Apparently they had learned of our imminent arrival from the reconnaissance troops and had walked here from a nearby town, carrying armfuls of flowers.

We were stunned. For the past two months German civilians had met us with silence, occasional weeping, and sullen, hostile stares. What a startling, refreshing change! It seemed unreal, dreamlike, and I experienced an eerie feeling of déjà vu. I knew that conquering Roman legions had sometimes been greeted in this manner, and I had a very real vision of the Teutonic ancestors of these people greeting victorious Romans two millennia ago.

My déjà vu passed, and in a moment we all had recovered from our surprise, and we began smiling and waving in return. It was a beautiful, sunny, slightly cool spring morning. Many of these Fräuleins, in their colorful dirndls and peasant blouses, were extraordinarily pretty. The war was nearly over, and the retreating Wehrmacht seemed to have disappeared into thin air. It was hard to feel animosity toward anyone.

As the pleasant sounds of our unexpected welcome faded behind us, we picked up speed and continued southward. We had apparently lost all contact with the retreating German forces. We came out of the woods lining the Inn River and saw spread before us a countryside of breathtaking beauty. It was an area of rolling hills, green patches of woods, sunlit fields, hamlets, and farms. The sweet smell of newly cut hay perfumed the air, and in the distance a great range of the Alps rose majestically above the lesser hills.

Years after the war I would wonder how this beautiful little country, this fairy-tale land, could have produced two of the most evil men in history, Adolf Hitler and Adolf Eichmann—one a mad, hypnotic demagogue who plunged the world into the worst war in its history and the other his lieutenant, who supervised the extermination of millions of people, who planned and directed the rail system that funneled those people to the death camps, and who helped develop the chief means of those mass murders, the gas chamber.

Hitler had been born in Braunau, not far from where we were right now. Eichmann came from Linz, a picturesque town about sixty miles east of Braunau, also on a river, the Danube. In 1945 few people in Germany, and fewer still outside, had heard of Adolf Eichmann. He seemed to have deliberately kept a low profile, avoiding publicity and avoiding being photographed. It was as if he had instinctively known that he might someday become a fugitive.

In late afternoon we pulled into the hamlet where we would spend the night. For nearly two months Headquarters Battery had spent almost every night in a different town, in the homes of civilians. We saw no reason to change this practice now, even though we were in a more friendly country. As we had done in Germany, we simply picked out houses we wished to occupy and evicted the inhabitants. But we did try to be a little more polite now that we were in Austria.

In Germany we simply knocked loudly on the door of a house, and when someone timidly answered, usually a woman or an elderly man, we would hand that person a piece of paper. On the paper was a typewritten paragraph in German, stating that the occupants had ten minutes to get out, taking with them whatever they could collect in that time. If we were in a generous mood, we sometimes gave them more time. If we were in a bad mood, we sometimes gave them less.

It was tranquil and almost eerily quiet that first evening in Austria. I have long since forgotten, if I ever knew it, the name of the village. It looked like most Central European hamlets—a picturesque cluster of houses dominated by the onion-dome spires of a church, nestled in the foothills of the mountains. It must have been in the western part of Upper Austria, somewhere north of Salzburg.

To our surprise and great satisfaction, the survey section found itself in a house that apparently belonged to a well-to-do family. It was an unusual house to find in a rural setting, not large but tastefully and expensively furnished. One member of the section headed immediately for the cellars of the homes we occupied and kept us well supplied with excellent wine, much of it originally looted from France by the Germans. We were enjoying some of that wine now, as we relaxed in the attractive living room.

Much to our surprise, the power was still on in the area, and as darkness fell we turned on lights, and more from force of habit than any real danger, we pulled down shades as a precaution against German artillery. The sergeant was in the kitchen, heating the rations for our evening meal. He would have delegated this chore, but apparently he was enjoying the luxury of a working stove.

The section was fortunate in having two excellent leaders, the sergeant and the lieutenant. They performed their jobs with efficiency and dispatch and required us to do the same, while maintaining what seemed an ideal level of discipline, not too much and not too little. Like the rest of us, they were citizen soldiers, not career men.

In spite of a few minor instances of friction, the lieutenant and I liked each other and got along very well. We had shared a number of escapades in the past two months, some humorous, some harrowing. On one occasion we had been lost, on a very dark night, in a rural area between the rapidly changing front lines. It was a dangerous place to be lost. Ordinarily we would not be driving at night, but this was an exception. We were trying to find our way by the jeep's blackout lights, which threw a faint glow about twenty feet in front of the hood. The lieutenant was crouched in his seat, holding a flashlight over a map, frantically trying to determine where we were.

Suddenly, above the sound of our own engine, there was the sound of other engines, monstrous engines, coming toward us. In a panic we turned off quickly into the adjacent field, stopped, turned off the blackout lights, and seconds later watched with pounding hearts as four huge tanks clanked past only yards away.

"Sir!" I said hoarsely. "Those tanks have low silhouettes! They're—"

"German!" he interjected in a shaky voice. (When we were scared, we used the word German. Otherwise it was always Kraut.) Panic-stricken, we waited until that frightening rumbling had faded in the distance, then returned to the road. We proceeded at about twenty miles an hour in the direction from which the tanks had come, expecting to be fired on at any moment. At the next intersection we turned, still lost, and eventually, miraculously, we were back with the battalion, relieved, exhausted, and shaken.

One day the lieutenant shot and killed a German soldier. It was a situation in which he had no choice but to do what he did. After being ordered to halt, the man panicked and ran. If he had stood still and put up his hands, he would have lived. If he had escaped, as he nearly did, he could have taken with him information damaging to us, and he himself could have killed Americans later. But the incident preyed on the lieutenant's mind, and for days he hardly spoke to anyone. Up to that time I had wanted a chance to use my rifle against the enemy, but after that I changed my mind.

Although the battalion's howitzers caused casualties among the enemy almost daily, by the very nature of artillery we were behind the lines most of the time and did not have a clear idea of the violence at the front. But on one occasion I saw something an artilleryman doesn't often see. I saw what we were shooting at.

Once, about four o'clock in the morning, one of the gun batteries was dug in on a hillside overlooking a narrow valley in the Harz Mountains. The enemy was in sight, or would be, with the first light of dawn. Across that valley, perhaps a quarter of a mile away, about a hundred German troops were reportedly asleep in a large wooden building, some sort of factory or warehouse. In the darkness we could just make out its faint outline. Incredibly, our gun crews had dug in and prepared the guns for firing without the enemy's hearing them, although that dark valley was absolutely still.

Unless they intended to leave before dawn, when we could fire accurately, or unless we accidentally gave away our presence, the enemy troops were doomed. They were trapped, without even knowing the were trapped. They were sleeping the last hour of their lives. Those Germans were remnants of a once-elite SS division we had been pursuing and decimating. Perhaps sheer exhaustion on their part had enabled us to come this close without being detected.

The lieutenant and I stood with a group of officers, behind and to one side of the battery. We had nothing to do but observe. Everyone spoke in a hushed voice. All was in readiness. A shell was in the chamber of each of the four howitzers, with more shells stacked behind them.

Finally the dawn came, and with it an extraordinarily clear light, so clear that small details could be seen at a great distance. Then it began. A few quick, quiet commands to the gunners peering through their sights, and all four gun barrels moved slightly, staying parallel with each other. The executive officer stood like a statue, his arm raised. The section chief of number two stood the same way, while the man with the lanyard was also poised and ready. Then came the hushed, tense command: "Number two, one round! Fire!" The arms came down, the cannoneer pulled the lanyard sharply, the howitzer roared and leaped, and the first, adjusting round was on its way. It fell a little short, a puff of white smoke a few yards in front of the building, followed by the dull thud of the explosion. I saw two tiny figures run out the front door. Probably they were the only ones to escape.

A quick command to adjust the battery, and the four gun barrels elevated slightly. Then the shouted command: "Battery! Six rounds! Fire at will!" In a moment all four 105s were firing, as twenty-four high-explosive shells began to bracket the target. Explosion after explosion rocked the building. The officer standing next to me offered me his binoculars; perhaps he didn't want to see too clearly what was happening. Through the glasses I could see debris being blown into the air, silhouetted against the reddish orange of the explosions and flames. Horrified, I saw that some of that debris was unmistakably in the form of human bodies. "Oh, my God!" I thought. I handed back the binoculars. "Those are SS men!" I reminded myself. "The scourge of Europe! They deserve to die!" Still, it was an unnerving sight.

One the fourth of May we ran our last surveys. The gun batteries were placed in the positions we surveyed, but I don't think they ever fired from them. The war was winding down rapidly. To our great relief the retreating enemy continued southward and eastward, across relatively open country. There had been an ominous rumor that some German units might turn westward and make a final, suicidal stand in the Alpine Redoubt, a rugged area that would have been very costly to attack. But that didn't happen. Now they would be squeezed between the 7th and the 3d armies (our own 71st would be the most eastward division of all the Western armies when the war ended on May 8), the Russians moving west from Vienna, and the British 8th and American 5th armies coming northward from Italy. It was almost over.

The section came back glumly from the survey that morning to the hamlet in which we had spent the past day and a half, but not to the same attractive little house. Instead we went to the larger, rather drab house from which headquarters was operating.

As we pulled up and stopped, we were mildly surprised to see a German soldier sitting on a low wall. A member of headquarters section explained that the man had just surrendered, and he was our prisoner until the MPs came for him.

I felt a moment of empathy with that forlorn-looking figure. He wasn't young—perhaps about forty—and he looked small and frail and harmless with his horn-rimmed glasses and an overcoat that seemed too large for him. His uniform showed him to be a Luftwaffe corporal. He looked rather scholarly to me, and I thought perhaps he had been a university professor in civilian life. "Poor fellow," I thought. "He shouldn't even be in uniform." Because of his frail appearance, I assumed he had had some sort of desk job.

We waited in two vehicles while the lieutenant and sergeant went into the house to report to the battalion commander. We paid little attention to the German sitting a few yards from us, and he paid little attention to us. The sky was overcast, and rain seemed imminent. In a few minutes the sergeant came out and ordered us all inside. He assigned my friend Dick, the Californian, and me to bring in the prisoner and take charge of him until the MPs arrived.

I grabbed my carbine, got out of the jeep, approached the man, and said, "Kommen Sie mit uns!" That brief sentence represented a major part of my German vocabulary.

"I speak English," he responded in a heavy accent and with a sharp edge in his voice that took me by surprise. It was unmistakably contempt. He stood up slowly and arrogantly, looking at me with a mixture of derision and condescension. Startled, I took a closer look at our prisoner, and I was rather unnerved by what I saw. His features were ordinary, except for a thin face and sharp nose. He was a couple of inches shorter than I was, and behind those studious-looking glasses were the coldest eyes I had ever seen in my life. As disconcerting as the eyes was the strange, faint smile on his lips. It was not a friendly smile. It was a smile that seemed to say that its owner had a secret, a secret that he had no intention of divulging but that was a source of great amusement to him. The sergeant told us to take him to a room on the second floor.

"Upstairs!" I said, indicating with my carbine that he should follow Dick up the narrow steps. Again, as he had done outside, he waited a moment, obviously to let me know he wasn't going to jump at my command. As we started up the steps, he gave me another contemptuous glance with those cold eyes and that unpleasant little smile. It seemed to irritate him to be ordered about, and yet, in a perverse sort of way, it also seemed to amuse him. This was a puzzling situation. No other prisoner I had dealt with had acted this way. I was beginning to believe we had a rather unusual person on our hands. And I was beginning to regret having felt a moment of empathy with that person.

As we went up the stairs, one possible reason for his odd demeanor suddenly occurred to me. "This guy acts as if he once had a lot of authority," I thought.

The upstairs room was big and cluttered with furniture. Other members of the section were already there, sprawled in chairs or on the floor. We took the German to one end of the room, and Dick, pointing to a chair, said, "Sitten Sie!" As he sat down, the man gave Dick the same hostile, arrogant look he had been giving me, but my friend didn't seem to notice.

I asked a couple of the others to watch the prisoner for a few minutes and took Dick outside. I felt I had to share my suspicion with someone. "Dick," I

Adolf Eichmann, in an undated Nazi file photograph.

said, "there's something odd about this guy! He acts very haughty, very superior. He acts more like an officer than an enlisted man. I have a feeling he isn't what he seems to be."

Dick shrugged. "Kraut noncoms have a lot of authority. Privates have to salute them and call them 'sir,' I think. He doesn't like being ordered about by privates—that's all it is. He's just obnoxious. That's not so unusual."

I was unconvinced, but no one seemed concerned by the fact that the German prisoner had no identity papers. What more could be done? If I had gone to anyone of higher rank with my doubts, the answer surely would have been "Let the MPs worry about it!"

So we went back and sat down near our charge. For some reason, one of the more suspicious things about him seemed to have escaped our attention. That was the fact that his uniform didn't fit very well. I suppose we didn't wonder about it because, in the last weeks of the war, we were used to seeing people in all kinds of unusual and ragged apparel, both refugees and members of the Wehrmacht. But our prisoner's clothes weren't unusual or ragged; they just didn't fit. Somehow it never occurred to us that he might be wearing someone else's clothes.

Another odd circumstance did occur to me, but I didn't attach much importance to it. That was the fact that he had surrendered by himself. This was unusual. The enemy almost always surrendered in groups—squads, platoons, companies at the beginning of the offensive and, near the end, battalions, divisions, armies—but almost never a single soldier.

Outside a light rain had begun falling. Our prisoner sat in a chair at one side of a desk, one arm resting on the desk, the sly, enigmatic smile still on his face. I noticed that his hands were clean, delicate, and manicured, like the hands of a woman.

We sat there in silence for a while, glancing at

each other occasionally, and then, since this person spoke English, I asked if he thought the German army might make a last-ditch stand somewhere. He said he was certain that wouldn't happen; the war would probably end in a few days. Dick joined in, remarking on the scenic beauty of both Germany and Austria, an observation with which the prisoner naturally concurred. He then asked us what our ethnic backgrounds were, and when told both of us had British and German ancestors, he seemed pleased.

The conversation turned to the post-war period. I asked what he thought should happen after the war. He suggested that what he termed the Aryan countries—Germany, Great Britain, the Scandinavian countries, the Netherlands, and the United States—form an alliance against the rest of the world, the non-Aryan world. Such an alliance could and should rule the world, he insisted. We thought this idea was preposterous and told him so. He was extremely displeased by our reaction, and the conversation died away.

After many minutes of silence he suddenly asked, "Are there any Jews in your company?"

My first impulse was to correct him and tell him that because we were artillery our basic unit was called a battery, not a company. My next reaction was a very uneasy feeling, one of dread. From the suddenness of the question, from something in his voice, and from the question itself, I got the strong impression that this man was obsessed with Jews. I decided to answer him civilly, to see where this topic might lead.

"Yes, there are a few—five or six, I think," I responded.

"Do you like them?" he asked sharply, almost accusingly.

"Yes, I like them!" I answered irritably. "Well, there's one I don't like very much, but it has nothing to do with his being Jewish. Why do you ask?"

There was a long pause, as if he were considering his answer very carefully. Finally he muttered, "Oh...no reason."

And that was the end of our conversation. It was as if he had suddenly realized it might be wise for him to stop.

Nevertheless, the brief exchange had made me recall something I didn't like to think about—the liberation by the division of the Nordhausen concentration camp. It had happened about a month earlier, in central Germany. Reconnaissance troops and infantry had come upon the place late one April afternoon, and we in the artillery learned of their discovery soon afterward. Nordhausen, a name unknown to most people, held about eighteen thousand prisoners, mostly Hungarian Jews. There were no gas chambers at Nordhausen; the people there were simply worked and starved to death. I learned later that the work they did was on the rocket weapons sent against England. When they died, their bodies were thrown into the ovens, which burned around the clock. The camp was populated by what appeared to be thousands of living skeletons.

The lieutenant got permission to go into the camp. He left most of the section in a farmhouse about half a mile away and went off with the sergeant and two of the corporals. I begged him to take me also, but he refused. I was angry as I watched them drive off without me.

So we had simply waited impatiently for our comrades to return. The owner of the house, whom we had permitted to remain, skulked about, doing his chores. He was extremely nervous and would not look at us directly. He knew what had been found half a mile away. There was an odd, sweet odor in and around that house that, though faint, was extremely offensive. It seemed to be unrelated to normal rural smells. We realized later that the odor came from the ovens and chimneys of the camp, from the smoke of incinerated human bodies, and from a huge pile of rotting corpses in the nearby woods. That smell was, literally, the smell of death. And in that foul-smelling house there was a clammy, greasy film over everything that must also have come from the smoke.

The others came back around ten o'clock. They were very quiet and at first would say nothing about what they had seen. In the pale light of a kerosene lantern their faces were ashen, and we realized we were looking at men almost in a state of shock. After the others were asleep, one of the corporals began to talk to me. He was a person I regarded as a tough, hardened individual, but his voice trembled with emotion as he told me of the camp—of people so thin it seemed impossible that they could be alive; of the overwhelming stench, which almost made him faint; of recoiling in horror as a group of inmates tried to show gratitude for their liberation by touching him with skeletal hands that frightened him; of corpses still in bunks among the living, because no one had the strength to move them; of the ovens, still with bones and skulls in them; and finally of the monstrous pile of bodies in the woods. I had trouble getting to sleep that night.

In the morning we started for the town of Nordhausen in convoy. This time we were near the end of the column. Somewhere between the camp and the town we came upon an incredible sight. Hundreds, perhaps thousands of the former inmates were walking toward the town in a great mass, though the fields on either side of the road. They were almost totally silent. The only sound they made was the rustling of their long, ragged coats against the grass of the fields. They looked like an army of scarecrows, a phalanx of living cadavers.

It was unclear why they had left the camp, where

Army medical personnel were already beginning to help them. Perhaps they just wanted to breathe clean air again and walk in the open as free men. Perhaps they were simply after food in the town. Or perhaps they wanted to confront their tormentors and murderers. I never learned what happened when they reached the town. We gave them what food we could from our rations as we drove slowly through their ranks.

At one point along the road there was a dead horse, probably killed by artillery fire the day before. Two of its legs stuck rigidly into the air, and its entrails lay spilled on the dusty ground. Men were swarming over that dead horse like giant flies, ripping off pieces of flesh with their hands, and eating it. "My God! Look at that!" the sergeant exclaimed. "How hungry do you have to be to do that?"

"Mighty goddamned hungry!" muttered the corporal. Of the four of us, I suspected he was the only one who might have experienced hunger during the Depression.

A little farther along, our slow-moving convoy came to a complete halt. We had been stopped only a few minutes when we saw two boys approaching from the direction of the town, walking leisurely, defiantly along the other side of the road. They appeared to be about fifteen years old, and each wore the brown uniform of the Hitler Youth. They were blond, pink-cheeked, and healthy-looking. As they passed along our column, they were watched with silent hostility, contempt, or indifference. They paid little attention to us, except for an occasional arrogant glance in our direction.

When they were almost opposite my jeep, they suddenly saw the vanguard of the starving Jews, who were coming up behind us and were now walking on the highway. The two boys stopped in their tracks, utter amazement on their faces. Then, incredibly, they began to laugh. They nudged each other, pointed at the Jews, made comments, and continued to laugh uproariously.

It was as if the devil himself were hurling a final insult at those tormented people. We were dumbfounded and enraged. In desperation I turned to the lieutenant. "Sir! What should we do? Shoot them?"

"Are you crazy, Shields? That would be murder!"

"We ought to do something! They're the murderers! They whole goddamned country are murderers!"

Those two young Nazis probably never realized how close they came to dying on that road. I know others in that column were considering using their weapons to stop that laughter. I thought momentarily of shooting over their heads, to shut them up. Then I decided I would get out of the jeep, cross the road, and begin bashing in their faces with the butt of my carbine. But at that moment the convoy began moving again. The last I saw of this drama was the two boys and the army of living skeletons approaching each other. I have often wondered what happened when they met.

Soon we were in the town, driving along the main street. It appeared to be one of the older, more picturesque towns, the kind one sees on postcards, with high-gabled, medieval-looking houses flanking the street. As in all the other towns we had entered that spring, white sheets hung from upstairs windows as a sign of surrender. But something was different in Nordhausen. The people here behaved differently. They saw the ugly mood of their conquerors, and they knew what had caused that mood. Instead of congregating along the main street, as was done in other towns, most remained indoors and watched our entrance silently and furtively from upstairs windows. In the other towns I had seen a variety of emotions on people's faces as we drove past them: fear, anger, hatred, anxiety, shock, dismay, and occasionally even friendliness. But on the faces of the people

of Nordhausen I saw a single emotion, one I hadn't seen before in Germany: guilt.

There were pretty girls in those windows of Nordhausen. Blonde, shapely girls wearing colorful peasant outfits. A month earlier, when we first entered German from Alsace, we had regarded all Germans with hostility. Then, as the weeks passed, we had begun to relax a little, reacting to attractive members of the opposite sex in a more normal way. We would stare at them, smile at them, whistle at them, and occasionally make lewd remarks, in English and in German. But we did not smile at the girls of Nordhausen.

As we neared the center of town the unnatural silence was broken. Ahead of us we could hear angry voices, and we could see some sort of commotion. Uniformed men were milling about in a little park-like area up ahead on the right. As we got closer we could make out three kinds of uniforms—MP, infantry, and some unfamiliar green ones without insignia.

We were extremely puzzled. We had never encountered anything like this before. Then we began to distinguish the words being shouted. "Kill them! Kill them! Torture them! Beat them up! Give them to us. We'll take care of them!" As we got closer we could see that the MPs were halfheartedly trying to protect the men in green, while a group of infantrymen were striking at them with rifle butts and fists.

Suddenly I realized what was going on. "Sir! Those must be guards from the camp!"

In a moment we were abreast of the melee. The lieutenant and corporal remained stoically silent as we passed the ugly scene, but from the back seat the sergeant, his face contorted with rage, shook his fist and shouted, "Kill them! Kill the bastards! Kill the murdering sons of bitches!"

Something seemed to snap in my mind. I reached in front of the startled lieutenant and shook my fist. "Kill them!" I cried. "Kill them! Kill them! Kill them!" A few minutes later we were again outside the town, in the quiet countryside, headed south. I knew I would remember the name of Nordhausen the rest of my life.

Having asked the questions that reminded me of these recent, grim events, our prisoner remained sunk in silence. After about an hour someone came up the stairs and said the MPs had arrived. Dick and I took the prisoner downstairs and out to the front of the house, where two MPs were waiting. They put him in their jeep and drove off. We said nothing to him, and he said nothing to us as he departed, but he gave us one final, chilling look with those cold eyes and that mysterious little smile. We both were relieved to see him go.

Exactly fifteen years later, in May 1960, I saw that face again and almost immediately recognized it, staring coldly from television screens and from the front pages of newspapers, beneath headlines saying Eichmann captured!

The man I guarded for about an hour that day, and spoke with briefly, was surely Adolf Eichmann.

Army records show that we were in the area in which Eichmann, according to sketchy biographical and autobiographical accounts, surrendered to American troops, on the day he said he surrendered. He said that he surrendered alone and in disguise, that disguise being a Luftwaffe corporal's uniform. In the last days of the war I saw thousands of surrendering Germans, but of those thousands I remembered only one face, and that one was identical to the face in the rare photographs of Adolf Eichmann. The ill-fitting Luftwaffe uniform had proved to be one of the great disguises of history and had earned for its wearer fifteen years of uneasy freedom, seventeen more years of life altogether. Fifteen years later that name and that face would be known by much of the world, but on that spring day in 1945, in that peaceful Austrian hamlet, there were only two who knew the terrible secret. There were only two who knew that behind that ordinary face with the icy smile there was unspeakable evil. There were only two who knew that the blood of innocent millions dripped from those manicured hands: Eichmann himself and his Creator.

—Stephen Shields is a writer living in Chagrin Falls, Ohio.

NO ANSWER

In 1945 I was a member of a super-secret Army intelligence unit attached to the Manhattan Project, which produced the atomic bomb. We were sent to a desert camp called Trinity, northwest of Alamogordo, New Mexico; our assignment was to cover the area within a hundred-mile radius of zero point so that we could remove residents quickly if the mushroom cloud blew toward them spewing radioactive dust.

The blast was scheduled for July 16, 1945, at 4:00 a.m. A fellow agent, Harold Jensen, and I drew Socorro, a little town northwest of ground zero, as our vantage point. A soaking thunderstorm was in progress as we parked our car outside town to avoid attracting attention at that early hour.

We waited until four-thirty. Then until five o'clock. Strangely, nothing happened even after the storm had abated. Had there been a postponement? We drove into Socorro to call from a pay phone in the lobby of a small hotel—we had been given codes so that we would not reveal the secret—but there was no response from the operator. The phone was dead.

We knew that all telephone communications from Los Alamos to the desert test site went through Socorro, and it was vital that scientists and engineers in Los Alamos and Santa Fe communicate with authorities in the desert who were preparing the test.

We had to find out what had happened to disrupt communications.

We tracked down the telephone exchange by following overhead cables. The switchboard turned out to be in a private home, as were many in small towns back then. From the porch we could see scores of lights flickering, indicating that officials were frantically trying to get through.

Unaware of her key role in the momentous test, the operator was sound asleep on a cot beside the switchboard. I pounded on the door. She came out rubbing her eyes. I nodded toward the switchboard, and she sprang to work, putting through the calls.

That did it.

Jensen and I returned to our outpost and sat on the front fender of the car to watch the show. At five-thirty the detonation took place: no sound at first, just a giant, bright, yellow fireball like a super-sun that hurt the eyes. In a few moments came the sound of a drummer striking a huge drum, but we felt no concussion or strong wind.

Like everyone else, Jensen and I kept the explosion secret until August 6, 1945, when President Truman announced "the most terrible destructive force in history."

—Al Bennett lives in Everett, Washington, and is the retired managing editor of the *Everett Herald*.

Scientists and workmen rig the world's first atomic bomb to raise it up into a 100-foot tower at the Trinity bomb test site in the desert near Alamagordo, New Mexico, in July 1945.

ASLEEP AT THE CREATION

I was a young war bride in the summer of 1945. A slap-happy one, recently wed to my college sweetheart, a football star from Hardin-Simmons University, for whom I had waited while he flew twenty-five dangerous missions over Europe as a B-17 bombardier. That had taken at least a year; now he was back, we'd had our war wedding, and we were stationed at a base in Alamogordo, New Mexico. He was busy every day from dawn to sunset, training crews in the new B-29 bombers for the invasion of

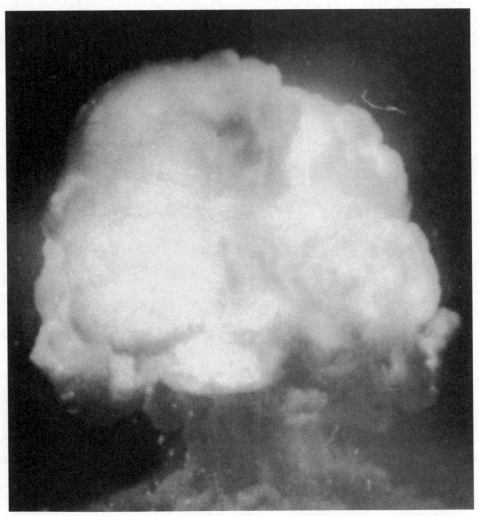

The first U.S. atom bomb explodes during a test in Alamogordo, New Mexico, in 1945.

Japan. I worked all day as a secretary in something mysterious called air inspection. My life consisted of shopping for privileged goods in the PX, flirting with handsome grounded officers who couldn't fly for one reason or another, and meeting my captain at night in the officers' club for dinner and too many drinks. Sometimes we would go out to the White Sands at night, to bury bottles of beer deep in the ice-cold gypsum sand and sit on the dunes, watching the moon rise. It was a romantic, thrilling, mindless time. My husband wanted to forget the horrible things he'd experienced in the 8th Air Force. He never talked about his memories. He made lots of cynical wisecracks, such as "The last time I saw Paris, the sky was full of flak." The truth was he had survived where others in his crew had not. He never mentioned Japan, but I knew he was dreading it.

I was too young, silly, and addle-brained to take anything—even his possible death—seriously. To me, Hitler, Mussolini, and Tojo were cartoon characters who would easily be vanquished by American right and might in the end. My life was fun and games: getting gasoline coupons and keeping up with all the latest swing music, plus playing Myrna Loy in real life, without too much success.

In the predawn of July 16 a shattering blast literally blew us out of bed in the little frame house we were sharing with an Air Force officer named Moskowitz and his glamorous former Copacabana showgirl wife. (The house had been divided into two apartments for the housing shortage.) We all ran outside in our nightclothes but couldn't see what had happened. Later the Air Force issued a formal statement that an ammunition dump had exploded. We thought no more about it but learned that the blast had shattered windows eighty miles away in El Paso.

Three weeks later, on August 6, all was revealed. We had been present, asleep, in fact, at the creation. The first atomic bomb had been exploded in the Los Alamos desert near Alamogordo. The Manhattan Project, which none of us knew existed at the time, had reached fruition. My husband said musingly, "Remember, I told you there was something out there in the twelve-mile area of the White Sands desert that they forbade us to fly over when we were training. It must have been the site of the bomb. I wondered what could be in that danged desert that was a secret."

Now President Truman had ordered that one of the only two other atomic bombs in existence be dropped on Hiroshima, and in that terrible moment of epic tragedy we only knew it was good news. It meant my husband and thousands like him would not have to chance death in the invasion of Japan. We had never heard of John Hersey, radiation sickness, the apocalypse; but it was the end of innocence, and there was no turning back. We simply celebrated the end of the war.

Years later I went back to Alamogordo, a dusty, unassuming little town where only the bowling alley and the post office seemed to matter. I was surprised to find that the residents had proudly posted on the outskirts of town a sign reading alamogordo: home of the atom bomb. By then I had learned that this was a dubious distinction. I was already living through what Margaret Mead came to call "the real Generation Gap." She said it consisted of those born before and after the invention of the Bomb. She was right, of course.

—Liz Smith has been a national syndicated columnist since the 1970s.

BIT PART IN A BIG THEATER

It was the summer of 1945. The fighting was over in Europe, Japan was on the brink of collapse, and I was on the island of Tinian in the Marianas, putting out a mimeographed newspaper and worrying the war might end before I got anywhere near the action. But in the coming weeks I found myself an obscure player in three immense events: the birth of the atomic age, the surrender of Japan, and the start of the Cold War.

One afternoon early in August I sat sweating in a Quonset hut complaining about distribution problems of the Tinian Times to Capt. Joe Buscher, an intelligence officer with the 393d Bombardment Squadron, a somewhat mysterious B-29 outfit. Buscher seemed preoccupied, and he interrupted our talk with a strange suggestion: "If I suddenly have to leave, why don't you follow me, stick right with me, and if anybody asks who you are, tell them you're with me. It'll be something you'll never forget."

A few minutes later Buscher stiffened, grabbed his cap, and bounded out the door. I was right behind him as he rushed up to a truck that was discharging a group of men in flying gear. Out of the corner of my eye I noticed a gaggle of U.S. Army Air Forces brass greeting the fliers and recognized one of them as Carl Spaatz, commanding general of the Army's Strategic Air Forces in the Pacific. Buscher pounced on one of the airmen, who was carrying a bulky instrument that proved to be a camera, and hustled him away from the group in the direction of another Quonset hut. I was two steps behind them as they entered what turned out to be a darkroom. The man with the camera quickly unloaded the film and deposited it in a tray of chemicals. Everybody crowded around him. No one

Yamada (second from left) learns of the surrender from Lieutenant Reifsnyder.

spoke as the film was developed, dried, and put into an enlarger.

Finally the airman held up an eight-by-ten print, still dripping with developer. In the faint red glow of the darkroom's safelight I beheld what would become one of the most memorable images of the twentieth century: the mushroom cloud rising over the city of Hiroshima. There was a collective gasp and mutterings of wonder from the group. My own reaction included bewilderment, since I had not been in on the atomic secret. The airmen, of course, were members of the crew of the Enola Gay, fresh from their historic mission. The 393d Bombardment Squadron was part of the 509th Composite Group, and the date was August 6, 1945.

My second brush with history began a few weeks later and had a comic-opera touch to it. It was prompted by Emperor Hirohito's August fifteenth radio address announcing Japan's surrender and ordering servicemen who had been bypassed by the twin American offensives across the Pacific to lay down their arms. Just off the southern shores of Tinian was the island of Aguijan, a fortress-like rock with sheer cliffs all around, topped by the overgrown remnants of a sugar plantation. We knew a reinforced infantry company was stranded there, along with a hundred or so Japanese civilians, mostly families of the soldiers who had been part of the garrison on Tinian before the U.S. invasion the year before. We assumed that they would have had no way to hear the emperor's speech since their battery supply would have long since been used up.

The island commander on Tinian, Brig. Gen. Frederick V.H. Kimble, borrowed a shallow-draft Coast Guard patrol boat and a Navy lieutenant who spoke fluent Japanese and ordered him to arrange a surrender.

I decided this would make a good story for the Tinian Times and invited myself aboard. On Friday, August 20, the little craft set off and slowly circled Aguijan, with Lt. John G. Reifsnyder calling to the Japanese commander of the island over a loudspeaker.

"Yamada, oshee," he bawled over and over again, using the name provided by Naval Intelligence. Occasionally Reifsnyder would add a phrase or two about the bombing of Hiroshima and Nagasaki and the emperor's directive. But nothing stirred on the island. We saw no sign that our message had been heard, or even that a human soul resided there. At nightfall we quit and sailed back to Tinian. The effort resumed the next day and continued for almost a week until, on the afternoon of August 26, somebody on the boat spotted a white cloth waving from the top of a pathway cut in the cliff. Reifsnyder decided it was too late in the day to do anything except tell the Japanese over the loudspeaker that he would return the next morning.

A thick fog enveloped Aguijan as we approached the next day. We could just make out the dark gray bulk of the island looming ahead when our boat stopped and a small landing craft pulled up alongside, ready to take Lieutenant Reifsnyder ashore. As sailors tried to steady the two craft, he gingerly climbed down into the waiting boat. I was leaning over the rail as he clambered past me with a grim look.

Then a totally unexpected thing happened, something that might be called an out-of-body-experience. A khaki-clad wraith-like figure suddenly vaulted over the railing and into the landing craft. I seemed to be watching in amazement until I realized that it was I who was Reifsnyder's unbidden fellow traveler. A startled Reifsnyder looked at me with what seemed like relief as the boat headed for a rock formation that served as a landing at the base of Aguijan.

On the escarpment looming above us we could

see the snouts of several Nambu machine guns aimed in our direction. Three gaunt figures, Japanese officers in tattered uniforms, began descending the trail as we scrambled frantically onto the slippery rocks. When they arrived, the three awkwardly saluted, and instinctively I stepped aside and took a picture. The conversation between Reifsnyder and Yamada began slowly, with expressions of bewilderment showing on the faces of the Japanese, who said very little. Curious, I tugged on the lieutenant's sleeve and asked what was happening. He explained that he was trying to get them to understand what the atomic bomb had done to the two cities it had struck. Then he resumed his dialogue with Yamada. Occasionally I asked for further clarification of the one-sided discussion. Finally the Japanese commander's side of the conversation began to expand, a smile of satisfaction crossed Reifsnyder's face, and the talks ended.

On the way back to the Coast Guard vessel, Reifsnyder told us that Yamada wanted time to talk to the civilians on the island and that he would have an answer the following day. The lieutenant added, "While these talks continue, I'm afraid you're going to have to keep being my partner. When I kept stopping to fill you in, they got the impression I was your interpreter and that you are demanding their surrender. I figured I might as well leave it that way."

Although General Kimble was not happy about it, he allowed me to play this role as we continued the negotiations. We brought Yamada's two deputies to Tinian to listen to a Signal Corps receiver that pulled in Radio Tokyo and the emperor's voice to the satisfaction, and profound sorrow, of the two officers. I sat in on discussions with Yamada about details of the surrender ceremony, which was planned to coincide with the big one aboard the USS Missouri set for September 2 in Tokyo Bay.

After some interservice wrangling it was decided that an admiral from Guam would formally accept Yamada's surrender on a destroyer off the coast of Aguijan. At that point I offered some advice based on informal conversations I had had with Yamada. "The officer gets seasick," I said. "He is very worried about that possibility and would like to sign the papers on land." My suggestion was ignored.

Getting the actual surrender document from Washington caused a delay, so we were two days behind the Tokyo ceremony. Also, the waters surrounding the island were found to be too shallow for a destroyer. Finally, on the morning of September 4, with our Coast Guard boat anchored off Aguijan, an admiral's gig arrived bearing a stern-faced rear admiral named Marshall Greer, dressed in summer whites, resplendent with campaign ribbons and gold braid.

When Yamada climbed aboard from a landing craft, his greenish pallor matched the color of his faded uniform. He looked even smaller than he had at our first meeting, encumbered as he was with an outsized dispatch case. The confined deck space on the slender vessel posed a problem: where to place the surrender documents for the signing. Finally the skipper of the Coast Guard boat suggested using the cover of a ventilator just behind the wheelhouse, and that was where the parties arrayed themselves, the Americans on one side and the three Japanese on the other. Nobody invited me to be part of the U.S. contingent, so I positioned myself directly behind Yamada.

After someone read the contents of the surrender document, the signing began. In the meantime I had noticed Yamada occasionally bending over his big dispatch case. I knew he was ill, but the rest of the group was oblivious of any impending disaster until the Japanese 2d lieutenant leaned forward to inscribe his name on the document. He threw up, loudly and spectacularly, spewing the stuff on the papers and the Americans directly across from him, including the admiral. Thus did World War II formally end for the garrison of Aguijan Island.

There was one postscript. Several days later, as had been agreed by the parties, the evacuation of the soldiers and civilians from Aguijan was scheduled to get under way. A number of large landing craft were anchored close to the landing, and a small party of officers huddled there, deciding how to manage this complicated logistical maneuver. I had tagged along, and while the group conferred, I headed up the pathway to the top of the cliff. When I got there I found the Japanese standing in two orderly groups, the soldiers on one side, the elderly men, women, and children on the other, rifles and automatic weapons neatly stacked between them.

Yamada was standing in front of the two groups, and as I approached him, he called me by name, bowed, and presented me with his sword. I detected a knowing smile on his usually somber face. The formal ceremonies of the other day notwithstanding, Yamada was surrendering his island to me.

I had one last brush with history in those momentous final weeks. Ever since my arrival on Tinian I had been asking people for a ride on a B-29. Finally, early in September, I was told that I could have it if I were to report to a certain building on North Field at midnight. When I got there, I was ushered into a brightly lighted hall crowded with flight crews. At the front of the room, before a huge map of the western Pacific, a briefing officer explained what this extraordinary flight—coming just a week or so after the Japanese surrender—was all about.

"We have pulled together all the operational B-29s in the Marianas for this mission," he began. "All the planes will be armed (most of them had had their machine guns removed earlier for the expected flights back to the United States), and aircraft commanders have permission to fire on any bogeys (unidentified aircraft) they see. We will rendezvous here (he pointed to a spot in the Sea of Japan), form a tight formation, and fly at low altitude across Korea along the thirty-eighth parallel, turn, and fly back. Then the formation will break up for the return flight to the Marianas."

The officer went on to explain the purpose of this foray. When Russia had declared war on Japan a few weeks earlier, many of the million-odd troops massed along the Manchurian border with Korea had pushed down to the thirty-eighth parallel. This had been expected—indeed, agreed upon by President Truman—but now that they were there somebody in command wasn't happy about it, and we'd been asked to put on a show of strength for the Soviets. "It's the biggest nose-thumbing in diplomatic history," is how our briefer put it.

So our armada droned menacingly over Korea. No bogeys were sighted, but the Russians knew we were up there flexing our muscles at them. Thus the mission could be regarded as one of the first manifestations of what would become known as the Cold War.

I left the military soon after, well satisfied with the bit parts fate had given me.

—James Holton was vice president of NBC.

Winston Churchill address a crowd in Strasbourg, France, in August, 1949.

CHURCHILL WEEPS

It was V-E Day, 1945. By common consent the Office of Strategic Services staff in London was taking the day off, but somehow the whole occasion seemed anticlimactic. We recalled those flickering newsreels of Armistice Day in 1918 and wondered where those frenzied mobs were now. Piccadilly Circus was crowded but tame. At Buckingham Palace the king and queen—two tiny specks—dutifully waved from a balcony, and we dutifully waved back.

We wandered down Birdcage Walk to Whitehall and Parliament. It was growing dark now, but I was aware of a group of musicians apparently waiting for something. Suddenly, onto a floodlit balcony directly overhead strode Winston Churchill, complete with cigar. A great shout went up, and in a few seconds the whole street was packed with people. When the din had died down, Churchill briefly assured the crowd, "This is your victory," and made his famous V sign. The effect shattered one of my pet theories. I have always held that no song falls as flat as "For He's a Jolly Good Fellow," whether at a birthday, wedding, or political rally. Somehow it never goes over and always trails off in awkward embarrassment. I now know that it can succeed perfectly in certain rare circumstances—namely, if it is sung by thirty thousand people, accompanied by a ninety-piece band, on V-E Night, to a triumphant war leader, standing on the floodlit balcony of a flag-draped building. Under these conditions it can even move a crowd, including me and Winston Churchill, to tears.

—Walter Lord is a historian and author, most recently of *Night Lives On*.

BOMBS AWAY

In 1945, with George Ball, Paul Nitze, other notables, and a staff of several hundred, I was assigned to the study of the effect of strategic air attacks on the German war economy—the United States Strategic Bombing Survey. The results were impressive. Great and extremely costly attacks on ball-bearing plants raised no enduring difficulty for the Germans. After the great RAF raids on Hamburg there was an easing of the labor supply as workers in banks, restaurants, shops, and places of entertainment that were not destroyed became available to the shipyards and submarine pens. After major attacks on all the German aircraft plants in 1944, aircraft production was promptly reorganized and in ensuing months greatly increased.

These findings were seen by the Air Force as deeply inimical to its mission. As a consequence, though published after acrimonious discussion, they were ignored. The further and historically important consequence was that strategic air attacks went forward on North Korea and North (and South) Vietnam with similar but perhaps even greater military inconsequence.

—John Kenneth Galbraith is Powell M. Warbug Professor of Economics Emeritus at Harvard University. His most recent book is *The Nature of Mass Poverty.*

The Goddess of Victory statue stands before the rubble of the Frauenkirche, a Protestant cathedral heavily damaged by the Allied bombing of Dresden, Germany, in the final months of WWII.

MY BRUSH WITH BETTY

My most vivid brush with history was so slight that although the incident produced one of the most popular photographs of World War II, my presence in the shot is always cropped out.

There were many canteens in America offering servicemen entertainment, but the one held on Saturday afternoons in the ballroom of the National Press Club in Washington, D.C., was unique. For one thing, it offered free beer. Also, in addition to visit-

President Harry Truman with the actress Lauren Bacall.

ing movie stars, many important politicians came to entertain. The movie actors were well received, but I suspect the troops rather preferred the beer to the politicians.

I was one of several sons of reporters pressed into service as volunteers. My war work, which consisted of bringing beer and hot dogs to servicemen and then clearing away the glasses, may not have ranked with rolling bandages at the Red Cross, but it was enormously enjoyable. I once helped the great swing-band drummer Louis Bellson, then in the Army, bring his gear onstage. Bellson gave me a quarter. Ordinarily I would not have taken a tip from a soldier, but I was crazy about Bellson's music and accepted his coin as a prized souvenir.

Schedules were not published, and we never knew who would appear on any given afternoon. The beefcake movie star Victor Mature, whom I had always thought of as something of an overstuffed turkey, put in an appearance and proved to be so self-effacing in a parody skit making fun of his great lover image that I became one of his most ardent fans.

Vice President Harry Truman showed up on one Saturday afternoon in the winter of 1945, causing something of a stir. Truman had gotten into trouble a few weeks earlier for going to the funeral of the Missouri political boss and his one-time mentor Thomas Pendergast. The old man had been sent to jail for tax evasion, and there was some editorial carping over the propriety of the vice president of the United States appearing at the funeral of a convicted felon. At the age of thirteen, however, I was full of solemn, obvious judgments and decreed that it took an O.K. guy to stand up for a pal just out of the

pen, and I was glad to get a look at him. The vice president did a small turn for the audience, and when he found there were sailors in the room from the cruiser Marblehead, he said the name of their ship reminded him of some of the senators he had to deal with. It was a pretty feeble gag, but the audience was indulgent, and he got a reasonable laugh before sitting down at an upright piano to play a few tunes.

I was hustling a tray of beer glasses when the spectacularly sexy Hollywood star Lauren Bacall arrived by a side door. I was so startled by her sudden appearance I lost control of the tray and sent several glasses crashing to the floor, splattering Miss Bacall's ankles with beer in the process. Horrified at my clumsiness, I swiftly tried to dry her legs, but Miss Bacall said she thought she could handle that herself.

Miss Bacall swept into the room to great cheers, and in an inspired gesture—inspired, I found out years later, by her press agent—she clambered on top of the piano and lay with her glorious legs crossed as a bemused Vice President Truman continued to play.

The picture got a huge play in newspapers all over the country. Although I was standing near the piano, I am not seen. A wire-service photographer told me he thought I was at least partially visible in his original shot but was apparently lost in the trimming.

I may have missed out on being famous. But at least I'm not a trivia question: "Who is the dopey-looking kid wearing an apron in that picture with Lauren Bacall on top of Harry Truman's piano?"

—Peter Andrews is a contributing editor to *American Heritage* magazine.

BRAIN DRAIN

During the coverage of the thirtieth anniversary of the moon walk, the media also ran stories on the pioneering Soviet cosmonauts Alexei Leonov and Yuri Gagarin. That reminded me of Herr Doktor Hans Kuepfenbender.

The original Zeiss Optical Works had been in Jena, Germany, which in 1945 became part of the Soviet zone of occupation. Renamed Zeiss Industries, the enterprise was re-established in Oberkochen in the American zone, in an area covered by my 516th

Military Intelligence Detachment. Dr. Kuepfenbender was the Betriebsleiter, the head of the operation.

The Vogt industrial complex in the vicinity had closed, and the U.S. Military Government had requisitioned the firm's Arbeitersiedlung, a worker's housing area of more than one hundred single-family homes, to quarter German rocket scientists and technicians and their families awaiting "political" clearance—screening for past membership in the Nazi party—before being sent to the United States to work

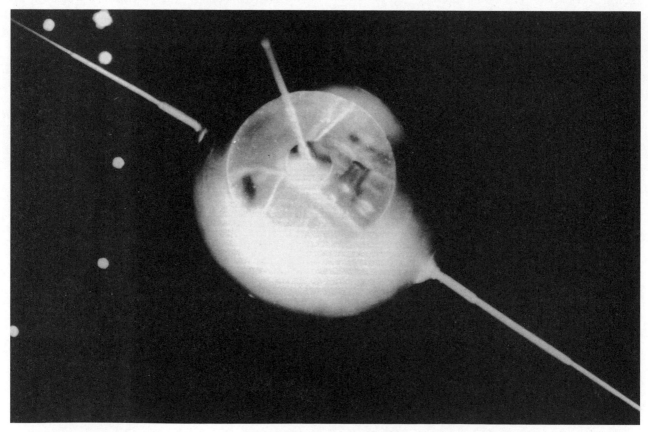

A model of the Soviet satellite Sputnik 1.

with Wernher von Braun. (We found that losing the war had engendered a nation-full of Germans who had been immer dagegen, always against Nazism. German cabaret comics had a field day with parodies on the subject: Ich war immer dagegen.)

My periodic meetings with Dr. Kuepfenbender revealed that the German "guests" at the housing complex had been disappearing regularly, with their families, apparently to Moscow. Since they were officially neither prisoners nor detainees, they were free to go. It would have been reasonable to assume that the unit (not mine) responsible for the scientists would have known of the defections. It did not.

But why would Germans leave American jurisdiction for the totalitarian, oppressive Soviet Union?

Shortly after the end of the war, many German space and rocket scientists went, or were dragged, to the Soviet Union, where they worked on rocketry, were well paid, and were treated like members of the nomenklatura—with dachas, abundant food, wine, women, and song.

These scientists wrote to their colleagues who were under American "supervision," describing their luxurious existence. At that time food allowances in the Allied areas had been as low as nine hundred and fifty calories per person per day, and many items were not even obtainable; indeed, practically the only

thing unrationed for a German just then was a deep breath. So when scientists with expertise in specific fields were invited to join their colleagues in Russia, they regularly disappeared in the postwar parody of the Drang nach Osten.

From the spring of 1947, when I discovered what was going on, until August, 1948, when I left Germany, I reported the situation weekly to my superiors, giving names and specialties, often in less than deferential military terminology, expletives not always deleted. (Reprimands were usually telephonic and merely cautionary.)

Why did we lose the services of the world's best space scientists? This is my explanation for the debacle. After May 8, 1945, the principal mission of many military personnel left over from the war was going home. No one anticipated extraordinary situations like that of the Oberkochen scientists. The higher-ups at headquarters, nominally in charge of intelligence field operations, simply did not know what to do about a circumstance not specifically provided for in their manuals or directives.

And that is why Sputnik and then Gagarin got up there first.

—Arnold J. Lapiner spent twenty years in the army before
he retired to teach social studies.

THE PRINCE AND I

Three of us Pacific war correspondents decided to give ourselves a vacation from the military and to get away—if only for a few days—from the frightful and chilling devastation all around us in Tokyo.

I was a war correspondent for Time-Life magazines in the Pacific and had flown a few days earlier from Manila to Atsugi Field, near Yokohama, with others attached to the MacArthur command. We were there to be aboard the battleship Missouri for the surrender ceremonies on September 2, 1945.

The papers were signed, and suddenly the war was over.

We wanted to see the countryside and small

Crown Prince Akihito at the Peer School in Japan.

towns and villages in a part of Japan untouched by war, at least physically. We settled on a train trip to Nikko, a lovely temple and shrine city in the mountains ninety miles north of Tokyo. Because several of the most magnificent shrines and temples in Japan were in a national park bordering the small city, it had been spared by the B-29s.

Money had little meaning to the Japanese at the moment. They were destitute. A can of Spam or a bar of GI chocolate carried more weight in the market than a hundred-dollar bill. In preparation for our trip we filled three knapsacks with candy, food, and cigarettes purchased at a post exchange and several bottles of Scotch whiskey.

We had a long walk up the main street from the railway station, lugging our bags to the Nikko-Kanaya Hotel. Not many people were in sight to see these three tall strangers chug uphill, and I hoped that they had heard the war was over, for I felt like Gary Cooper walking to his destiny in High Noon.

Shin Kanaya, the charming, bespectacled owner of the hotel, which was just across the road from the sacred bridge leading to the temples, said we were his first American guests since Ambassador Joseph C. Grew, who had vacationed there during his nine years in Japan, came for a weekend visit just before Pearl Harbor. We shared with him our whiskey and sent candies to his wife, who was ill.

Later that afternoon Mr. Kanaya came to my room. "The keeper of the emperor's trout streams would be pleased to bring you each a trout for dinner." Pause. "A small consideration would be most appropriate, say, a package of cigarettes," said Mr. Kanaya.

That night we dined on trout. Cost: three packs of Camels. After months of Army rations it was a near-sensual experience.

Mr. Kanaya had one further suggestion. "If by chance you can spare some sweets, I have several small boys who have not had candies for a long, long time. You might wish to surprise them with such a gift, and I would be glad to arrange a small presentation."

He continued. "All the princes from the Peers School, including the crown prince, were brought here several months ago to get away from the fire bombings. They have been at school in the building across the way." He pointed to a small white two-story building beyond a grove of trees.

The next morning at precisely eight-thirty the three American war correspondents, led by Mr. Kanaya, walked onto the graveled playing field of the school. A dozen small boys were standing in a line at youthful attention but in complete silence. Standing a few feet in front of them, in his role as the future emperor of Japan, was another small boy, Crown Prince Akihito, in shorts and white shirt, round-faced and solemn. We were the first Americans that many of these small boys had ever seen.

Mr. Kanaya told the children who we were and why we had come to this beautiful city of Nikko, and said that Mr. Clayton had a presentation to make. The night before, the three of us had pooled several pounds of chocolate bars and hard candies.

I stepped in front of the boys. I don't remember what I said, but I do know that when I handed the crown prince the bag of candies, we did not shake hands. I bowed, and in return he bowed.

End of ceremony.

The boys stood at attention until we walked to the edge of the playground and turned into the hotel. As we walked up the steps, I heard shouts and laughter coming from the playground.

We left shortly after for Tokyo.

—Bernard Clayton, Jr., a food and travel writer, lives in Bloomington, Indiana.

General Douglas MacArthur disembarks from the USS Nashville in the South Pacific during World War II.

BENEVOLENT BARTENDER

Watching television recently, I saw a documentary about Douglas MacArthur. It explained something that had puzzled me for more than fifty years.

Just after the Second World War, I was a young cameraman in the Philippines working for the Army Pictorial Service, a branch of the Signal Corps. One day the assignment desk in Manila directed me to the harbor to photograph some general. The general turned out to be Douglas MacArthur. In those months just after the war, everyone was trying to relax, and five-star generals were no exception. MacArthur had organized a short cruise and party on Manila Bay. At the last minute someone decided that photographs of the excursion were needed.

Out around Corregidor the assignment began to get grim. Never before had I been bothered by seasickness, but a choppy Manila Bay was doing its dirty work. Old Navy salts claimed that watching the horizon for a while would make the queasy feeling go away. Rather than embarrass the general's guests, I reported to him to explain my problem and how I planned to solve it.

"Son, I think we can do better than that," he replied. He put his arm around my shoulder and ushered me into the bar. He ordered for both of us. To my twenty-two-year-old palate, the resulting concoction tasted like brandy with a dash of this or that added for good measure. Whatever it was, it did the trick. I finished the assignment with no more trouble.

But over the years, I did wonder at his consideration of my plight—until I saw that documentary. At one point, it noted that General MacArthur was plagued with the tendency to become air or sea sick, and it was a great embarrassment to him.

Now I knew! That old rascal was in the same shape I was in on that cruise, and I was his excuse to alleviate his condition.

I photographed General MacArthur many times in Manila and in Tokyo over the next year. I always had the feeling I was extended a benevolent generosity not given to other photographers. And that, too, I now understand. We were two souls plagued with the same malady.

—Dave Wallis is semiretired from running his own advertising firm.

THE MAN

Stan Musial, the great St. Louis Cardinals outfielder, was close to murderous with a bat in his hand. His fellow Hall of Famer and opposing pitcher Warren Spahn said, "When Musial came up to hit, your infielders were in jeopardy." He was known as "the Man," a name given him by groaning Brooklyn fans convinced that whenever the Cardinals took on the Bums, Musial appeared at the plate in every pressure situation. "Oh, no. Here comes that Man again."

But I remember him as the Man for a different reason.

Nineteen forty-six. Wrigley Field, Chicago. August. Musial and his Cards were in town to play the Cubs. The Cubs has won the pennant the year before with World War Two rejects: youngsters and might-have-beens and old guys who soon went back to running their retirement gas stations. But now the big boys were back from the war, and the Cards were playing hard for big-league stakes, trying to catch the leading Brooklyn Dodgers.

My buddies and I were there early as usual, hanging over the low wall between home and first where we could watch batting practice, pepper games—and beg for autographs. The great Enos Slaughter was playing pepper close by. "Hey, Enos! Sign my scorecard!" No response. "C'mon, Enos! What're you, stuck up?" No response. Slaughter was a big man. Muscular. Heavy legs. Not a young man. He wouldn't look at us. He seemed like an old man in a boy's game (Slaughter was thirty in 1946). He was there for the money, nothing else. Signing autographs wouldn't get him a World Series check, and he wouldn't even look around. We got on him with the razz. We started to rhyme Enos with the only rhyme we could think of. It became a chant. Eleven-year-old kids acting stupid. He never looked our way.

But one guy did. And he walked over to us. We knew who he was, and we shut up. It was Stan Musial. He wasn't as big as Slaughter, but to me he was bigger than God. When he spoke, his voice was as quiet as a man come to pay his respects.

"You boys shouldn't be yelling at Mr. Slaughter that way. Mr. Slaughter is fighting for a pennant. He's very tired. We're all very tired, and we have a lot of work to do. Mr. Slaughter is trying to play baseball. He doesn't have time to sign for everybody. You boys are fans, you should be able to understand that. Now, if you want an autograph, maybe I could sign one for you. My name is Stan Musial, and I could put that on your scorecards for you, if that would be all right." It was all right. It was more than all right. It was the Tabernacle. I had Billy Nicholson's autograph. He led the league in homers in 1943-44. I had Phil Cavaretta's autograph. He was batting champ in 1945. I had a lot of names on a lot of pieces of paper. None came close to Stan Musial.

The Cardinals finally beat the Dodgers. Then they beat the Boston Red Sox in the World Series. Slaughter made a throw that's still shown on film clips of "Great Moments," and his heavy old legs beat Johnny Pesky's throw to the plate in what should probably be called "Greater Moments."

Musial did well too. Musial always did well. But it isn't his play I remember so much now. Now, forty-six years later, that's reduced to statistics on a cold page. His generous gesture, though, his gesture and the warmth of his words, remain vivid.

—Tom Bohnen now lives in Kettenpom Valley, Zenia, California, where there is no electrical service.

Stan Musial congratulates Enos Slaughter as he crosses home plate after hitting a home run in 1945.

A COOL HAND

As a young bachelor in New York in the years immediately following World War II, I was fortunate to be frequently an "extra man" at the small dinner parties of Judge and Mrs. Learned Hand in their house on Sixty-fifth Street (later the residence—speaking of brushes with history—of Richard Nixon). Judge Hand was a great man, the greatest it has ever been my privilege to know, and I hung on his beautifully articulated phrases. One night when I arrived, always the first, I found him reading a letter from Bernard Berenson, his friend of many decades, with whom he maintained a regular correspondence.

"BB wants to know why I always subscribe my letters to him in such hyperbolic terms as 'Your devoted pupil' or 'Your disciple in art' or 'Your constant admirer.'" The judge put away the letter and glanced at me with his great, bushy eyebrows raised. "He asks why I never sign myself simply 'Affectionately yours.'"

I paused, but I knew I had my cue. "Well, sir, why don't you?"

"Because I don't like him!"

Nor did he ever joke in such matters.

—Louis Auchincloss is a lawyer and author,
most recently of *The Rector of Justin*.

Judge Learned Hand, Circuit Judge of the United States Court of Appeals, travels aboard the S.S. Carolina in 1949.

WHISTLE STOP

uring the golden Indian summer of 1948, I was an eleven-year-old aspiring journalist in Shell Lake, Wisconsin. My parents owned the local weekly newspaper, the Washburn County Register. I was the sports editor, printer's devil, and errand runner.

We had received an unending barrage of press releases from the local Democratic party proclaiming that President Truman would be in Spooner, whistle-stopping on his campaign across the Midwest. My father, a staunch Republican, refused to print such rubbish, claiming that he would not allow his paper to provide political propaganda for a discredited administration. Somehow my mother and I persuaded him that the president's visit in a town only six miles away was a genuine news event. He insisted on rewriting the press releases, but in the end he ran the story on the front page under big headlines. Then, to our surprise, Dad announced that we would cover the president's speech. He had been convinced by our argument that history should prevail over partisan politics.

As we drove north to Spooner in our ancient Model A Ford (the weekly newspaper business was not exactly lucrative), my father regaled us with his familiar repertoire of Truman insults, from "To err is Truman" to "bankrupt haberdasher." In those more casual times press credentials were nonexistent, but fortunately the station agent recognized us and directed us to a choice spot right along the railroad tracks. The train of course was late. To an impatient rookie reporter the delay seemed like hours, but it may have been only forty-five minutes. As we waited, the crowd grew steadily larger. The party faithful later estimated it at ten thousand people; my father saw fewer than twenty-five hundred.

At last the great moment arrived, the high school band played "Hail to the Chief," and the president appeared at the back of the train, looking remarkably similar to his image in the Movie Tone newsreels. I couldn't see over the heads of the adults who pushed forward, so to my mother's consternation I climbed up a nearby coal pile for a better view. The speech was short and incisive: Truman blasted the do-nothing Republican Congress and the selfish Wall Street capitalists and urged us to turn these rascals out. His constituents applauded loudly and exhorted him to "Give 'em hell, Harry." After one final swipe at those rich robber barons and their Republican cohorts, the president introduced his daughter, Margaret, and the "Boss," his wife, Bess. The train was ready to head north for Superior when Truman pulled a note out of his pocket, glanced at it, and then raised his hand to quiet the crowd. In his Missouri twang he thanked everyone for coming and said he was astonished that so many people had turned out. "I would particularly like to thank the Sheas, who featured my stop here in the Shell Lake Register. Would they please step up here so that the Truman family can thank them personally?

Who cared if he didn't get the name of our paper right? My parents waved me down from the coal pile, I tried frantically to brush off the black dust, and we boarded the train. Father explained that the story was my idea. "Well, I have two Shea votes, young man, but you'll have to wait a few years," Truman said. "I think I can carry Wisconsin with your help." He shook my hand, Bess hugged me, and I think Margaret may have kissed me on the cheek. The crowd cheered (not really, but memory is not an exact science). Mother was ecstatic, although she worried that the president might have gotten coal dust on his hands.

An aide gave Mom a small package, we stepped down off the platform, and the train thundered out of Spooner on the most successful of all whistle-stop campaigns. The package contained an autographed Truman photo and a pair of presidential cuff links. I don't remember what happened to the cuff links, but the photograph was still in Dad's office when he sold the newspaper years later.

Fast forward to 1965, the year before my father died. Despite my promising debut, I had abandoned both journalism and politics and gone to law school. Dad, still a skeptical newsman, was asking my opin-ion of the Warren Commission, saying, "John Kennedy was far too liberal, but I thought an Irish Catholic should have the chance. He was the only Democrat I ever voted for."

"What about Harry Truman, Dad? You and Mom seemed awfully happy when he beat Dewey."

Dad just smiled. "You don't think I would be per-suaded by an old pol just because he invited us onto his railroad car and gave me some cuff links, do you?"

I still think my father voted for both Harry Truman and John Kennedy.

—Jeremy C. Shea is an attorney with the Quarles & Brady law firm. He lives in Madison, Wisconsin.

Harry Truman, his daughter, Margaret, and wife, Bess, campaign from the rear platform of a train in Bridgeport, Pennsylvania, on October 7, 1948.

THE INTERVIEW

During the late 1940s I lived in Rowayton, a small Connecticut village, with my wife and two small children. I was the art director of Columbia Records, a job I dearly loved. In my work I had many opportunities to meet the musical celebrities of the day, Frank Sinatra, Benny Goodman, and Duke Ellington among them, and I considered myself a fairly cool cat.

Fate had blessed me with Roussie, the world's most delightful daughter. At the time she was some-

Aleksandr Feodorovich Kerensky, prime minister of the Russian provisional government of 1917, delivers a salute during an inspection of his troops.

where between four and six and my regular weekend date. Every Saturday we did the chores together, visited the post office, and wound up in the town's only drugstore.

Soybel's pharmacy was a true drugstore—no greeting cards or eyelash curlers. In the rear of the shop the druggist filled prescriptions and sold patent medicines. The front was given over to a small, gaudy soda fountain with four or five stools. George Soybel's counter was a gathering place for the town cognoscenti, and the stools were almost always filled.

One cold wintry Saturday Roussie and I had finished our errands and went to cap the morning with a visit to Soybel's. We were in luck. Only one stool was occupied. A gentleman in a heavy black overcoat and a natty Borsalino hat was nursing what seemed to be a ginger ale float. I sat next to him and hoisted my daughter onto the stool beside me. While she and I were deciding what to order, George Soybel emerged and greeted us.

"Jim, I want you to meet a new resident in Rowayton," George said. I turned to the stranger, who had a pleasant, angular face, and extended my hand. He took it.

"This is Aleksandr Kerensky."

ALEKSANDR KERENSKY!

Was this the Aleksandr Kerensky who had been the first premier of the provisional Russian government after the 1917 revolution? The Kerensky who had held the fate of the world in his hands? The man who could have ushered Russia into the twentieth century, avoided the murderous regime of Stalin, saved the world from the Cold War? Who might even have been such a benign and powerful influence on the 1920s and 1930s that Hitler could never have risen to power and World War II might never have happened?

As if he could read my thoughts, he smiled and nodded several times in confirmation. Pictures of the revolution flashed through my mind. Kerensky was thirty-six in 1917, and here he was, three decades later, wrinkled but recognizable, and rather handsome.

A dozen questions stumbled behind my tongue. Why had he not been more forceful when he had the reins of power in his hands? Why had he failed to prevent Lenin from entering Russia? Why hadn't he seized and imprisoned him? What should I ask first? I opened my mouth.

"How do you like Rowayton?" was what came out.

Kerensky proceeded to tell me how happy he and his American wife were in our town. He enjoyed the peace and quiet he found here and was finding time to write, et cetera, et cetera.

A woman appeared at the door.

"I'm ready," she said, and Kerensky hopped from his stool, shook my hand, and exited.

The trouble with history is that it has a habit of rushing by us so swiftly that we don't recognize it until we see the taillights receding in the distance.

—James Flora lived in Connecticut.

HELP FROM ON HIGH

In the early summer of 1949 my psychological life was not tightly held to reality by the usual tethers. On June 19 I married the woman I loved, and a few days later I prepared to consummate a dream that I had concocted over the preceding months—to privately charter an airplane to fly forty-six students and my wife and me to Europe. My plan had been developed during the busiest year of my life: It was my first year of medical school, and I was simultaneously courting my fiancée at a campus 120 miles away. That I survived the rigors of medical school and long-distance courtship is a marvel matched only by the story I am about to tell.

Actually, my airplane idea was not mine. In the summer of 1948, as a member of the Experiment in International Living, I was one of the earliest American students to enter Germany after the Second World War. That summer all of the available passenger boats traveling to Europe quickly filled up. Somehow the American Youth Hostels procured reduced-fare air space at the last minute for student travelers, and I was one of those few who flew to Europe for the price of boat travel. It registered in my mind that I was witness to an important economic event. For the first time in history travel by air was as cheap as third-class steamer, and an additional half-month in Europe fell into the bargain! I promised myself that I would look into that in the fall.

Just before the Christmas vacation of 1948, I got a free afternoon in Chicago. With barely more than the slightest idea where to begin, I started at the top—Pan Am, TWA, and Air France. Looking as honest and grown-up as I could, I asked: "Sir, could you tell me if there would be any fare reductions available if I could fill one entire airplane with students going to Europe early in the summer and returning a couple of months later?" A negligible group discount was offered from the $800 full fare, leaving a price that was more than three times what I had paid the summer before. Discouraged, I turned to the yellow pages of the telephone book, where I discovered a number of airlines I had never heard of. I made a list of addresses starting with 'A' and headed for Chicago's Loop. My first stop was Alaska Airlines and, as it turned out, I went no further.

The modest Alaska quarters more resembled the offices of a trucking company than those of an airline, and that was an appropriate analogy, since I had stumbled onto an air-freight carrier whose freight was only occasionally people. I asked my question, and the manager complimented me by taking me seriously. He asked me a few questions, consulted a scheduling chart, and said I could have an airplane that could accommodate forty-eight passengers leaving Chicago for Paris on June 23 and returning sixty-two days later for $10,500.

"$10,500 total for both flights?"

"Yes." Quick math: The round-trip price per passenger was slightly more than $200.

"I'll take it!" About five minutes had passed since I had come into the office. Generous terms were arranged. I had several months to recruit my student passengers before I had to pay Alaska anything more than a modest deposit. I floated out of the office an astonished, engaged-to-be-married medical student in the travel business.

I spent forty-three dollars on advertising in three college newspapers and filled our airplane within two weeks. I was married on June 19 and went off to a nearby resort hotel as stage one of our honeymoon.

Stage two was to be Europe. We returned to Chicago on June 22, the day before our flight was to leave for Paris. I called Alaska Airlines to make sure everything was O.K. It wasn't. Our airplane, routed toward Chicago from the West Coast, had been denied permission to land at Chicago's Midway airport. In 1949 the Civil Aeronautics Authority (CAA) regulated and directly controlled all air traffic. The people at Alaska didn't know why permission had been denied, but they suspected that it had to do with the student passenger cargo. Why? No one knew. What to do? No one knew that either. All my passengers

The author's passport.

were planning to be at the airport for an 8:00 a.m. departure the following morning. Distraught, I took to the telephone to report our awful situation and promised to do everything I could to resolve the problem: "Don't call me, I'll call you. And stay near the phone." The race had already begun.

I called Alaska Airlines every twenty minutes all afternoon and into the evening. I called the airport every twenty minutes. I called the CAA repeatedly but couldn't find out anything. I called my parents. No one knew anything, and nothing was happening. Late in the evening we opened the first bottle of wine. What was most frustrating was not being able to get information of any sort as to why the CAA had denied the flights. The Alaska Airlines officials guessed that it had to do with what was most obvious—charter travel drastically undercut commercial airfares and would ultimately threaten the large carriers. Best to quash the competition early if possible. We hated to think that a federal agency was vulnerable to such machinations but had to allow that possibility. And if that was so, then the only remedy was to exert our own pressure.

We were forty-eight students: We had to have some leverage somewhere. But where? I had never before had the occasion to petition my governmental representatives. I wasn't even sure who they were. By now it was well past midnight, but the hope lingered. I began my efforts at political influence by calling the mayor. No one answered. I called the Chicago Tribune to find the names and phone numbers of my state legislative representatives and called them. No one answered. In the middle of our second bottle of wine I realized that Washington was the answer; that's where the CAA was.

Back to the Tribune for more telephone numbers. Operators deflected the calls to my congressional representatives and instructed me in polite detail how to reach them in the morning. Then, in a moment of slightly drunken inspiration, I came upon a solution that matched my desperation. I'd call the president! Even though it was about 4:00 a.m. Washington time! So what!

I'd made all my calls through the same person-to-person, long-distance operator, and by now she had become involuntarily involved in our plight. When I rang her once again and told her I wanted her to reach President Harry Truman, I was heartened by the fact that she didn't ring off immediately. Dutifully she called the information operator in Washington to get the telephone number of the White House, then dialed it. I held my breath and at the edge of my mind registered surprise that the call wasn't answered on the first ring as had been the calls to Congress. On the third ring a man answered in a slow, deliberate voice that twanged with an unmistakable Midwestern accent.

Operator: "This is the long-distance operator in Chicago, Illinois, with a person-to-person call for President Harry Truman."

"This is Mr. Truman. Who is it that is calling?"

"Mr. Justin Simon, in Chicago, Illinois."

"What is the nature of Mr. Simon's business."

Me: "Operator, tell Mr. Truman that I need his help. Forty-eight ambassadors of good will, college students from across the country, are stranded in Chicago because the CAA has denied permission for our chartered airplane to land here in Chicago and take them off for the summer in Europe."

"Operator, ask Mr. Simon why that happened. Well, Mr. Simon, since you're on the line, you can just tell me. Why did the CAA do that?"

"That's why I've bothered you in the middle of the night, sir. I'm terribly sorry to have bothered you, but we can't find out why the CAA did that. We've tried everything we can to find out what the snag is, and we can't. All these students are stranded here and most of them can't hole up for very long, and we just have to get our airplane or a whole lot of plans are about to be ruined, and lots and lots of American good will aimed for Europe will go down the drain."

"Well, I don't much mind that you've called me. I was up anyway. I don't know anything about this, but if you'll call Mr. Rogers in my Department of Transportation at eight-thirty Washington time"—he gave me the phone number—"I'll do what I can to see that he can tell you something. Well, it might be best if you didn't call him until about a quarter to nine. He'll know something by then."

"Thanks, Mr. President."

"Oh, you're welcome."

Sleep was out of the question. The call to Mr. Rogers at the appointed time rendered the news that all the problems were resolved and the airplane was on its way. I called the passengers and then met them at the airport, and we watched together through a chain-link fence as a dot in the western sky grew into our airplane. It landed and then carried us to Europe. Our relief and elation were unbounded, but the enduring effect of the crisis was the one created by Mr. Truman. This is what responsive and responsible governance is all about, but in a detail so miniature as to be far beneath the call of presidential duty. But not the way Mr. Truman defined it. He not only saved our summer, he also instilled an optimism about government that resides in my heart to this day. I'm deeply grateful for both gifts.

—Justin Simon is a psychoanalyst in private practice in Berkeley, California.

President Harry Truman talks on the telephone in his office, Washington D.C., 1945.

BOTTLE BLONDE

One evening in November 1950 my mother asked me to pick up a bottle of sherry on the way back from work in my hometown of Green Bay, Wisconsin. She needed the wine to pour over the several fruitcakes she had baked for Christmas and which were now lying on a shelf in our fruit cellar awaiting that little touch of alcoholic aroma to bring their flavor to a peak. She wanted the least expensive sherry I could find.

I went into a drugstore near where I worked, picked out a bottle (I remember it cost sixty-nine cents), and brought it up front to pay. The clerk, the brother of the proprietor, knew me and also knew that I was twenty—a year below the legal age for purchasing alcohol. He refused to sell me the wine:

"But it's only for my mother's fruitcake," I said.

"Can't help it. You're too young. The feds are in town checking up, and we could lose our license."

I began to lose my temper. I demanded the bottle of wine, citing a long (nodding) acquaintance with the proprietor, my father's (nonexistent) influence with the proprietor, and my mother's fruitcakes' (dubious) utter need for that sherry.

During this heated argument neither of us noticed a small, middle-aged lady with what we then called bottle-blonde hair who was picking out some small items and listening to our conversation with some amusement. She approached the checkout counter with her purchases and interrupted the yelling match.

"Look," she said, "would it be all right if I bought the bottle of wine and gave it to this young man? I'm late, and I want to get out of here."

"No way, lady," said the clerk. "That would be contributing to the delinquency of a minor."

The lady muttered something under her breath and then turned to me. As she did, I began to realize that I had seen her somewhere before.

"Why don't you wait for me outside?" she said.

And so I went out and waited on the sidewalk while she paid for her purchases, including my bottle of wine. And then, as she came out the door in the gathering twilight, I suddenly knew who she was. She was Sally Rand. I had seen her photo in an ad in the local paper the previous day. She was appearing in Green Bay for a few nights. My father had commented on it. It was Sally Rand all right. It had to be. She certainly looked older than her picture, but there was no doubt in my mind. And boy, was I excited!

For the benefit of those readers below the age of fifty or thereabouts, Sally Rand was an exotic dancer who had first achieved fame at the 1933 Chicago World's Fair by riding a horse from the downtown Loop of the fairgrounds, dressed as Lady Godiva. She had been trained in ballet, but hard times make for hard choices, and she made her living as an exotic dancer. She appeared onstage clad in nothing but two fans of ostrich feathers, fore and aft, from behind which she would let the audience see bare portions of her anatomy—a leg here, a shoulder there, perhaps a glimpse of derriere or the shadow of a breast. No one knew if she was really naked, and her appeal lay largely in the eternal hope that by chance or design she would drop one of her fans. After the fair was over, she organized a dance troupe and toured the country. She became something of a byword for the 1930s definition of naughty and was the subject of dozens of off-color stories and snickering jokes told by ten-year-olds of all ages (sample: "Calling all cars, calling all cars, be on the lookout for Sally Rand with a hat on. That is all!").

So when she came out of that drugstore, I was more than a little impressed. She handed me my bottle of sherry and waved away the money I offered her.

"You're Sally Rand, the bubble dancer, aren't you?" I blurted out.

"Fan dancer."

"I meant to say fan dancer, but it came out wrong." I could feel my ears getting warm.

She smiled. "That guy in there sure was a big jerk, wasn't he?" Then: "Have you seen my show?"

I confessed that I hadn't.

"Well, it's a pretty good show, if I must say so myself. And you don't have to be twenty-one to get in."

I said I would think about it, and thanked her for buying me the wine.

"It was nothing. Like I said, that guy was a real jerk."

And then her face lost all its animation, and she looked tired and old, and I noticed that she wore heavy makeup. I thought, "Being in show business must be one hell of a way to make a living."

"Well, so long, young fella. If you get the chance, see the show." She turned on her heel and headed in the direction of a hotel just down the block.

I never went to see Sally Rand; I was afraid of what my parents might think. I don't know what motivated her to come to my aid. Maybe it was boredom, or the desire to put an officious clerk in his place. All I know is that she was to me a warm and kind person. And she got me my bottle of wine.

—John J. DuPont was, until 1992, the editor of *The Conservationist*, published by the New York State Department of Environmental Conservation.

Sally Rand in 1933, dressed for her "Fan Dance."

THE PRIVATE JACK BENNY

In the fall of 1951 I was twelve years old and living on the island of Okinawa. My father, an Air Force colonel, was the public information officer for the 20th Air Force, headquartered at Kadena Air force Base there. At that time the 20th was flying bombing missions from Okinawa to Korea.

Conditions on the island were not ideal. We lived in a Quonset hut, and because of the "night soil" fertilizer used locally, we didn't have fresh produce or dairy products. We used canned vegetables, cold-storage eggs, and reconstituted milk. There was no television, and the sole radio station was run by the armed forces. Few permanent structures existed, since the island had been virtually destroyed during

Jack Benny (center) performs for the troops at a base in the South Pacific in the Summer of 1944.

the war. For a twelve-year-old boy, though, it was a neat place. With all the aircraft activity and countless battlefield sites to visit, I was enjoying it.

One day it was announced that Jack Benny would visit Okinawa and give a show at Kadena. To me, as to most youngsters who grew up during the radio age, Benny was a big star. Our family would gather and "watch" him on the radio each week; it would be a thrill to see him in person.

Since my father was the public information officer, it was his job to meet Jack's troupe upon arrival at the base, and he said I could go with him as long as I didn't get in the way. The flight arrived somewhat late, but finally the C-54 taxied to where we were standing. The usual military and civilian officials had gathered to meet the plane, and I had a tough time getting a good view. I did manage to see my father shake hands with Mr. Benny. I was somewhat taken aback by the fact that he looked much older than he had in the movies, but then I realized that he was not wearing his famous toupee. Too soon he was in a staff car and gone. I was disappointed not to have gotten a closer look.

On the way home Dad said he had to stop by General Stearley's quarters. Maj. Gen. Ralph Stearley, the commanding general of the 20th Air Force, was my father's boss. While my father went inside, I sat down to wait on a comfortable rattan chair on the general's screened porch. His quarters, although not plush, were great by Okinawan standards. The porch looked out on the South China Sea, and I was enjoying the view when I heard the unmistakable voice of Jack Benny from inside. I realized that he must be staying at the general's quarters.

Suddenly there he was. He walked through the door from the house to the porch, saw me sitting there, and came over and sat down right across from me. He looked tired and began to relate how strenuous the trip had been, how rough it had been traveling through Korea, moving mainly by helicopter and jeep. He went on for several minutes, and I couldn't help thinking, "This is like having a conversation with my uncle. He's not funny at all."

But then I grasped something that helped me years later when I became a newspaper reporter and had occasion to talk to a few celebrities. People are just people. Their public images do not necessarily reflect their real personalities.

After a short silence I could almost sense that Benny was realizing he was talking seriously to a kid who had expected something funny. Just then General Stearley appeared in the doorway and asked Benny if he would like a drink. For a second Benny looked at me, and then, in his "on air" voice, he asked, "Well...how much are they?"

"Jack, they're free," the general said, smiling.

And with that unbelievable timing, Benny replied, "Then I'll have two."

I felt Jack Benny had performed just for me.

—John E. Condron, Jr. is retired from the newspaper and printing business and lives in Fort Wayne, Indiana.

THE SCENT OF FAILURE

Rocky Marciano is the only heavyweight champion who ever retired without losing a professional fight or even boxing to a draw. Time and again on his way up, Marciano was in danger of losing when his mighty right pulled it out. While a youth, in Brockton, Massachusetts, before becoming champion in Philadelphia on September 23, 1952, he worked as a dishwasher, short-order cook, landscaper, and as a floor sweeper at the Stacy Adams men's show factory.

In 1952 I was a men's shoe salesman at Marshall Field's in Chicago. That summer I took a busman's holiday, visiting a number of men's shoe suppliers in Massachusetts. While I was talking with Arthur Luce, Stacy Adams's Brockton comptroller, Rocky Marciano walked in with his father, who had recently retired after working twenty-one years on a bedlast machine at the Stacy Adams factory.

Marciano gave Luce a plain paper grocery bag containing the pair of boxing gloves he had used the previous Saturday. Rocky said he thought Arthur might like to hang them on his office wall as a trophy. Then Rocky explained that this shoe factory was partially responsible for his continued success as a boxer. "When I worked here, I couldn't stand the smell of wet leather—it nauseated me—but I had to have the job. Whenever a boxing match isn't going my way, I can smell my sweat on my opponent's leather gloves—continually hitting me in the face—and I think to myself, 'If I don't turn this fight around, I'll have to go back to work in that shoe factory.' I then give the fight that extra effort and I win."

Arthur looked down at the shoes Rocky was wearing and asked where he got them. "Over at Sears," he replied. Arthur said that Rocky was now a famous representative of Brockton, and it wouldn't be right for him to go to press conferences without wearing Stacy Adams shoes—especially since it was possible his father had worked on that very footwear before his retirement.

Arthur turned to me and he said, "We have here a shoe fitter from Marshall Field's in Chicago, and I want him to take you to our stockroom and fit you with several pairs." Rocky agreed: he would proudly wear Stacy Adams, he said. Then he added, "The first thing to go on a fighter are his feet." I still remember that Marciano wore size 9D in the Savoy last, a broad-toed shoe.

—Allan Nelson continued working in the
footwear industry for twenty-five years and then
taught high school. He is now retired.

Rocky Marciano, undefeated in 49 professional bouts, annouces his retirement in New York on April 27, 1956.

Dylan Thomas, photographed in 1946.

CANCELING THE POET

In 1952, my junior year at Wellesley, it was common knowledge among English majors that an assignment to interview the visiting poet was a reward for excellence. Only you wouldn't have known it from the way my poetry professor, Roberta Grahame, presented it to me. "Remain after class," she instructed, and later left me standing before her desk for a full five minutes while she read a student's poem.

Although I knew nothing of Miss Grahame's background, I perceived her to be one of a breed: a New England spinster educator—careful, aloof, impassive. She wore the requisite tweeds and no makeup and had written a slim volume of poetry, entitled *Last Bell at Midcentury*.

She told me to report to her office at six the following evening and we'd go together. "I assure you, you'll find it interesting. Extremely interesting," she remarked cryptically.

When I arrived at the appointed hour, Miss Roberta Grahame sat just as I had left her, but this evening she was crying, her face blotchy, her eyes streaming with tears. When she saw me, she blew her nose vigorously in a Kleenex and announced, "We're not going. They've canceled. They've sent him away."

"But why?" I blurted out.

Miss Grahame shrugged; her answers were choked and fragmented. "I'm not certain of the details. There was a party. Some of our people were there. He was inebriated. He's still young—only in his thirties. He touched a breast. Who knows?" She paused and then continued but in a voice I'd never heard before, one suffused with emotion. "They're fools. They don't know what they're doing. The man's a genius!"

I was too taken aback, too abashed by her unexpected passion and distress, to say anything appropriate. "Maybe they'll let him come back later. Maybe next year," I said.

But by the next year Dylan Thomas was dead.

—Barbara Goldsmith is the author, most recently
of *The Age of Suffrage, Spiritualism, and
the Scandalous Victoria Woodhull.*

JOE MCCARTHY VISITS BILL BUCKLEY

It was Labor Day 1952, and Sen. Joe McCarthy had come up to Stamford, Connecticut, to have lunch with me and my wife and with Brent Bozell and his wife (my sister). Bozell and I were doing research for our book on McCarthy.

During lunch the phone rang for the senator. He took the call and came back to the table, obviously concerned. "What's the matter, Joe?"

"Well, that was the head of the Republican party in Massachusetts. He wants me to go to Boston and give a speech for Cabot Lodge. Trouble is, that's hard to do. Joe Kennedy has always been on my side, and he contributed five thousand dollars to my own reelection campaign. If I go to Boston, Jack Kennedy will lose to Cabot Lodge, no doubt about it. That's why they want me."

We resumed lunch. And about fifteen minutes later McCarthy rose, excused himself, went to the phone, and was back in about five minutes, smiling broadly.

"Well, I took care of that one all right! I told his manager, 'Sure, I'll give a speech for Cabot. But he'll have to ask me to do it.'" Big laugh. "Cabot Lodge would never ask me publicly. He'd lose the Harvard vote."

And so John F. Kennedy beat (narrowly) Henry Cabot Lodge for the Senate and, in due course, became president.

—William F. Buckley, Jr., is editor in chief of *National Review* and an author, most recently of *Elvis in the Morning*.

Joseph McCarthy and his wife, who were famous for their social lunches, dine with the columnist Constantine Brown and his wife.

LEARNED DISCUSSION

As an eighteen-year-old in the summer of 1953, I sometimes served as a driver for my eighty-year-old grandmother, Constance Parsons Hare. On one occasion I drove her into Manhattan for a luncheon she had arranged for about twenty of her oldest friends at the Colony Club. As we sat down, at different tables, I noticed

that I was the only person present younger than about sixty. This observation did nothing to diminish my teen-age argumentativeness and distaste for polite conversation. Having recently written a prize-winning school essay on McCarthyism, I was eager to educate my elders about the evils of the senator from Wisconsin. After a few confident sentences, it was

Judge Learned Hand, shown here with Senator Paul H. Douglas and Senator George Aiken.

apparent that all but one of those at my table considered McCarthyism an inappropriate topic for luncheon conversation. My resolve only strengthened by this cool reception, I focused my efforts on an elderly gentleman who showed interest by pressing me to clarify and justify my opinions. With each new question, my rhetorical juices flowed stronger. This old fellow, I told myself, needs to learn something about the importance of civil liberties. The longer this one-sided conversation went on, the more pained became the expressions on the faces of the others at the table, but to my puzzlement no one interrupted, and the old gentleman remained serenely attentive.

On the drive home my grandmother was horrified to hear my account of the conversation. She told me that the "old gentleman" I had been attempting to enlighten on civil liberties was Judge Learned Hand, the most respected American jurist living. After scolding me thoroughly, she explained that she and Learned Hand had been friends since they were painfully shy teen-agers standing together on the sidelines at summer dances in Lenox, Massachusetts.

—Peter H. Hare is Distinguished Service Professor Emeritus of the philosophy department at the State University of New York at Buffalo.

Senator Joseph McCarthy confers with Roy Cohn during a televised Senate subcommittee meeting.

JOE MCCARTHY AT THE LIBRARY

In 1954 Sen. Joseph R. McCarthy, accompanied by Roy Cohn, flew to Madison to deliver a lecture at the University of Wisconsin. I was his student host and met him at the airport. He and Cohn were drunk; they continued drinking from a whiskey bottle as we drove to the campus. On arrival, I told the senator he had an hour before his talk; I asked if there was anything he would like to see.

The card catalog in the library, he replied. I took him there. He marched to the M section, pulled out three drawers covering works by and about Marx, and demanded to see the director. I took him there. He and Cohn all but threw the drawers down on the director's desk.

"This is a goddamned outrage," the senator roared. "The good children of Wisconsin shouldn't be exposed to this crap. I want all these books burned."

"I can't do that," the director replied calmly. "Those books are state property."

The senator was taken aback but recovered. "Well," he sputtered, "well, you have a dirty-book section, don't you?"

"Yes."

"Then lock up these books where they belong." (In those days, pornography was kept under lock and key; you could read the books only in a closed room in the library.) The director agreed.

I checked a few weeks after the senator left. The Marx books were still in circulation.

—Stephen E. Ambrose is Boyd Professor of History at the University of New Orleans and the author of *The Wild Blue: The Men and Boys Who Flew the B-24s Over Germany.*

"HOPPED-UP COUNTRY"

As a teenager I liked the sound of guitar music, and I practiced until I was fairly proficient at picking out tunes. Later I got an electric guitar, and lots of noise became my best creation, musically. After graduating from high school, I moved to Shreveport, Louisiana, and worked days and picked nights. I met Hank Williams, Sr., and saw Hank, Jr., as a diaper baby in Bossier City, across the Red River from Shreveport. Later they moved to Nashville.

A couple of years later, with delusions of grandeur, I too went to Nashville, intending to pick on the Grand Ole Opry. I soon learned that the city was overrun with guitar players who could beat me, and most of them were starving. I went back South, got a real job, and just picked for fun. I moved to Arkansas, worked for American Oil, and did my picking on KELD radio in El Dorado and at various PTA and church functions.

In 1954 KELD called and asked if I could pick onstage that night with a young man trying to make a start in rock 'n' roll. They offered to pay me seventy-five dollars. Were they kidding? That was more than I made in a whole week at my full-time job.

The stage was on one side of a football field, and a tent had been set up for the star. I was escorted backstage to meet him and get prepped for the show.

By this time I was getting nervous. I was twenty-five. This kid was nineteen, dressed in a pale lavender suit, and hyper as a mule colt.

I started trying to back out of the deal, and he started trying to put me at ease. He didn't smoke, drink, or curse, and he answered my questions "Yes, sir" or "No, sir." When I told him I'd never picked rock music, he said, "Sir, my stuff is just hopped-up country."

We went onstage and started the show. Fifteen minutes later he didn't have a dry thread on him, and only two strings remained on his Martin D-18 guitar. The crowd was making so much noise they couldn't hear my mistakes. After about an hour the singer said, "You did good," and I headed home.

When I walked in the door and laid my money on the table, my wife asked how it had gone. I told her I played terrible but nobody heard it; they were screaming, fainting, dancing, and deaf. I told her about the kid, his good manners. I told her he had an energy that the crowd loved. I predicted he would make a million dollars in the next few years if his body could stand it. "Who was he?" she asked.

"He called himself Elvis Presley," I said.

—Bob Festavan works for Cahaba Maintenance and Construction Co., in Alabaster, Alabama.

A young Elvis Presley plays hopped-up country in a 1956 publicity photograph.

MOSCOW MEMORIES

Delta-Bravo-Zero-Four-Black were our code words in Moscow that summer of 1954. The Cold War was on, and, despite our adolescence, we were right in the middle of it. Armed with Defense Department charts that showed the silhouettes, names, ranges, and blood-red stars of Soviet military aircraft, we scanned the skies and reported any unidentified sightings to our uniformed handlers at Fairchild Air Force Base. We peered through government-issue binoculars, watching for a sneak attack on Moscow—a small, rural, college town surrounded by contoured wheat fields in the panhandle of northern Idaho.

We belonged to the Air Force Ground Observer Corps, and were among 375,000 Americans who, in organized shifts, monitored horizons all over the country, reporting directly to the Air Force. According to the promotional materials from the Defense Department, the Soviets had the bomb and the planes to drop it, but America's DEW line—the distant early-warning radar system—could not reliably detect low-flying bombers and their escort MiGs, especially in the Pacific Northwest, where we lived. With the United States so vulnerable, the Air Force operated the Ground Observer Corps for some nine years in the 1950s, enlisting private citizens to operate observation posts and act, it was said, like modern-day Paul Reveres.

Between the seventh and eighth grades, when Doris Day was singing "Secret Love" on the radio and adults were talking about the Army-McCarthy hearings at the dinner table, members of my Boy Scout Buffalo Patrol took our first loyalty oath, promising not to overthrow our government, and were formally inducted into the Ground Observer Corps. From the Air Force recruiter came promises of shiny silver wing pins, a subscription to Aircraft Flash magazine for photos of military jets with billowing contrails, and viewings of fun Air Force movies about the earth slowly turning red, like a Sherwin-Williams paint commercial.

A more effective pitch came from veteran sky watchers in our scout troop. Hidden behind the Soviet-aircraft identification chart in the observation shack was, we were told, a legendary book containing unprecedented carnal scenes not found in any available literature of the day. But that was not all. Supposedly the fastest girl in the eighth grade had signed up for the Ground Observer Corps, giving titillated Buffaloes all manner of sexual double entendres to snicker about when discussing the observation shack.

Because of where we lived, it didn't take much to recruit us. According to adolescent folklore, Moscow, Idaho, was unquestionably the number-one Soviet bombing target. Although the town's high school team was the Bears and one of its colors was red and there was even an annual May Day parade led by obscure Hollywood actors almost everyone pretended to have heard of, there were not, to our immense pride, any real similarities between the Moscow in Idaho and that other one. After all, we were the free Moscow, and that comparative fact was always cabled to the Kremlin as part of our May Day festivities, baiting the Reds and brazenly giving them yet another reason to obliterate a small Idaho town first. There was another crucial difference: unlike the Russian Moscow, ours openly celebrated Christmas and did so once with a large banner over Main Street that read, with undetected irony, "Put Christ Back into

Trying out the family bomb shelter in Bronxville, New York, in 1952.

Christmas—the Moscow Chamber of Commerce."

We began our patriotic observations after a perfunctory training session at the volunteer fire department, and once a week we climbed three flights of stairs, up a ladder, and through a trap door into an unfinished plywood shack on top of Whitworth Junior High School, one of the highest points in town. Overlooking an orderly grid of wide streets, thick maple trees, and quiet middle-class homes, the shack came furnished with one set of perpetually unfocused binoculars, a Soviet-aircraft identification chart, a log book for sign-ins and sightings, and a direct phone line to Fairchild Air Force Base in Spokane.

On duty for the first time in the observation shack, the Buffaloes hastily found the dirty book beneath the Soviet-aircraft identification chart. Even more quickly, we riffled straight to the dog-eared pages, which, though utterly unremarkable by current standards, were enough in those days to draw pubescent patriots up three flights of stairs and a ladder and into four hours of weekly service to their country. To the collective regret of all the Buffaloes, however, the other sign-up incentive proved to be a hoax: except for brief glimpses of her in a rakish Chevrolet driven by a high school boy with glistening black hair, we never saw the alluring eighth-grade girl anywhere that summer.

Once, after weeks of tedium atop Whitworth Junior High School doing nothing more for America than watching crop dusters drone overhead, it happened: I spotted what had to be a Soviet MiG, streaking low across the distant wheat fields. Frantic to confirm my sighting, I grabbed the binoculars, slammed them to my sockets, and furiously twisted the infernal focus knob. Sure of what in reality was only an indistinct, fast-moving speck, I called Fairchild Air Force Base, blurted, "Delta-Bravo-Zero-Four-Black," and reported my observation with as much technical jargon as I could hurriedly read from the Soviet-aircraft identification chart, which was not, at the moment, hiding the dirty book.

"O.K., kid, we'll scramble," came the laconic reply. Hyperventilating, I leaped outside to the railing and watched intently for the F-94C Lockheed "Starfires" that our trainers had promised. Squinting, listening, straining, I waited. But, as the minutes dragged on, the Starfires never came. Neither did anything else, except for some wounding stabs of humiliation. After slowly putting the dirty book back into its well-publicized hiding place and then signing the log book without any mention of the debatable MiG or the promised scramble, I left the observation shack and the Ground Observer Corps for good.

A few weeks later I returned to Whitworth Junior High School, not to read dirty books or to watch for Soviet aircraft but to attend eighth grade. Back in school, I read in my issue of Junior Scholastic about a revolutionary new Supreme Court case that had banned something called racial segregation. There was also a newsreel about a Communist military victory over the French in a part of the world that I had never heard of before: Indochina, at a place called Dien Bien Phu. My personal Cold War was over. Other, more difficult, battles loomed unseen.

—Peter D. Baird is a lawyer living in Phoenix, Arizona.

CELESTIAL TACT

If journalism is, as has been said, the first draft of history, a foreign correspondent has many professional brushes with history. But I won't bore readers with mine. In fact, I won't even mention how as a reporter for a newsmagazine, living in Paris and later in London, I shared a urologist with Charles de Gaulle and my wife a gynecologist with Queen Elizabeth. No state secrets escaped from either. But I did learn something when I was sharing a guitar teacher with the future emperor of Japan.

The time was the mid-1950s, the place Tokyo, where Crown Prince Akihito, as he then was, and I were taking classical guitar lessons from the same teacher—obviously, not together. One day, after I'd gone through another fumbling bout with Bach, I asked my teacher, by way of conversation, how the prince was as a musician. There was a pause. Loyalty to the Son of Heaven was clearly competing with candor in the teacher's mind. "Saaa—" he began, sucking in his breath and letting it out in that long Japanese sigh of deep thought. Then, brightly, "He's just as good as you are."

—Curtis Prendergast, of Bethesda, Maryland, is a former foreign correspondent for *Time* magazine.

Japanese Crown Prince Akihito handles one of the television cameras while visiting New York's Radio City in 1953.

MY DAY WITH HEMINGWAY

In early 1955 I was a first lieutenant in the United States Air Force stationed at Charleston Air Force Base, South Carolina. Our base's basketball team had been invited to Havana to help the Cuban national team prepare for the Olympics. Having no qualifications for anything relating to the game of basketball, I had nevertheless managed to get myself assigned to go along as team "trainer." I had no idea what duties that entailed, nor did I care. There were few places in the world as exciting as pre-Castro Havana. I was going. That was enough.

I was vaguely aware from a recent story in the press that Ernest Hemingway lived near Havana, but that fact held no significance for me. Celebrities, as a rule, did not go to great lengths to seek out the company of lowly lieutenants; but fate was about to change the rules.

In 1955 Ernest Hemingway was at the pinnacle of his fame, probably the most celebrated author on the planet. He was besieged by admirers wherever he went, and the relentless adulation had by now driven him into retreat at his estate, Finca Vigía, on the outskirts of Havana. He had become one of the world's most reclusive and inaccessible celebrities.

We landed at Havana Airport to a tumultuous reception. As we taxied into the terminal, cheering crowds waved Cuban and American flags. We waved back, graciously accepting the unexpected honors.

"Damn," I exclaimed, "they must love basketball in this country."

We did not learn until we reached the terminal that the airplane taxiing in front of us carried Richard M. Nixon, then vice president, on an official goodwill visit.

Our reception at the Vedado Club was exceptionally friendly. We were put up in a first-class hotel downtown. Maj. Jack McKinnon, who had arranged the trip, was not directly involved with the team, so I found my duties as "trainer" to be even less demanding than expected. We deemed it sufficient that I could be reached by phone if the need arose, the phone being located conveniently at the end of the Vedado Club bar.

One gentleman in particular seemed dedicated to making our stay as memorable as possible. His name was Mario Menacol, and his grandfather, I was later told, had been president of Cuba at the turn of the century. He was also a close friend of Ernest Hemingway and one of the few people in the world who could drop in on the novelist.

One day Menacol casually asked us over lunch if we would like to take a drive in the country and meet a friend of his. We accepted.

About ten miles from the club we arrived at a fenced compound with a large wrought-iron gate. As we drove up, a servant approached, and we learned, with a shock, the identity of our host-to-be.

"Mr. Hemingway is expecting us, José," said Menacol.

I had read most of Hemingway's novels and short stories, and I admired him enormously. I was thrilled beyond imagination and, indeed, a trifle terrified.

After letting us in the gate, José accompanied us up to a large Spanish-style house, situated on a hilltop commanding a magnificent view of the wooded countryside. A four-story tower was attached, rather incongruously, to the otherwise conventional structure.

We were led into a long, rectangular living room surrounded on three sides by glass-paned French doors. As we entered the room, dozens of eyes stared solemnly down at us from the heads of hunt trophies that Hemingway had collected from around the world. The remaining wall space was covered with several decades worth of photographs of famous people, places, and events. And there, seated on a chair set on a raised dais, was the great man in the flesh, of which a good deal was exposed. He was wearing nothing but khaki shorts and sandals, a wet towel draped over his large belly. He sat facing the single wall, ignoring the lovely view through the French doors.

As we introduced ourselves, he did not rise, explaining that he had suffered a ruptured disk in the first of his two recent plane crashes. I was surprised, since the injury had not been reported in the press. He was in constant pain and rose only once in the course of the afternoon—to take us out on the veranda to show us the tower where he did his writing when in Cuba. Hemingway waved us into chairs arranged about the dais; his own chair placed him head and shoulders

above us, so that he seemed a plump Buddha surrounded by his disciples.

The first order of business was clearly a matter of serious concern to him. "Gentlemen," he said, gravely addressing Major McKinnon and me, "I want you to give me your word, as officers, that you will not reveal your visit here to the press."

Apparently satisfied with our pledge of secrecy, Hemingway visibly relaxed. Here, it occurred to me, was a lonely man, held hostage by his legions of fans. He seemed actually looking forward to a good bull session.

"Gentlemen," he said, "let's have a drink!" We had several.

Happily for me, Major McKinnon's interests inclined more to sports than literature. And Menacol seemed content to sip on his rum and soda and listen. I would have Ernest Hemingway virtually to myself!

My first comment was to congratulate him on his recent award of the Nobel Prize. "Thanks," he said,

Ernest Hemingway consults during the filming of The Old Man and The Sea *in 1956.*

"but I can't get my hands on the money. The god-damned American ambassador [who had accepted the prize on his behalf] is holding it. He wants to come out and 'present' it, and I don't want the son-of-a-bitch in my house!" Why, he did not say. "My taxidermist in Nairobi is holding up my trophies, and I need the forty thousand dollars!"

I found it hard to believe that Ernest Hemingway could need money, but he seemed perfectly serious. How he finally collected the prize I never found out.

I was eager to steer the conversation around to Miss Redmon's class in American literature at the University of North Carolina. I had always been a bit skeptical of her ability to see into the minds of authors and extract hidden meanings that routinely went over my head.

I recalled vividly one lecture in which she had explained the exquisite symbolism she discerned in this brief preface to The Snows of Kilimanjaro: "Kilimanjaro is a snow covered mountain 19,710 feet high, and it is said to be the highest mountain in Africa. Its western summit is called the Masai 'Ngàje Ngài,' the House of God. Close to the western summit there is the dried and frozen carcass of a leopard. No one has explained what the leopard was seeking at that altitude." Could we not see, she wondered, the beautiful metaphor therein expressed: the leopard, sensing impending death, climbing the mountains as if reaching out to God? Hemingway was alluding to the bond that exists between God and nature. I quoted Miss Redmon as best I could remember and asked Hemingway if this was what he had in mind.

"Bulls—!" he said. "She doesn't know what she's talking about! I just thought it was a hell of a good story, that's all. If you ever see her again, Lieutenant, you tell her what I said."

As we talked, Hemingway noticed that our eyes were drawn to his beard, which he scratched incessantly.

"Damn beard itches," he said.

"Why don't you shave it off?" offered Major McKinnon, happy to find a way into the conversation.

"Got a skin problem. Shaving only makes it worse," Hemingway replied.

I asked every question I could think of, from serious to frivolous. I even asked if, after his acquaintance with Ava Gardner in the filming of The Snows, he believed the tabloid reports of a torrid affair that she was said to be having with Sammy Davis, Jr.

"No, Lieutenant," he said. "Those people write that crap for one reason—money. Truth has nothing to do with it." Ava was a sweet Southern girl, he said, and he just didn't believe the story.

As the sun sank into the hills, shadows began creeping up the wall, and Hemingway suddenly became acutely aware of the time of day.

"José," he shouted, "come get this damned rum out of here. Can't you see it's martini time?"

Perhaps understandably, I cannot remember how many martinis we stayed on for. Fascinating hours slipped by and darkness fell. I do recall that at one point our conversation was interrupted by a disturbance outside.

"Mr. Hemingway, Mr. Hemingway," a female voice yelled. "Are you at home?"

"José," he hollered irritably, "get her ass out of here!"

Finally we sensed that it was time to take our leave. Reluctantly—and unsteadily—we said good-bye, and my brush with history was over. The forty years that have passed have surely released me from my pledge.

—Wallace Paul Conklin was an Air Force lieutenant colonel who lived in Ft. Walton Beach, Florida.

JUST ANOTHER WEAPON

The year was 1955 and the U.S. Army had embarked on a program of developing relatively small tactical nuclear weapons that could be used on the battlefield. A series of atmospheric tests in Nevada had convinced military scientists that properly trained soldiers could not only survive such explosions but also take part in maneuvers planned to exploit these weapons.

These hypotheses, however, had never been tested, and the atomic bomb had taken on very frightening connotations. So to demonstrate that the weapons were "safe," the Army decided to run a test with live soldiers. The purpose of the test was to teach troops that the bomb was just another weapon of war.

Test participants were selected from various units across the United States. I had just been promoted to captain and was stationed at Fort Bliss, Texas. I considered the opportunity to see a nuclear explosion a once-in-a-lifetime experience and was the first in my unit to volunteer. Not only was I selected to take part, but I was put in charge of the entire 4th Army contingent, a group of two hundred and fifty officers drawn from posts throughout the Southwest. I knew one man slightly. The rest were strangers.

Our group assembled at Fort Bliss and began a two-day train ride to Las Vegas, Nevada, about an hour's drive from the test site. During the trip I established a simple organizational structure, placing each of five lieutenants in charge of about fifty people. Together we prepared a handwritten list of the participants. Our morale was high. We all looked forward to a unique military experience as well as a chance to do a little gambling.

Our train arrived in Las Vegas so late that it became apparent we would have no supper that

US marines take part in a tactical exercise a few seconds after an atomic bomb was detonated during the 1952 Operation Tumbler-Snapper, in Yucca Flats, Nevada.

evening. However, a call to Camp Desert Rock, the tent city at the Nevada test site where we would sleep during our planned three-day stay, brought assurances that hot coffee would be waiting for us when we arrived around midnight. It was not. Nor had our group been assigned particular tents. We were instructed to find cots wherever we could until more permanent arrangements could be made the following day.

That plan might well have worked if one of the most violent storms in recent Nevada history had not struck at about three o'clock in the morning. It blew away every tent in Camp Desert Rock, soaking everyone and their personal belongings. Our personnel list disappeared. I found I was responsible for two hundred and fifty wet, hungry, disgruntled soldiers whose names I didn't know and who were scattered throughout the countryside.

A noontime breakfast got everyone back together, and by evening a modicum of order had been restored—just in time for everyone to board buses for the big city. The return buses left Las Vegas at 1:00 a.m. and arrived at camp an hour later. At 4:00 a.m. we were awakened for a dry run of the test. We boarded buses and drove for about an hour into the desert, where a series of trenches about eight feet deep awaited us. We climbed in, crouched for about an hour, and then returned to Camp Desert Rock, arriving about 8:00 a.m. We had the rest of the day to enjoy the 118-degree temperature in open tents in the middle of the desert.

Little did we know this would be our normal routine for the coming week. The test, called Apple II, was scheduled for the day following the dry run. However, after we settled in our trenches, wind conditions were pronounced unfavorable and the test was postponed. This sequence was repeated on the next five mornings. By this time only a few had money left to go to Las Vegas. However, those who did learned

that each evening a light on one of the buildings downtown indicated to the local populace whether there would be a test the next day. A blue light meant no test; a red light meant there would be one. Apparently our superiors hadn't bothered to check the light each evening.

On our seventh morning we learned that the light had been red the previous night, so we felt confident that this would be the real thing. Our trenches were just over a mile from ground zero, the point immediately below the nuclear device. (No one ever used the term "bomb".) We were told that the test device was roughly the same size as the bombs dropped on Japan and was located in a tower several hundred feet above the ground. We were also told there would be a bright flash, followed by a wave of heat. Next would come the ground shock. Finally there would be a rush of air as the blast wave passed over us. At that point we would be able to leave the trenches and walk up to an area near ground zero where we could see the effect of the explosion on various types of military equipment.

Since I knew that the blast wave would travel at the speed of sound (eleven hundred feet per second), I calculated that it would hit the trenches about six seconds after the explosion. If I allowed a second for the blast to pass and an extra second's margin, it would be safe to stand eight seconds after the initial flash. This meant that if I counted carefully, I would be able to view the fireball much sooner than my colleagues, who would be waiting for the official word to stand up.

As the time for the explosion approached, we all crouched in the bottom of the trenches with our arms over our eyes. We shivered slightly in our field jackets; the desert is cold at six o'clock in the morning. Finally the countdown started—sixty seconds, thirty seconds, twenty, ten, five, four, three, two, one—and then came a flash of unbelievable intensity. In the brilliant light I saw through my jacket—and through my arm—the pebbles at the bottom of the trench. (For many years I thought this must have been some type of optical illusion. However, I have recently learned that this is a real phenomenon, apparently caused by X rays induced by the explosion.) Contrary to my expectations, the flash lasted for a considerable time, more than a second. As I was recovering from the flash, the temperature changed from morning cold to well above that of the hottest day I could remember.

Then, as I was reconciling myself to the blast of heat, the earth suddenly jumped what felt to be about six feet in the air and then fell back and began to tremble violently. The thought rushed through my mind: They've miscalculated and blown up the whole world. After what seemed a very long time, I finally had convinced myself of the world's probable survival when suddenly a tremendous freight train roared directly over my head. This lasted about a second, and then all was quiet—until a few seconds later, when the train roared back going the other way.

Now all was quiet. I lay quivering at the bottom of the trench, the counting of seconds long forgotten, when the announcement came that it was safe to stand up. By now several minutes had gone by since the initial explosion, and the fireball had spread considerably. Even so, it was a remarkable sight. A thousand colors, shining and mixing and changing and migrating—like tiny, colorful lightning flashes—appearing, disappearing, and appearing again. All of us stood in awe as the cloud expanded, gradually losing its colors and turning into a vast brown-gray balloon. The broad, dirty stem connecting the cloud to the ground slowly dissipated, and the now colorless ball of debris drifted away into the distance. The show was over.

About half an hour after the explosion, we were allowed to walk toward ground zero, stopping about two hundred yards from the actual spot. Along the way we saw an assortment of obliterated military vehicles, weapons, and dummies. The most impressive item was a heavy battle tank that had been split in two by the blast, with the turret blown one way and the main body the other.

Contemplating my experiences in the trench, I realized that I was no longer concerned about nuclear weapons. I was now terrified by them. Later in my military career I took part in many map exercises and maneuvers in which commanders simulated the use of nuclear weapons, often rather casually. I listened to a number of armchair war hawks, as well as some very prim and proper ladies, advocate that we drop a couple of nukes on Hanoi or Baghdad or Pyongyang to show those people we meant business. I feel confident their opinions would have been different if they had been in the trenches at Apple II.

My last assignment in the Army was with the Defense Atomic Test Command in Albuquerque, New Mexico, where I was the test-group director for two underground nuclear tests. After I retired in 1970, I got a Ph.D. in nuclear engineering from the University of Texas, and taught it there for several years before leaving to start my own business. At present I am in great health and, to the best of my knowledge, I have suffered no ill effects from Apple II, or my other work in the field. My wife and I have three healthy, intelligent children and four world-class grandchildren, with probably more to come.

A few years ago there was some concern that participants in the Nevada test might have suffered long-term health effects. The Army responded that it had no way to evaluate the impact of the test; it had kept no record of the people who had taken part.

—Dr. John H. Vanston is the chairman of Technology Futures, Inc.

ME 'N' ELVIS 'N' NATO

In the spring of 1956 a kid out of Memphis with a greasy pompadour and a semipermanent sneer, who belted a raucous and rowdy brand of what was then known as rockabilly—a combination of Nashville country and gut-bucket Mississippi Delta blues—was drawing swarms of local belles to his appearances at the "Louisiana Hayride" in Shreveport. That, in turn, drew numerous lonely young airmen from nearby Barksdale Air Force Base, like sharks to schooling tuna.

Late one Saturday evening, after fruitless cruising at the Hayride, several other sharks and I stopped for a final cup of coffee at the Kickapoo Inn in Bossier City, just across the Red River from Shreveport. It was the last all-night café on the way out of the area, a final stop for truckers and travelers heading out.

As we sat bemoaning our lack of female companionship, a mob of honking cars roared into the parking lot, accompanied by the shrieks of what seemed to be several thousand teenage girls. The door burst open, and four hulking escorts entered, forming a wall around a somewhat flamboyant late-middle-aged man dressed like Burl Ives and a sallow, handsome kid in his late teens or early twenties.

Elvis Presley seemed polite, deferential to his elders, and gracious in signing autographs for the few fans who managed to evade the front-door security. As we finished our coffee, I looked toward his table, nodded, and raised my cup in a toast. He nodded in return and lifted his cup. My friends and I departed the Kickapoo and for several months regaled the local girls with imaginative tales of how we'd had coffee with Elvis himself! Whether or not it was a successful ploy, we did seem to have better luck arranging dates.

Almost four years later, happily married and the father of two, I was assigned to a small Air Force weather detachment at Heidelberg Army Air Field in West Germany. Our job was to provide support to the Army and, when necessary, to deploy to the field and furnish weather data from primitive airstrips. In January 1960 the largest post-World War II military exercise yet held in Western Europe was scheduled under the title Winter Shield I. A quarter of a million troops from every nation in NATO were deployed across the sprawling Grafenwöhr armored training center near the East German border. For weeks in deep snow with low, threatening overcast and generally miserable conditions, we froze and worked around the clock, subsisting on C rations.

Finally, in some small act of compassion, the generals decided on a stand-down midway through the exercise. All the troops were staged into the main post at "Graf" for a hot shower, a change of clothes, and some hot food at the cavernous old Wehrmacht Kaserne (mess hall). My first order of business was a steaming shower, followed by clean underwear and a layer of fresh clothes. Feeling like a millionaire, I strolled over to the mess hall with visions of steak and potatoes.

The line of hungry GIs snaked from the parade ground through the wide doors. The men were coming out as fast as they got in, and the expression on their faces was not one of satisfaction. When I reached the door and peered inside, I realized why. A long line of cooks were fishing the familiar cans out of boiling vats and clanging them onto metal trays. C rations!

I overheard the guy ahead of me talking to his buddy. "— this —," he said. "I'm goin' over to the PX snack bar."

Suddenly the thought of a great big juicy cheese-burger, heaped with onions, tomatoes, lettuce, and mayo, and chased by a thick strawberry milk shake, was what I was really fighting the make-believe war for. I put down my tray and hurried over to the PX.

A double line of Brits in baggy field coveralls, French, Dutch, Danes, Turks, Greeks, Italians, Belgians, and West German Bundeswehr in Feldgrau all had had the same idea.

I was in a quandary. My truck back to the airstrip was due to leave in another two hours. It was obvious that unless some miracle occurred, I would get

no cheeseburger and milk shake to carry me through another week of C rations. And then, bless him in whatever rock-star Valhalla he may now inhabit, Elvis again came into my life.

The low mutter of voices in the line suddenly changed to calls of "It's Elvis!" A dirty jeep with two filthy GIs coasted slowly up the street in front of the snack bar. The long line melted away. Suddenly there wasn't a soul between me and the PX door.

When his Selective Service number had come up, Elvis, like millions of young Americans before and after, had dutifully reported. Now he was serving

Elvis Presley is the center of attention at a restaraunt in the 1950s.

as a rifleman with a scout platoon in an armored division in West Germany.

I strolled into the now empty PX snack bar as though I were the only man left in "Graf." Behind the counter two middle-aged Fräuleins were bouncing up and down like frantic terriers: "Alvis!...Alvis!" But they subsided long enough to fill my order for "two cheeseburgers, with everything, and a large strawberry milk shake, bitte." There was no delay. The unclaimed burgers and shakes ordered earlier by the horde were there for the taking. Only an older non-commissioned officer, unimpressed by "the King," nursed a beer at the corner table and muttered about how the Army had gone to hell since Korea

The mob began to filter back in as I finished the last of my burgers, and I strolled out onto the snow-covered front steps with the remainder of my milk shake. At about the same time, Elvis's jeep began to inch through the crowd of autograph seekers.

As he passed by me, only a few feet away, our eyes met, and I raised the milk shake in a salute. I looked into his sleepy-lidded, tired face, grimy with dirt and stubble, and felt a kinship, born of weariness, bad food, little sleep, and bone-aching cold. We nodded, and he drove out of my life.

In 1977, as we were preparing to send our youngest off to her first year of college, the radio interrupted its normal broadcast to announce the sudden death of Elvis Presley at his home in Memphis. As a Depression baby I was a little too old to be a fan of rock 'n' roll, but I always had a soft spot for Elvis. I've often wished I'd had the opportunity to personally thank the King for improving a young airman's romantic life and for giving him the opportunity to grab a couple of cheeseburgers and a strawberry shake one cold day when they really mattered.

—Jack DuBose is deputy director of the Arkansas Department of Management. He retired from the Air Force after a 27-year career.

THE WINNERS

From 1954 to 1957 I was a starting guard on the University of Kansas basketball squad. My career was fairly unremarkable until the fall of 1956, when a young Philadelphian named Wilt Chamberlain joined our team.

Over seven feet tall with the quickness and agility of someone a foot shorter, Wilt was easily the greatest player any of us had ever seen. He could score and rebound almost at will, and his incredible ability to dunk a basketball left everyone gaping. In his debut performance, Wilt scored fifty-two points, and immediately we were picked to win the national championship.

Just two years earlier, in 1954, the Kansas forward Maurice King had become the first black starter for a Big Seven team. Fortunately, Maurice had a Jackie Robinson temperament, because he was subjected to outrageous indignities on a daily basis.

Then Wilt and his brash talent came along, and racial tensions—particularly in the traditionally Southern states like Missouri and Oklahoma—escalated. It seemed everywhere we went we heard "nigger," "nigger lover," and worse. Officials would often ignore blatant fouls committed against black players, and opposing schools waved Confederate flags and played "Dixie." Of course, now I know that what I saw was just the tip of the iceberg. Dick Harp, our idealistic young coach, tried to protect all of us as much as possible, and Maurice and Wilt were too proud to admit how bad things really were.

But none of us could have imagined the atmosphere awaiting the team at the 1957 Midwest Regionals, held that year for the first time in Dallas, Texas. The tournament hotel refused to accommodate blacks, so we stayed at a dingy motel miles away in Grand Prairie. No restaurant would serve us, so we took all our meals together in a private room.

Our first game was against our hosts, the fifth-ranked (and all-white) Southern Methodist University Mustangs. SMU was undefeated in its new field house, and it was easy to see why. Their crowd was brutal. We were spat upon, pelted with debris, and subjected to the vilest racial epithets imaginable. The officials did little to maintain order. There were so many uncalled fouls, each more outrageous than the last, that Maurice and Wilt risked serious injury simply by staying in the game, and, incredibly, they responded with some of the best basketball of their lives. We escaped with a 73-65 overtime win.

Naively I thought the worst of our crowd problems was over. But the next night SMU fans adopted our opponents, the all-white Oklahoma City University Chiefs. OCU's flamboyant coach, Abe Lemons, encouraged the support, and soon emboldened OCU players were throwing themselves on the floor, trying to take blacks out of basketball—permanently. Our ordinarily mild-mannered coach had a few choice words for Lemons, and the two nearly came to blows.

Before long, however, we were winning easily, and OCU's frustration became desperation. Wilt in particular appeared at the free-throw line over and over again. Infuriated fans hurled food, seat cushions, and coins at the court, and the field house rocked with racial slurs and threats. Someone stopped the game, and I was afraid Coach Harp was pulling us off the court for our own safety.

But the officials had finally had enough. They threatened OCU with a forfeit if fans didn't settle down, and reluctantly SMU's athletic director took the microphone and appealed for better behavior.

The crowd howled, but eventually we were allowed to resume play. The final score was Kansas, 81-61, with Wilt named to the all-tournament team. Armed police officers escorted us off the court and all the way back to the airport.

Less than one week later, on March 22, the National Championships (now called the Final Four) began in Kansas City. Kansas had almost a home-court advantage: Three of our starters (including myself) were Kansas City natives, and the tournament site was only forty miles from campus. Our semifinal opponent, two-time defending champion San Francisco, fell easily, and the stage was set for a matchup against the undefeated and top-ranked North Carolina Tarheels.

Emotions were running high—perhaps too high. We fell behind early, and only Wilt's incredible ability kept us from digging our own graves. We spent all of the first half (and much of the second) playing catch-up, but with two minutes to go we were ahead by five. Then inexplicably we went into a slowdown game, completely at odds with our usual run-and-gun style. The score was tied 46-46 when the buzzer sounded.

Both teams began playing nervously and cautiously; no one wanted to make a mistake that could cost a national championship. Each team scored only once in the first overtime, and in the second, neither scored at all.

By this time the crowd noise was deafening, the court was blanketed in thick cigarette smoke, and the tension was almost unbearable. The pace picked up. With six seconds left in triple overtime, we led 53-52, and Carolina's Joe Quigg was called to the free-throw line. He sank both shots, and Carolina was up by one.

Everyone in the stands—and certainly everyone on the court—knew Kansas would try to get the ball to Wilt. The only question was how. We knew Wilt would be double- or perhaps triple-teamed. North Carolina's best defensemen would be swarming over Gene Elstun, our number two scorer, and Maurice, our top ball handler. Coach Harp figured that would leave six-foot-six forward Ron Loneski almost unguarded. Granted, Ron was not the best passer in the world, but he was so tall that presumably he could lift the ball over our opponents' heads and in Wilt's general direction. Wilt had such great hands that he could take it from there.

I took the ball out of bounds at mid-court and had little trouble passing in safely. But North Carolina's defense, playing on pure adrenaline, trapped Ron out of position. He was forced to make a shaky pass inside, and somehow, unbelievably, horribly, the ball landed in Carolina hands. The buzzer sounded, and the game was over.

What is now considered the greatest college basketball game ever played had for us deteriorated into a nightmare. Stunned, we watched Carolina celebrate, and somehow we made it through the awards ceremony dry-eyed. But as soon as we passed through the locker-room doors, we all broke down. The long bus ride back to campus was completely silent.

Now almost forty years later I look back on my college basketball career with more pride than bitterness. To this day we are ranked in the top twenty-five teams ever to play college basketball, and I know our regional title in the segregated South did more for the game than any national championship has ever done. I'm glad I had some small role in challenging the inequities of the day, and I'm honored to have been associated with some of the bravest men ever to don a basketball uniform.

I just wish we could have won.

—John E. Parker Jr. lives in Overland Park, Kansas.

Wilt "The Stilt" Chamberlain, while a center at the University of Kansas, leaves the floor after scoring 45 points to lead the Jayhawks to the title in the 11th annual Big Seven invitational tourney.

LOOKING FOR ADLAI

It was 1956, and Adlai Stevenson was running against Dwight Eisenhower for the presidency. People who supported Stevenson tended to feel an almost personal emotion for him, and I felt as if a beloved relative were running.

Sometime during the summer I heard that he was making a swing through the state and would give a speech in a hotel in Vancouver, Washington. His itinerary would take him from Spokane in the far east over to the Columbia River and then many miles west along a winding road outstandingly beautiful but narrow, not a road good for anyone in a hurry.

On the day that Mr. Stevenson and his party wended their way to Vancouver, I happened to be driving into the next county on the same Evergreen Highway. My children and I watched like hawks all the way up the river. It was close to four o'clock in the afternoon when we started back, and we thought it a reasonable hour to spot them. The speech was scheduled for eight o'clock, and they might be on the last leg of their trip as we drove home. We were weary of watching and of all the false alarms when we finally came to the suburbs of Vancouver.

The Evergreen Highway goes straight through to the city center, but I turned off at the outskirts for some shopping and then took a main street that crossed Evergreen. As we approached the intersection, we had a moment to realize something was going on. Motorcycle police were at the head of a long line of traffic.

Suddenly I realized this must be them. We were the first in the traffic line, and my eyes filled with tears as I saw the great limousines, one of them almost certainly his car. Suddenly carried away, I rolled down the window of our shabby old station wagon, leaned out, pounded on the door with my open hand, and shouted at the top of my voice, "I hope you win." There must have been a number of puzzled people stopped at the light. I realized a stately funeral cortege was making its way across the intersection.

—Margaret Abbott lived in La Center, Washington.

Presidential candidate Adlai Stevenson (left) gives the victory sign with running mate Senator John Sparkman at the 1952 Democratic Convention.

THE BIBLE LESSON

I was a young reporter in Chicago on the day in 1956 that Harry Truman turned the tables on me. He gave me the most memorable interview of my reporting career, but I was too embarrassed to turn it in to my editor.

I was working for the Chicago American, covering police headquarters from midnight to 8:00 a.m. At about 6:00 in the morning, I got a call from my editor, directing me to go to the Sheraton-Blackstone Hotel and interview Truman before he checked out at 8:00. Truman, who had been out of office for about four years, was in the Chicago area making a halfhearted campaign speech for the Democratic presidential candidate, Adlai Stevenson.

I rushed to the hotel and bluffed my way past the front desk by showing my press credentials. (Security was looser in those pre-Kennedy-assassination days.) I went to the fourth floor and rang the bell of the hotel's Presidential Suite.

The door was opened by a big, burly middle-aged man. I told him I was there to interview the president. He told me: "The President made a speech last night in Gary, and all the other papers were there. Why weren't you?"

I had no idea why my paper hadn't covered Truman's speech, so I made up a story. I said, "The reporter who was assigned to cover the speech was suddenly called away to a fire."

"Well, the president said everything he had to say last night," said the man. "But if you go sit by the elevator, we'll be checking out in about fifteen minutes. You can ride down with us."

I thanked him profusely and went to sit by the elevator. A few minutes later he walked down the hall and said, "The president will see you now."

President Harry Truman waves from the back of a limousine.

I gulped hard and followed him back to the suite. As I entered, there stood Harry S. Truman, the former president of the United Sates, beaming from ear to ear. He was wearing a gray three-piece suit. (I had on khaki pants and a red checked wool shirt; midnight police reporters seldom covered anything more formal than a murder or a fire.)

"How are you, young man?" he asked, shaking my hand vigorously. The other man left the room. We sat on settees facing each other in front of a fireplace. My mind was racing, trying to think of something that might draw out the famous Truman temperament, and I recalled that the civil rights plank in the Democratic platform was very weak. So I asked him, "Do you think civil rights will be an issue in this campaign?"

"My boy," he replied, "civil rights has been an issue ever since Nebuchadnezzar."

I wrote furiously, trying to think of a follow-up question when he demanded, "You know who Nebuchadnezzar was, don't you?"

"Of course," I shot back. My mind was now in overdrive. The name was vaguely familiar from my Sunday-school days, but I just couldn't place it.

"Well, who was he?" Truman asked.

I was devastated. "I give up," I said. "Who was he?"

Truman threw back his head and roared with laughter. "Hey, Al, I'm giving this young man a Bible lesson," he called to the man in the other room. Then, turning back to me, he said, "I won't tell you. You look it up and tell me the next time I come to town."

I asked a couple more inane questions, and then the bellhop arrived for the luggage. We rode down in the elevator and walked through the lobby together. I was still trying desperately to think of who Nebuchadnezzar might have been.

Truman got into a big black limousine. Then he rolled down the window and beckoned to me. I leaned down. "Now don't you misquote me," he said, waggling a finger, "or I won't talk to you next time I come to town."

As the car pulled away, the first line of an old spiritual popped into my head. "Neb-u-chad-nezzar was the king of Babylon . . . Shadrach, Meshach, Abednego. . . ." Of course! He put the children of Israel into the fiery furnace for refusing to worship a golden idol.

Truman's car was just turning the corner at the end of the block. I wanted to yell, "Wait! I've got the answer!" But it was too late.

When I phoned my editor, I told him, in my embarrassment, that Truman hadn't said anything newsworthy. It was several years before I was able to tell my colleagues what had really happened. I never saw Harry S. Truman again.

—Bruce S. Odom is the president of Blue Moon Communications, Inc., which publishes *Out of the Blue*, a newsletter for former IBM employees.

QUIZ SHOW

hat I'm about to record is true, including the parts I've forgotten. Seeing the movie Quiz Show disinterred a memory almost half a century old. On the way back there, though, I must pause first at 1958, when Charles Van Doren was holding forth on the tube and piling up all that money on the "Twenty-One" show. Being something of a snob at the time, I hadn't acquired the habit of watching television. Besides, I was a book editor, and my evenings were spent reading manuscripts.

But I did watch Charlie. His sister Ann lived two doors down Bleecker Street from me, and he and I were nodding acquaintances. Also, I myself had won some money as a contestant on a quiz show back in

Contestants Vivienne Nearing and Charles Van Doren compete on the populer quiz show Twenty-One in 1957.

the dark ages of radio. So week after week I watched—with empathy, with a degree of jealousy (radio quiz winners won hundreds, not hundreds of thousands), and with growing skepticism; those long, agonizing pauses as the contestants searched their souls in the isolation booths began to seem awfully studied. Their depiction in Quiz Show was certainly among the movie's best effects and vividly recalled for me my own brief moment of stand-up glory and my early basic training in how broadcasters control who wins quiz shows and why.

In the 1940s, radio shows were produced by advertising agencies. Four days after my discharge from the Army late in December 1945, my godfather, Pete Barnum, a Madison Avenue advertising executive, arranged to get me on a quiz show, of which there seemed to be dozens on the air. This one was so sparsely produced, and its emcee so uncelebrated and free of charisma, that I have forgotten its name, and his.

As instructed, I turned up an hour and a quarter before the broadcast at the production office in the Times Square district. Two men in suits were huddled with two young soldiers in the back of the big room, and another functionary was talking with a girl (as a woman was then called) over in a far corner. These, I gathered, were the other contestants.

A shirtsleeved man, maybe forty years old, who turned out to be the announcer/emcee, approached and greeted me by name. "You must be Max," he said.

"Close," I said.

The contestants would be assigned different categories of questions, he told me. Mine was to be the dates on which notable events of the year just past had occurred. He would name an event, and I was to guess, within thirty days, when it had taken place. It wouldn't be fitting for him to lay it all out for me, he said stuffily, but for starters it might be a good idea if I brushed up on V-E Day, and on just when Charlie

Chaplin's paternity suit was brought or settled or hit the headlines.

I told him I had been overseas for the entire year and was rusty on domestic news events. But I was already planning to make a beeline to a back-issue magazine store on Sixth Avenue, and I recall my flush of annoyance when he made the suggestion I visit such a store to catch up on the year's happenings. Thinking back, I suppose each of us carried some shoulder chips as baggage into our colloquy. He probably resented my being sponsored, as it were, by an advertising honcho, and I resented his obvious relish at being able to dispense or withhold information of value to me.

As the announcer and I talked, I could not help noticing that the two soldiers seemed to be getting walked through their routine more exhaustively than I, an observation I was not shy about mentioning to the announcer.

"I may as well tell you," he said, "one of the soldiers is going to be the winner."

I don't know why he told me, and I don't expect he was supposed to. Perhaps it was because he thought I, a known nepot, ought to be sophisticated enough to understand the logic of the decision. Perhaps he just wanted to rub my nose in this foregone conclusion.

"How come?" I asked him.

"They're in uniform. It's as simple as that. The audience will be rooting for them."

I, feeling the natural contempt of a twenty-three-year-old overseas veteran toward teenage stateside recruits, pointed out that their tunics were unadorned by any mark of rank or length or theater of service, and they in fact gave every evidence of having been in the Army approximately long enough to get their teeth fixed at Fort Dix, whereas the uniform I had taken off four days earlier had born sergeant's stripes, a YANK patch on the shoulder signifying my status as a combat correspondent on the Army weekly, plus ribbons signifying Pacific Theater, Air Medal, and, yes, the Good Conduct Medal over the left breast pocket.

"If I'd worn it, would I have had a shot at being the winner?"

"We couldn't have three soldiers," he replied, all sweet reason. "Also, if you're a veteran, how come you're not wearing the ruptured duck?" This was the universal nickname for the gold-colored lapel pin issued to all discharged servicemen.

I shrugged. "I'm just not." I wasn't about to articulate to this patronizing oaf my feeling that the ruptured duck was uncool—or corny, as I probably thought of it then.

"By the way," he said, "how do you want to be billed? How do we introduce you?"

I told him I was goofing off while awaiting word of acceptance to Harvard graduate school. It was true enough, but it sounded a bit stuffy and elitist to us both. He suggested "college student."

If the audience was into soldiers, I wanted whatever piece of that action I could get. "How about 'recently discharged veteran'?"

So we decided he'd combine the two designations.

I was making a move toward the door when one of the men who'd been talking to the soldiers detached himself and walked over to say something to the announcer, who immediately raised his hand to summon me back. The other man called me by name, my right name, and introduced himself as the show's producer. He made affectionate mention of Pete Barnum and indicated the announcer that accidentally neglected to remind me of one matter that could come up on the program on which they wanted to brief me: They wanted me to remember the date of April 12. "It's the date of FDR's death," he said, "and it's a date we think every American should know. The audience will want you to hit it right on the head—no thirty-day leeway. Listen, you do well, there's no reason you couldn't win second-prize money, O.K.? See you back here no later than quarter to eight."

I was not too proud to thank him, and as I left for the back-issue store, I thought over what I'd been told. The same dynamic that sealed the fate of Herb Stempel on "Twenty-One" was, of course, at work even in 1945. The producers would have been crazy not to have tilted the decision to one of the GIs. The uniforms wouldn't be visible to people listening on their radios, but radio shows drew their energy from the enthusiasm and applause of the studio audience, and back then soldier was a synonym for winner. A guy in a suit meant nothing.

Notwithstanding, I schemed for a way to upstage the two rookies as I speed-read my way through a stack of old Newsweeks.

When I returned to the office where I'd been briefed, I passed the main entrance to the theater. Then, as now, it didn't take much to attract a crowd in New York. It was a cold night, but there was a big gang out front, waiting for the doors to open so they could file in and watch our little gavotte.

Inside there was a podium. There were bright lights and a standing mike. The contestants took turns at the mike, and the audience was obediently enthusiastic as questions were asked and answered. I looked over at the deadpan faces of four or five men behind the glass of the control booth, and one of them gave me a perfunctory high-sign wave. It was the producer.

I have no recollection of how the girl did or of just how things were arranged so that one of the soldiers did indeed wind up with the most points. I answered all my questions correctly enough, and I did win second-prize money. The other questions are long forgotten, but I got Chaplin right. The memory I still carry with me is of my final exchange with my interlocutor.

"What day did President Franklin D. Roosevelt die?"

I paused, eyes cast upward, as if the answer lay in the flies above the stage. The studio audience's anxiety for me to get it right was palpable. Finally I spoke, and I was emphatic. "April thirteenth."

There was a collective groan from the audience. I was within the thirty-day limit, of course, but I'd been given the exact date, the date all Americans were expected to know, and I'd muffed it.

The announcer shot me a scathing look. I'd double-crossed him. "The thirteenth?" He made the word sound like sacrilege.

"No? Not the thirteenth? I could have sworn—oh-h-h." I said, and I raised my hand dramatically. "I know. Out where I was, in the Pacific, I was on the other side of the International Date Line. Back here in the States (I don't believe I added "for you civilians," but it was surely there in my tone) it was the twelfth, of course. But at the 73rd Very Heavy Bombardment Wing on Saipan it was definitely the thirteenth."

Immodesty compels me to admit the crowd went wild. I looked over and saw that even the producer and his cohorts in the control booth were laughing and clapping.

The emcee pulled me away from the mike and put his hand over it. "Pretty cute, Harvard," he whispered. "Pretty damn cute."

—Knox Burger is a literary agent in New York City and has been a magazine and book editor.

BOXER

I grew up in Louisville, Kentucky, back in the late fifties and early sixties. One day a few friends and I went to Columbia Auditorium. We wanted to learn how to box; we knew how to street fight. Street fighting and boxing were different, like night and day. There was this program called "Tomorrow's Champions," an amateur-boxing show on television every Saturday evening. We had told our family and our girlfriends we would be on television. All three of us won our first fight. We thought we were all that. So the next week we would be on again.

My friend Ronnie was to fight some kid by the name of Cassius Clay, Jr. We had seen this kid working out in the gym. He was always in the ring sparring around by himself. We thought, he's nothing: "Ronnie, man, you can take him."

Paul and I won our bout; then it was Ronnie's turn. The kid weighed just eighty-nine pounds. Ronnie was ninety pounds. The bell rang, and they both came out. Ronnie got knocked out, knocked cold. Paul looked at me. I looked at him. We couldn't believe it. Only later did we find out the reason this kid was sparring by himself was because nobody in the gym would get in the ring with him.

—Henderson Simmons was, at the time of writing, incarcerated at Northpoint Correctional Center in Burgin, Kentucky.

At twelve-years old, Cassius Clay (later Muhammad Ali) shows his best pugilist stance.

KENNEDY PACKS THE HOUSE

As a college sophomore in 1960, I had little interest in politics except that the woman I was dating was a member of the Young Democrats on campus. Democrats at Oregon State College in those days were a rare commodity, so when the presidential campaign got under way, our little group didn't expect to be much involved.

Imagine our surprise, then, when we were asked by the State Central Committee to help play host to Sen. John F. Kennedy when he made a campaign speech in Corvallis. I knew nothing about campaigns or electioneering, so I was given grunt work: nailing up posters, running errands, and stuffing envelopes.

On the day of Kennedy's arrival, I was relegated to helping set up the ballroom of the Benton Hotel in Corvallis, where the senator was to make his speech. We worked hard to spruce up the hotel's grand ballroom with the best red, white, and blue political trappings. I had just stepped back from hanging the last piece of bunting when someone asked me to drive two other young Democrats out to the airport to greet Kennedy's front man, who for this event was his brother Ted.

When Ted Kennedy got off the plane, he looked at the three of us and said, "How many of you are here?" I thought he meant Young Democrats, so I said there were two more of us back at the hotel. For a moment I thought he would get back on the plane and go home, but after we explained that we hoped to turn out a big crowd, he came with us.

At the hotel Ted Kennedy surveyed our lavishly decorated but cavernous ballroom and asked how many people we thought would turn out. The Central Committee folks said they hoped for fifty or sixty and explained that Corvallis was "pretty Republican."

Kennedy said that nothing looked worse than a poor turnout and made a decision: We would move the reception into the hallway outside the ballroom. It was a large hallway, but to my mind it was not big enough to hold fifty people plus the news media. I blurted out that there wouldn't be enough room for everyone. Ted Kennedy looked at me. "I know," he said.

This was all beyond me, but I pitched in to move the tables of punch and cookies out into the hallway and tried to string some of the bunting and crepe paper in appropriate places. Then Kennedy gave me an order: Close the ballroom doors, and under no circumstances open them to anyone.

Soon about thirty people had arrived, and then came the traveling press. Kennedy had arranged platforms at one end of the hallway, and he told the reporters that was their best vantage point for pictures.

I watched in awe. The newspeople swarmed onto their platform. Cameras and lighting equipment were much larger in those days, so the press took up a great deal of what I could see was becoming very cramped space. Also, the good citizens of Corvallis now numbered almost seventy-five (exceeding our wildest expectations) and began to overflow onto the sidewalk outside.

When Sen. John F. Kennedy and his entourage arrived, there was barely enough room for them to squeeze into the hallway. The crowd began to applaud, the camera lights came on, and the next president began to work his way through the crowd toward a small dais. As JFK approached my "guard post," Ted Kennedy introduced me and the other Young Democrats nearby as those who helped organize the event.

I shook the senator's hand, and he flashed me that incredible smile. "Boy," he said, "you sure know how to turn out a crowd." He went on to give his speech and munch on a few cookies, and then he left for his next event. After he was gone, someone remarked that there were almost a hundred people in the hallway.

The next day we all gathered around a television set to see how it was reported. The Corvallis stop didn't get much coverage on national television, but when the film came on I finally realized why Ted Kennedy had made us leave the auditorium. The commentator said something about an enthusiastic crowd at Corvallis while the film showed what looked like hundreds jamming a large area. Jack Kennedy was right. We had turned out quite a crowd, if not in person, at least on film.

—Mike Burton is the executive officer of Metro, the governing body for the Portland, Oregon region.

John F. Kennedy campaigns in Oregon in the Summer of 1960.

THE CONCERT

Louis Armstrong created a dilemma for me in the middle of Africa in 1960. I was the director of the United States Information Service in the three-state Federation of Southern Rhodesia, Northern Rhodesia, and Nyasaland.

One morning I received an unexpected message marked "urgent" from the State Department's Cultural Exchange Program in Washington: "Louis Armstrong and All Stars currently in West Africa. Department planning to extend Armstrong tour to additional countries in Africa. Advise soonest if you wish performances."

Who wouldn't want Armstrong? He was world-acclaimed, and I knew that both whites and blacks in

Louis Armstrong with the author's children in Africa.

the Rhodesias and Nyasaland listened to his jazz on the Voice of America.

The telegram went to American embassies in seven other African countries, where my colleagues could respond like gangbusters to its offer. They didn't have to cope with our situation—at that time the Rhodesias and Nyasaland composed one of the most racially segregated areas on earth.

How could the man known as "America's Goodwill Ambassador" perform in such an environment? Should Armstrong give concerts before segregated audiences, which was the entrenched local custom? Were segregated concerts better than no concerts at all? Or should I simply tell Washington to forget it and skip this place?

Or was there another way? My colleagues and I got together to talk over the State Department's offer. There were four of us on the senior staff, and we unanimously decided that a visit by Armstrong would be an opportunity to dramatically demonstrate where America stood on racial discrimination. "Our goal has got to be nonsegregated concerts if Armstrong is going to perform," summarized our political officer.

The next step was to win support for this position from our new boss, Consul General John K. Emmerson. He'd been on the job for only two weeks when the State Department telegram came in. He was fifty-two, well educated, and he asked sensible questions: "Will many whites come if seating is nonsegregated?" and "Are there apt to be any security problems?" We weren't sure that large numbers of whites would attend, we answered, but we thought so. Even if they didn't, I added, our promotion of the concerts on a nonsegregated basis would give the United States greater credibility with the black majority. As for security problems, we told him we weren't sure about this either, but precautions could be taken. Emmerson nodded. So far, so good.

Then he came to the tougher questions. "Should the United States be getting out front like this on the race issue here? Is this the right time for us to take such an initiative so publicly? Look," he went on, "is confrontation with the white leadership of the government any way for me to begin my assignment here? You gentlemen are asking me to go in and insist on changes by heads of government I've never even met yet."

Our political officer broke the silence that followed. "Well," he said, "who the hell is going to answer the boss's questions first?" He looked at me. "The Cultural Exchange Program is your baby."

I said, "The staff has given this Armstrong matter serious attention, and we all agree that this is a unique and important opportunity. We don't know how the local government will react, but we're convinced it's worth a try."

The discussion lasted an hour. In the end our consul general said, "O.K., let's bring Armstrong here. Helluva way for this new boy on the block to start things with the local authorities, but let's give it a go."

Elated, we bolted for the door to get started. "Hold it!" Emmerson motioned, right-hand palm in the air. "There's something you've overlooked—Washington. I'm not going to lay down a challenge to the leadership here without Washington knowing it and approving it beforehand."

A cable went back to Washington in an hour, and we got a reply three hours after that: "Concur in full." Our memo to the local government was hand-delivered the next morning. How they would respond was anybody's guess. We were mildly optimistic because at that time the government was slowly edging toward desegregation. The chief justice of the country, Sir Robert Tredgold, had asked us a few months earlier for American law books with cases showing how we desegregated public places in the United States, "including swimming baths." A few commercial hotels in the country had begun to open their doors to nonwhites, but big concerts with possibly thousands of people on a nonsegregated seating basis was a new issue.

The answer arrived in five days. It came in a phone call to me from the head of the Federal Information Department, Colin Black, a jovial professional: "The government has instructed me to say they approve. They have no problem with open-to-all concerts and nonsegregated seating. We'll send over confirmation in writing. It will be lovely to meet the fellow," Black concluded.

Clearly the government was intending to keep the matter at a low level, information officer to information officer, so as to convey the impression that its decision on the American position was not a serious political problem, no big deal, and that it was decided very quickly. But insiders told us later that there was sharp debate within the highest levels of the government.

We scheduled five concerts in a week in the Federation, three of them in Southern Rhodesia (now Zimbabwe), and published ads in the local press and put up posters announcing that Louis Armstrong was coming, that his concerts were "sponsored by the United States of America" and would be "Open-to-All." My black friends were ecstatic and incredulous; my white friends praised our initiative but questioned whether it would be successful.

I met Armstrong and his All-Stars on their early-evening arrival at Salisbury airport. He got off the plane holding his trumpet case and I offered to carry it. "Nah, man, thanks, this horn's my bread and butter. It never leaves me," he said. In the terminal he was immediately recognized. People clapped and requested his autograph.

In the car I asked him how the concerts had been going in West Africa. "Man, the cats were jumpin' everywhere," he smiled. "They had to stop the show in Ghana for a little while because the people were rushing the bandstand and might have turned us over." He was in high spirits, so I thought this would be a good time to introduce the subject of his concerts in this region of Africa. I told him we had pressed the local government and won approval for nonsegregated performances. Armstrong grew somber. "It's a good thing you won or I wouldn't be here!" The consul general's driver chuckled.

The opening-night concert was held in Salisbury, the capital city, in an open-air soccer stadium that seated twenty-five thousand people. The standard ropes separating blacks and whites were gone; blacks were everywhere, not just at the far ends of the stadium.

For the first time ever at an event of this magnitude in Southern Rhodesia, whites and blacks were sitting side by side completely filling the stadium: white government officials and business executives, black clerks, white farmers and black laborers who had come in trucks and buses from nearby rural areas, white and black students, white and black church leaders, white parliamentarians and black policemen, white army officers, and black troops—all of them cheek by jowl in the stands. When Armstrong appeared, everyone rose and cheered together.

Waving his gleaming brass trumpet and stopping to shake outstretched hands, he came striding down the middle of the field from one end to the other, where the stage was set up, a spotlight on him for the whole hundred yards. He beamed with pleasure all the way, nodding his head at the sight around him.

It was a warm summer night with a full moon in a cloudless sky. The atmosphere was one of warmth, too, as whites and blacks smiled at each other throughout the concert.

When Armstrong belted out "Mack the Knife," "Blueberry Hill," and "I Can't Give You Anything But Love," the audience knew the words and sang along with him.

"Yeah, you got it!" he shouted to the crowd. "Sing it, baby!" gesturing in a "come here" motion.

At the end of the ninety-minute concert, the audience simply would not leave. Finally, after a series of encores, Armstrong raised his arms over his head, like someone trying to stop traffic, and asked for quiet. "I gotta tell y'all something." He looked over the crowd, leaned closer into the microphone and spoke huskily but softly: "It's sure nice to see this." The audience knew what he meant and erupted in thunderous applause. With six words, Louis Armstrong had captured the mood of a historic, unprecedented night.

I watched it all with great relief. My stomach had been killing me for three weeks because I was worried, not really sure whether nonsegregated seating was going to work. More than ten thousand whites showed up, according to stadium officials.

After two filled stadium concerts in Salisbury, Armstrong gave his next performance in Bulawayo, the second-largest city in Southern Rhodesia. He seemed to have a knack for quick, often evocative one-liners. We were walking out of a hotel one morning when three local white journalists came up to him. One of them asked a typical question put to visiting celebrities:

"Well, Mr. Armstrong, how do you like Rhodesia?"

Without missing a beat, Armstrong said: "Y'all sure know how to keep little black children in bare feet!"

Armstrong's concerts sparked new impetus toward desegregation. Several months later the dismantling of segregation laws and regulations increased. One of the first barriers to fall in Southern Rhodesia was segregated seating in entertainment, including movie houses. Next came the lifting of color bars in athletic teams, sports competitions, and in spectator seating at sports events.

After Armstrong completed his tour of Africa and was back home in New York, we exchanged letters. On learning of the ground-breaking results of his visit to the Federation of Rhodesia and Nyasaland, he asked me what I missed most from the United States. I answered jokingly, "A pastrami sandwich on rye from the Stage Deli in New York." Two weeks later a big refrigerated package arrived at my office in Southern Rhodesia. It was a twenty-pound pastrami from the Stage. We enjoyed it for weeks.

—Mark B. Lewis was director of the U.S. Information Service in Ghana from 1962-64. He is a freelance journalist in Washington, D.C.

LAST TIME UP

On one damp and raw day in late September of 1960, I was in Boston's Fenway Park. A great player was "hangin' 'em up" for the last time at the end of the game against the Baltimore Orioles. I was there in the center-field bleachers in the bottom of the eighth inning when "Old Number Nine" stepped into the batter's box.

For the better part of twenty-two years he had been the star hitter of the Boston Red Sox. He had been through hardships and setbacks that might well have stopped a lesser man, including five years of wartime service in the Marines during the height of his career. Now it was all down to one last time at bat.

Fans stood and cheered for several minutes as the umpire held up the game. Nobody sat down. It might have been the ninth inning of the seventh game of the World Series. It seemed as if each fan was trying to savor these last few moments. The batter did not acknowledge the ovation. He never had since his first or second year in the big leagues.

Finally Jack Fisher of the Orioles delivered his first pitch. It was low and inside for a ball. Still everyone stood. The next pitch came in high, and with a Herculean swing the hitter missed the ball. It was not like him to swing at a bad pitch. He stood there grinding the bat in his hands like someone trying to wring out a wet mop. He was a picture of tense concentration as he stared at the pitcher on the mound.

How would all this end after such a colorful career that included being the last hitter to bat over .400, two MVPs, and six batting titles? So often he seemed to hit one out in the most dramatic situations. He had belted a three-run homer to win the 1941 All-Star Game in Detroit. He homered off a Dizzy Trout pitch in his last at-bat before leaving for the Korean War, and did it again his second time at bat when he returned. Now he was like a matador standing in the middle of the ring waiting for the bull's last charge.

Fisher was into his motion, and the next pitch was a fastball about thigh-high. The hitter, with a quick hitch and his fluid swing, made contact with the ball. It flew off the bat and headed in a straight line, almost in my direction. The Baltimore center fielder, already playing deep, slowly faded back and glanced over his shoulder to see how much room he had to the fence. He looked as if he had the ball in his sights and was ready to make the catch. Everything seemed to shift into slow motion. The ball hung in the air, the fielder's face was turned up, another step, another, and finally the ball sailed over the fence.

The batter raced around the base path with his head down, never looking up. This was typical of him.

For minutes fans stood and yelled for him to come out of the dugout, but he refused. A man to my right kept screaming "The old man is still number one!" The hitter wouldn't come out and wave good-bye. He had made a vow years before that he would never again tip his hat to the crowd. Only when Pinky Higgins, the Red Sox manager, sent him out to left field the next inning and brought him back in before the first batter stepped to the plate did he raise his head and look my way for just an instant. With his head down again, Ted Williams loped toward the infield, across the first-base foul line, and disappeared into the dugout and into baseball immortality.

—Paul Blandford lives in Ipswich, Massachusetts.

Ted Williams clouts his 521st home run in his final game on September 28, 1960.

POPGUN IN THE COLD WAR

It was March 1961, and I was a thirty-year-old cultural affairs officer with the U.S. Information Agency assigned to our embassy in Buenos Aires. My job had a faintly sub-rosa flavor. I was to induce Argentine publishers to produce Spanish translations of books that would reflect favorably on the United States. The inducement was a guaranteed purchase of perhaps a few hundred copies, which we would distribute to libraries throughout Latin America.

One day a liberal Argentine journalist came to my office with a copy of a small, dog-eared paperback in Spanish that resembled a nineteenth-century penny dreadful. I have long since forgotten its title. He told me that the book had been written by a disaffected former member of Fidel Castro's regime and that the amateurish publishing job had produced next to no distribution. He thought I might want to arrange a new edition. By this time Castro had declared his Marxist allegiance, had carried out drumhead executions of his enemies, was clapping political opponents into jail, and was fomenting insurrections outside Cuba. U.S. policy had hardened into the enmity that has persisted until this day.

My visitor left the little book with me, and I read it that night. It was well done. The books whose translations I had arranged thus far had painted a positive impression of the United States; this one worked the other side of the street, presenting an ideological foe in his worst light. The book did not fit my "white" propaganda program, but better distribution might promote the U.S. policy of debunking Castro. I had an idea. Here was a job for the CIA. During those peak Cold War years, the CIA had a tough, effective image rather than the battered face

it presents today. I must confess that my next steps were motivated by a curiosity about spying and the clandestine rather than any professional impulse. I made a discreet inquiry at the embassy and managed a meeting with an officer attached to the CIA's Buenos Aires station, a man described to me only as "Dutch."

At our first encounter, attended also by a couple of Dutch's colleagues, I noticed that I was steered deliberately to a particular chair, which I assumed was wired. I described the Cuban's book, its limited distribution, and its potential as at least a popgun in the Cold War. Through the agency's covert methods, I suggested, a mass-market edition might be underwritten. They were immediately interested but wanted to chew on the idea a bit, and we arranged a second meeting.

By early April we had met about three times, and another session was scheduled. Just before that day I received a cryptic call from Dutch. "Meeting's canceled," he said. "By next week we probably won't be needing this project. Good-bye."

Of course I did not realize at the time that I had just been tipped off to the CIA-engineered Bay of Pigs invasion by anti-Castro Cubans, which occurred on April 17.

I heard nothing more about the book project, but, obviously, the CIA, for better or worse, would be working its bag of tricks against Castro for the next four decades.

—Joseph E. Persico is the author of books of biography and history and collaborated with Colin Powell on the Secretary of State's life story.

In the spring of 1962, Fidel Castro blasts the United States with accusations of American assistance to counterrevolutionary elements in Oriente Province.

THE BEST PART OF THE HUNT

In the fall of 1961 I was an English major at the University of Virginia and William Faulkner was writer-in-residence there.

Mr. Faulkner was at that time finishing The Reivers, his Pulitzer Prize—winning novel that would be published the following spring. I was doing some rudimentary research into Shakespeare's Richard III for a paper that would never be published.

One day an announcement appeared on the English Department bulletin board stating that for the next six Thursday evenings Mr. William Faulkner would be pleased to hold a small symposium, open only to English majors and graduate students. The number of attendees would be strictly limited to the first twenty who signed on.

I had studied Faulkner the previous year under Joseph Blotner, one of the foremost Faulkner scholars, and had found Faulkner's work incomprehensible. However, many considered him America's greatest living writer, and the chance to learn from such a figure proved decisive. I signed on.

The next Thursday at the appointed hour, the small band of disciples and the curious gathered in a room in Cabell Hall to hear the great man. Faulkner was a shy person with unremarkable speaking abilities, and it soon became apparent that this evening symposium had clearly not been his idea.

The sessions were scheduled to last an hour but Faulkner's routine was to amble up to the lectern about ten minutes late, make a few desultory remarks, and then throw the floor open to questions. About the fourth session, when the speaker asked for questions, a dedicated young graduate student deep in a thesis on Faulkner, who always sat in the front row taking copious notes, raised his hand. "Mr. Faulkner, in paragraph (such and such) of section (thus and so) of your short story 'The Bear,' you make reference to (such and such). There has long been debate among scholars whether or not you were referring to the betrayal of Christ in that passage. Would you be so kind as to edify us on that point?"

William Faulker sizes up a horse in Oxford, Mississippi.

Faulkner stared at the earnest young man for a long moment. He then leaned on the lectern and a small smile appeared beneath his white mustache. "Young man, I regret I cannot edify you. You see, I haven't read that story in more than twenty years, and besides, I was dead drunk when I wrote it. I haven't the slightest idea in hell what I had in mind when I wrote the passage to which you refer."

Not too long after the incident in his symposium, I encountered the novelist on a chilly November morning at the punch bowl in the Farmington Hunt Club lodge prior to the call to horses.

Faulkner liked riding to hounds and would frequently join the hunt at the nearby Farmington Hunt Club or Keswick Hunt Club. It happened that I had friends who rode with both those packs, and I, too, enjoyed a good hunt on a fine fall day.

"Good morning, Mr. Faulkner," I said. He nodded and then appraised me more closely over his cup of brandy milk punch. "Aren't you in that goddamned Thursday symposium of mine?" he asked. When I replied in the affirmative, he said, "I thought you looked familiar. You're one of the few who never say anything. I wish there were more like that. Tell me, why did you sign up for the damned thing anyway? Are you one of those people who're majoring in me?"

I laughed and, to gain a little time, offered him a Lucky Strike and then lit one myself. He declined, indicating his pipe. "No, sir, I'm not majoring in you. In fact, I don't even understand most of what you write. I just thought it would be foolish not to take advantage of the opportunity."

"I like that, son. No bullshit. What's your name? I'm terrible with names."

I told him, and we had another cup before the call to mount. As we walked outside, he said, "Who are you riding with today?" I told him no one in particular, and he suggested we ride together. We went to our mounts, mine a kind chestnut mare that belonged to a friend and his a big brown gelding he had borrowed. Faulkner was a small man, not more than five foot six and not the most steady horseman. He needed assistance in mounting, and the big gelding nearly unseated him straightaway.

We were soon on our way in pursuit of the hounds and Faulkner made the first two or three jumps, but then his horse balked at a "chicken-coop" jump and its rider went flying. I was just behind and stopped to help. It was apparent that Mr. Faulkner wasn't hurt, but neither was he too keen to continue. After sending the others onward, he turned to me: "Dick, my boy, what say you we go back to the lodge and have us a punch. That's the only really civilized aspect of this damned sport anyway."

I concurred, and off we went. We had a most pleasant morning drinking brandy milk punch and discussing the old South, women, and maybe a little literature. We met one or two more times fox hunting, and I went to the last two of his "goddamned symposiums."

The following spring, when The Reivers came out, he appeared at a local bookstore signing first editions. I bought one and got in line. When it came my turn, he spoke to me cordially and even remembered my first name. He wrote in the book, "To Dick— Remember, the best part of the hunt is the punch." He signed it "William (Bill) Faulkner." In less than two months Mr. Faulkner was dead. I treasured that book (although I never read it) until it was destroyed in a fire in my apartment some years later. But maybe it doesn't matter, because the memory is just as keen as ever.

—Richard C. Latham is in the oil-and-gas business in Dallas, Texas.

THE SPY

The first thing you must understand in the story of how I was recruited to spy for Albania is that when I was eight years old, I never foresaw a time when I might be embarrassed to admit that I used to read Dennis the Menace comic books. But the truth is that before I discovered Superman or Batman, let alone Hemingway or Shakespeare, I loved reading about a kid my age who got away with things I never could.

The second thing you must understand about the story is where I lived at that time in the early sixties. Our house was near Peru, Indiana, on Capehart Street on Bunker Hill Air Force Base, now renamed Grissom Air Reserve Base after Indiana's native astronaut, Gus Grissom. Bunker Hill was an important base for the Strategic Air Command, the nuclear weapons branch of the U.S. Air Force.

Life on a SAC base was, for our fathers, a constant state of readiness to bomb the Soviet Union, for all of us made the assumption that the Russians would drop a hydrogen bomb or a missile on us at any time. For most people Stanley Kubrick's masterpiece Dr. Strangelove is a dark comedy; for me it is a home movie of my childhood. My classmates and I knew no other life, and it seemed perfectly normal at the time.

Bunker Hill was special in many ways. Peru was the unlikely but historic winter quarters for a number of circuses. Unlike military families, circus families put down roots in the area. Sometimes on the edge of a cornfield a family would set up a trapeze and teach their children the act while passersby watched the free show. Just outside the base, past the security fence and guarded gate, was a barn with a painted sign by the highway: free elephant manure.

Idyllic as it was, I had visions of the wider world. The inside cover of the Dennis the Menace comic book ran a list of readers looking for pen pals. For some reason I thought I would like a pen pal in Hawaii and sent a request to the magazine. After a time I received a letter from Dennis, promptly pasted in a scrapbook, telling me that he would run my listing. When the issue finally arrived in the mail, I was thrilled to see my name in print even though Bailey was misspelled as Badey.

Soon the letters started arriving, some from Hawaii but the majority from other parts of the country, including one from a woman in her twenties who assumed I must be a young airman on the base. I wish I could say that I made lifelong friends through the mail, but before long I lost interest in the project.

One day while I was at school another letter arrived for Greg Badey of Bunker Hill Air Force Base. This letter, I was told years later, was strange-looking, with foreign stamps and an Albanian postmark. Albania was at that point in the Cold War the most radical Communist state in Europe, having broken away from the U.S.S.R. to follow the Maoist line of Red China. The envelope alarmed my mother so much she opened it. Inside was a letter asking me if I would be the writer's pen pal. He asked me to send him photographs of my home, my pets, my school, and, if I wouldn't mind, photos of the airplanes on the flight line and the buildings around the base. My parents immediately took the letter to the Air Police, who confiscated it. My parents never heard any more about it, but I'm sure that somewhere in the bowels of the Pentagon or the FBI there is a

A Dennis the Menace *comic book from 1968.*

classified file on the Dennis the Menace spy connection recorded for history.

In time we were transferred to another base. My father retired after twenty-three years of active service and lived to see the end of the Cold War. Our former enemies are now friends or at least friendly rivals, and Albania threw off its shackles and is building a democratic state. Historians are now gaining access to the once-secret files of the Cold War and finding the answers to many mysteries. One mystery, however, may never be answered: What kind of spy reads Dennis the Menace comic books?

—Greg Bailey, an attorney in St. Louis, is a correspondent for *The Economist* and a freelance writer.

KERENSKY

As an undergraduate student at Stanford University in the early 1960s, I frequently saw on campus the stooped, shuffling figure of Aleksandr Kerensky, who had briefly headed the Provisional Government of Russia, which was overthrown in the Bolshevik Revolution of October 1917. Kerensky was then working on his memoirs while in residence at the Hoover Institution on War, Revolution, and Peace, which houses an outstanding collection of materials related to the Russian Revolution.

When I traveled to the Soviet Union with a student group in the spring of 1961, all the Russians to whom I mentioned seeing Kerensky insisted that I was mistaken. He was long dead, they explained—and he was, indeed, as dead to Soviet historical memory as were the political figures who had been crudely chiseled out of the mosaics that adorned various Moscow subway stations.

On returning to the Stanford campus in the summer of 1961, I found myself working at a campus job serving food in the cafeteria line at the faculty club. One day Kerensky appeared in the line, methodically pushing his tray along and selecting his lunch. I nudged the student working next to me and told him who the historical figure approaching us was. As it happened, my coworker was then enrolled in a course in Russian history and determined on the spot that he must conduct an interview with Kerensky.

Abandoning his place behind the mashed potatoes, he followed Kerensky into the dining room. No less derelict in the line of duty, I forsook the cubed carrots and followed. No sooner had the old gentleman settled laboriously into his chair than his white-jacketed interrogator loomed closely above him.

Without ceremony or even introduction, he put the question to a startled Kerensky: "Mr. Kerensky, to what do you attribute the downfall of the Provisional Government in 1917?" Kerensky ended the interview with a glance at his plate and a single word: "Myself."

—David M. Kennedy is a professor of history at Stanford University.

Aleksandr Kerensky, photographed in 1955, fifteen years before his death.

THE CONTACT

When I joined the U.S. Navy in January 1960, I was sent to Newport, Rhode Island, to learn Morse code and semaphore. I then reported to the USS Independence, and when I arrived in Norfolk, Virginia, my company commander sent me to officers' school to learn about radar air interception of unidentified aircraft. I was the ship's only enlisted man attending officers' school for air control.

During this training I was always on the radar's air picture when jet fighters were launched, but otherwise I was on the surface picture. To avoid collisions, whenever other ships appeared on radar, we would figure out CPA (closest point of approach)—time and distance.

When we left Norfolk Naval Base, we were sent to the Caribbean Sea, southeast of Cuba. This was during the naval blockade of the island in the fall of 1962, when high-altitude photographs showed Soviet missiles there, almost starting a war between

A Russian ship carries missiles to Cuba as tension builds in the fall of 1962.

the United States and the U.S.S.R. During that time I never left my radar set. I slept on the floor, and they'd bring my food up from the mess hall. This went on for five or six days. The officers would take over the air picture between 0800 and 1600 hours, and that's when I'd try to sleep. I never showered or shaved; I must have stunk to high heaven.

Also during this time, we would go from a thirty-minute standby to launch an all-out attack on Cuba, then to a fifteen-minute standby, and, on a number of occasions, down to a five-minute standby. One evening an officer told me that the ship was going into complete communications and electronic silence. We were launching a radar aircraft between Cuba and Haiti in the Windward Passage, and it would transfer its radar image to my screen on the ship so I could observe any nearby surface contacts.

Just before midnight I noticed movement along the coast of Haiti, a ship heading west on a course of 285 degrees at seven knots. I called the watch officer, who in turn called the captain and the admiral, who was on board. Other officers showed up. They watched me track the hazy contact on my radar screen and decided to send out escort destroyers to intercept the unidentified vessel before it reached Cuba.

As suddenly as the officers had come, they all disappeared. I was alone again, but now I was tracking our destroyers heading to cut off the mystery ship. The officers returned early the next morning, so I fell asleep for a few hours, until word came in that the destroyers had stopped a Russian freighter with nuclear missiles on board. The destroyers made it turn around and head back toward home. That was October 26.

The news made me feel good, and I went back to sleep with a smile on my face while the officers stood around congratulating one another. When I awoke, I never heard another word about what had happened. But I won't forget sitting in that quiet dark corner and finding that Russian freighter running along the coast of Haiti trying to make it to Cuba. It's a small part of history, but I made it.

—Douglas K. Gitchel worked at the Chrysler Corporation for thirty years. He is now retired and living in Arizona.

TOUCHED BY IKE

In 1962 Brown Military Academy in Glendora, California, was a boarding school modeled after the U.S. Military Academy at West Point. Like our counterpart on the Hudson, we endured the indignities of plebe year, stood countless inspections, and wore full-dress uniforms of a pattern first seen in the War of 1812.

On ceremonial occasions we stood resplendent in tight gray coatees, trousers, crossbelts, and white gloves, all surmounted by "tar bucket" shakos. Cadet officers merited the added glory of sabers, red sashes, and feathered plumes. Such splendor was not achieved without a good deal of effort.

Before parades we spent hours spit-shining our shoes and polishing the brass chest-plates and the countless buttons on our jackets. Nor did we neglect our M-1 rifles (much carried but never fired). I spent ages rubbing the wooden stock of my rifle with lin-

Eisenhower visits cadets at the Citadel in 1955.

seed oil in order to bring it to the requisite state of gleaming perfection.

There was, however, one problem. The stock would become so slippery with all that rubbing that I could not get a grip on it when I wore my white cotton gloves. At the command "port arms," my hand would rise to the prescribed position, but my rifle would slide through my fingers and crash to the ground. I remember standing in ranks, looking from my empty right hand to the rifle at my feet while my squad leader muttered dire threats.

I soon learned that if I soaked my gloves with water just before a parade, I could maintain a grip on my rifle. It was a crude expedient, but it worked.

Brown Military Academy held full-dress parades once a month. On those days the corps of cadets would pass in review. Promotions would be announced, and awards presented, by the reviewing officer, usually an individual of some renown. One day in the spring of 1962 the commandant informed us that the reviewing officer for the next monthly parade would be none other than former President Eisenhower. I learned that I would receive an award for scholastic achievement at that time.

The big day came. I donned my full-dress uniform, drew my rifle, dashed madly to the latrine, soaked my gloves full of water, and fell in line. The corps of cadets marched off to the strains of the "Washington Post March." The band played. The adjutant strutted.

The plumes on the cadet officers' shakos fluttered. I managed to keep control of my rifle.

Finally the command was given, and the adjutant bellowed, "All officers, colors, and persons to be decorated—center, march!" I passed my rifle to the cadet next to me and marched out to join the rank assembling before the corps of cadets.

We marched forward on line and halted before the reviewing stand. There he was: Dwight David Eisenhower, General of the Army, five stars no less, and former president of the United States. It suddenly dawned on me that I was about to take that august hand in my clammy glove.

"Cadet Private Grace, front and center!" With a sinking sensation I marched forward, halted, saluted, and clutched Ike's right hand in mine.

The former president started slightly, glanced down at our clasped hands, and suddenly broke out in his famous grin. I cannot be certain, but I swear he even winked at me. I saluted, faced about, and flew back to my place in the rank.

After the ceremony Eisenhower spoke to the school about his own days as a cadet color sergeant at West Point and joked about the demerits he had accumulated. His remarks were brief but warm. I like to think there was a pair of damp white gloves in his own past.

—William J. P. Grace lives in Portland, Oregon.

TEACHING THE BERLINER

From 1957 to 1980 I taught German at the Foreign Service Institute School of Language Studies, run by the Department of State in Washington, D.C. Classes were small, seldom more than four students, and I spent six hours every day with them, five days a week for five months. Following the school's unconventional method, I started by giving my students a short sentence, which they had to repeat again and again until their pronunciation was correct. Longer sentences followed, and as their speaking ability progressed, I gave them dialogues to memorize to help promote conversation within the group. Mark Twain once said that it takes thirty years for intelligent people to master the German language. It's too bad the Foreign Service Institute's method hadn't yet been tried; he would have admired its success.

One evening I received a phone call at my home in Maryland. "This is the White House calling," said the voice on the line. "I'd like to speak with Mrs.

Kennedy in Berlin on June 26, 1963.

Plischke from the Foreign Service Institute." I laughed and said, "I'll see you in the morning," and hung up. I was absolutely sure one of my students had tried to play a joke on me. But the following morning I was called to the dean's office and was told that the special assistant for national security affairs, McGeorge Bundy, had called the school. President Kennedy was planning a trip to Berlin, and he wanted to give a short speech in German. I was to go to the White House and meet with Mr. Bundy for further instructions.

I was quite nervous, but Mr. Bundy put me at ease by saying, "Don't worry, the president doesn't speak German, so you are in charge." He accompanied me to the Oval Office to meet Mr. Kennedy. I received a very friendly welcome. The president asked me what part of Germany I came from and if I still had family over there. When I told him that I was from East Germany, where my mother was still living, he asked if I had been allowed to see her. I was touched by his genuine interest.

The head of the German-language section at the Foreign Service Institute, Dr. Jack Chew, had put a few simple German sentences into phonetic spelling for the president to read so that I could test his pronunciation. When I handed the president the paper, he took a look and smiled, apologizing for not having any talent for foreign languages. But when he read them out loud, he sounded rather good. "What did I say?" he asked. I translated the sentences into English. He said, "That's insignificant. I'll write my own," and he turned to Mr. Bundy and asked him to write something too. They read their drafts to each other. Bundy complimented the president on his version, and Mr. Kennedy said, "I'll use mine." At the end of his script was the sentence "I am a Berliner."

The interpreter scheduled to accompany President Kennedy on the trip was there in the office. (He was a rather unpleasant man who complained bitterly that he had had to interrupt his vacation just to watch the president's mannerisms.) Right then and there he rendered the president's words into German, translating the definite article a into ein, even though most Germans would say, "Ich bin Berliner." When I pointed out this minor difference in usage, the president seemed a little startled. He must have discussed it with Mrs. Kennedy because the next day he said he wanted to leave the ein in the text. This was later criticized by people who did not like the speech, or the president, or his trip to Berlin. I had told the president it was all right because I remembered an old Prussian song, written in 1831 by Bernhard Thiersch: "Ich bin ein Preusse, kennt ihr meine Farben." No German would have thought that that was wrong.

We met five times to practice the text of the speech, but it was not easy to concentrate, for often we were interrupted by the president's secretary, Mrs. Lincoln, and by phone calls. I remember one call that was rather funny. The president was laughing hard. He repeated some names and at the end said, "I must tell Jackie all about that." It must have been about the Profumo-Keeler affair in England. He mentioned his wife's name almost every day.

It was very easy to work with President Kennedy, but he did not have enough time to memorize the speech he had written. I suggested that he concentrate on the last words, which were part of the following sentence: "Your courage and perseverance have made the words 'I am a Berliner' a proud statement." The president repeated the Berlin sentence after me until it sounded very good.

The president's trip to Europe that June had some memorable moments: the church service Kennedy attended with Konrad Adenauer at the Cathedral of Cologne, the speech to the Atlantic

Community in the Paulskirche in Frankfurt, the visit to the little house of his forefathers in Ireland. But when Kennedy stood in front of the Schöneberger Rathaus on June 26 and called out, "Ich bin ein Berliner," he electrified the hundreds of Germans in his audience. (He said afterward, "I wish these people were American voters.") I watched the event on television and was proud of his pronunciation and deeply touched by the response he received.

In July of 1978 I was called to the White House to meet with President Carter. He too was planning a trip to Germany, and he wanted to be able to pronounce correctly the names of German cities and politicians. He also planned to say a sentence from the poet Schiller's "Ode to Joy." He apologized for not having the time to study with me directly and asked if I could teach his secretary Susan Clough instead. I did my best, but when Ms. Clough read the German words in her charming Southern accent, her pronunciation did not quite match my tape recordings or the phonetic script.

Although I was unable to help President Carter with his German, I was grateful to have met another very kind American leader.

—Margarete Plischke now lives in San Mateo, California.

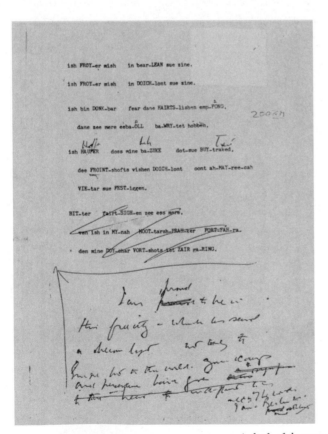
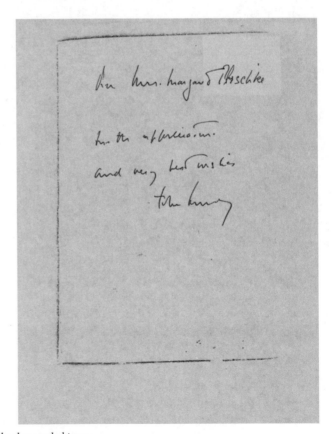

A draft of the remarks that made history.

A Fair Country Cook Meets the President

When I was the chef at the Hotel Cortez in El Paso, Texas, in the spring of 1963, word arrived that President Kennedy would spend a night at the hotel later that year. I would be preparing meals not only for his party but for the president himself. I decided to design a commemorative dinner, a menu strictly in JFK's honor, and after giving the matter lots of thought, I devised a meal composed of ingredients that were either grown or processed in the immediate vicinity of El Paso.

I never would have believed the amount of preparation necessary for an overnight stay by the president. We had a suite repainted and a local furniture company come in and outfit the rooms with French Provincial furniture. About a week before the visit the Secret Service moved in. They studied the route from the airport. They made a fire inspection and a security check of the hotel. They planned an escape route from the presidential suite through the main kitchen and included me in the escape plan, which flattered me to no end.

Two agents asked me to show them the kitchen facilities. I gave them a tour of the dishwashing department in the basement, the storerooms and walk-in refrigerators, the bakeshop, the salad department, and the main kitchen. They seemed impressed. Then they dropped the bombshell: "We will be bringing two Navy cooks out of Washington to cook for the president. We hope we can count on your cooperation and help."

I mumbled something as we continued to walk about. Then I began to get mad, so angry that I actually became calm. Having satisfied themselves that my kitchen would be adequate for the two Navy cooks, the Secret Service agents began to make their way to the exit. As we came to my office door, I asked them to step inside.

"Gentlemen," I said, "you are looking at an American chef who has worked for forty years to perfect himself in his profession. If the president of the United States comes to this American hotel, in the United States of America, where there is an accredited American chef, and he brings two Navy cooks along with him to prepare his food, then I am going to be insulted not only for myself but for every American chef in every American hotel in the country. What's more, as soon as the presidential party clears the hotel, I'm going to squawk loud and long to the press about the insult. If you want to have me relieved of my post, you are welcome to do so. However, that will not change my mind.

"On top of that," I concluded, "I'm a pretty fair country cook, and I don't believe you can bring anyone out of Washington who can beat me." They replied they were carrying out the policy of the agency; they were sorry, but there was nothing they could do about it.

I was miserable. This was the biggest letdown of my career. I felt I had to do something. Then, like a flash, it dawned on me. Why not bake a cake? I began to plan what would be on it: highlights of the president's political career; the name of every school he'd ever attended; sugar replicas of PT-109 and his book Profiles of Courage; a scale model of the rocking chair he used in the Oval Office; and on top a lop-eared Democratic donkey.

In the center of the lobby stood a defunct water fountain that had been dismantled and made into a table with settees all around it. I decided to put the huge cake on this table so that the president would be sure to see it.

I started frantically on the cake. All the sugar work had to be done ahead of time so it would dry and harden, and I didn't have many free hours in which to do it. A dozen times I vowed to forget the whole thing: If I wasn't good enough to cook for him, then I certainly didn't want to make him a cake. But in the end I found myself determined to make such a beautiful cake he would be sorry he hadn't let me fix

President Kennedy in the spring of 1963.

his meals. When the cake was almost done, I sent for Paul Burns, the Secret Service agent in charge during the president's visit, showed it to him, and told him what I had in mind. Paul nixed the idea.

"Why?" I asked.

"Because," he said, "if the president sees that cake, he'll spend thirty minutes in the lobby looking at it, and we just don't want him exposed that long. Put in on the mezzanine. At least the press corps will see it, and if we have a chance, we will try to take the president by it later on."

The mezzanine! My cake hidden on the mezzanine! This guy Kennedy was really hard to get along with.

The morning of his arrival I was preparing fresh fruit for the president when Paul Burns came up to me. "You know, Chef," he said, "we looked into your background pretty good, and we found out you are a pretty fair country cook. So if you promise that you yourself will take care of the president's food personally, we'll pull out of your kitchen and leave it up to you."

I finished the fruit bowls and set up the cake on the mezzanine. By the time I finished, there was cheering and whistling outside the hotel. I went to a window and saw the president getting out of his car. He waded through a sea of people shaking hands, passed under the marquee, and then he was walking briskly over to the desk to flatter the hotel with a token registration. Suddenly he looked up and saw the cake. Leaving his party, he bounded up the twelve steps two at a time and landed in front of me with his hand extended. He seemed fascinated with the cake. I explained to him how we made the sugar replicas. He asked, "Why is it that you see so few things like this anymore, Chef? Is this, like so many other things, becoming a lost art?" I replied that it was, that youngsters no longer had the patience to become proficient at it.

A few hours later George Thomas, the president's valet, called to say the president would see me in his suite to discuss his dinner. I took a copy of my commemorative menu, a copy of our regular menu, and a pad on which I had listed some other special dishes.

The president rose from his rocking chair, shook hands, and asked me to sit down. I had been expecting to stand at attention while the president of the United States gave me the order for his dinner. Instead I was asked to pull up a chair.

The president had a copy of the commemorative menu in his hand. "It says here," he began, "you designed this dinner especially for my visit. I am flattered and amazed at the ingenuity with which this dinner has been put together. Were all these items really grown or processed in this immediate neighborhood? It's hard to believe the land we flew over on our way from White Sands could produce any of these foods." He asked me where I was from, and when I told him, he said, "Franklin County, Virginia, is noted for the amount of moonshine whiskey that's made there and not for famous European sauces. During one year of Prohibition, Franklin County used more sugar than the rest of Virginia, North Carolina, and South Carolina combined, and 99 percent went into the manufacture of illicit moonshine whiskey. But some mighty fine people have also come from Virginia, including quite a few of the men who have held the office of president." I was amazed at the ease with which he talked to me.

Finally he said, "Let me tell you, I am going to enjoy this dinner that you designed in my honor." He hesitated a moment, as if searching for the right words. "But I must make a few minor changes for which I am truly sorry. I won't be able to eat the fruit salad, which sounds delicious. In its place I would like to have some plain chopped lettuce, with just a little French dressing. The breads intrigue me, especially the anadama bread, which I would love to try, and the Boston brown bread, which I'm sure you included in the menu out of respect for my New England background. But I'll have to forgo the pleasure in favor of a plain white roll with butter and, if you have it available, some apple jelly." All the while he talked I was making notes on my white pad.

"I will have five guests for dinner," the president continued, "and you may bring the dinner up as soon as it is ready."

In the galley my assistant and I went to work. When we had the food ready, we placed it on the plates, covered the plates with heated covers, and set them on tables. I wondered if the Secret Service agents would inspect the food. They did not. We delivered the tables and returned to the kitchen. I glanced at my watch; it was 9:15 p.m. I had now been working under intense pressure for about twelve hours. Later that evening I got a call from George Thomas telling me that the tables were ready to be picked up. He passed on the president's compliments and lifted the cover from the presi-

dent's plate; it was almost empty. The other guests had done a good job too.

The next morning I served the president breakfast (fried eggs, bacon, toast, and more apple jelly). He presented me with some souvenirs—a PT-109 tie clasp and a bottle opener from the White House. I promised to make a cake for his second inauguration. Then his party left.

As I looked back, I thought to myself that even if I'd had the power to do so, I wouldn't have changed a thing. I thought how lucky I was, yet I had to concede that it wasn't all luck. I had studied and worked very hard. My career suddenly took on the shape of a Horatio Alger plot: boy starts out washing pots and pans in a waterfront saloon and finishes by preparing dinner for the president. I made my way back to my office, the happiest chef in the United States of America.

—George Lowell Young, Sr., died in 1981. This account, written not long after the event, was sent to us by his granddaughter Charlotte Young Roby.

STORM WARNING

The saying has it, "There's no such thing as an ex-Marine," and in my case it's all too true, even though it's been nearly thirty years since those brief three I spent on active duty with the 2d Marines.

In what history will regard as peacetime just before the war in Vietnam, I served with a few men who became lifetime friends and many others who earned my deepest professional respect and admiration.

Far from the least of these latter was a young corporal. He was a Rifle Squad Leader in H Company, 2d Battalion, 2d Marines ("Horrible Hog" of "Two-Two") of which I was the executive officer for about six months in 1963.

During those six months I had the chance to observe this corporal at close quarters. He was a recruiting-poster Marine, tall, broad-shouldered, blonde, and, like most of us then (sigh!) very fit. But beyond appearance, his performance was truly outstanding. He had qualified every year as a Sharpshooter with the M-14 rifle. He led his thirteen-man squad by example, joining them in all the dirty work.

He was demanding in a quiet, efficient way, the sort of Squad Leader who, after spending Monday through Thursday training in Camp Lejeune's distant fields, forests, and marshes and then hiking fifteen miles back to the barracks, would remain in the squad bay with his men well into the evening, cleaning and squaring away gear and weapons until everything was absolutely shipshape. Then he'd fall his men in for a formal squad rifle inspection, a highly unusual event in any company.

Both his rank and the fact that he was married were extremely uncommon for a first-enlistment Marine. It was plain he loved the Marine life, and he made it clear that he intended to make the Corps his career. Other squad leaders and even platoon sergeants noted his performance, appearance, and his quiet, intelligent demeanor, and quickly strove to improve their own to avoid suffering by comparison. Because of all this, Horrible Hog was a very good company in which to work.

In August 1963 I transferred to H&S (Headquarters and Service) Company of Two-Two and joined the operations staff as battalion training officer—a nice, indoor job with very little heavy lifting or camping out in the rain. I began to lose contact with most of the noncoms from Horrible Hog.

In the fall the annual training cycle wound down and there was time to get caught up on courts-martial. There were three kinds, the commonest being the Special Court Martial, a panel of about five company-grade officers who heard the evidence, rendered a judgment, and passed a sentence, typically a reduction in rank and/or forfeiture of pay and benefits for a month or so, and sometimes confinement either to quarters or in the brig.

All the company-grade officers in Two-Two were assigned to one or another of the Special Court Martial panels, known as "boards," and cases were assigned to boards that did not contain the accused's supervisors. It was, then, a complete coincidence that in November 1963 the Special Court Martial Board of which I was a member was assigned to hear the charges being brought against the same young corporal from H Company whom I had so admired. The charges themselves were as unusual and unexpected as the identity of the accused. The typical

Special Court Martial heard charges of Unauthorized Absence (what other services call AWOL) over and over with boring familiarity, once in a while theft or brawling, but almost always UA, usually by a lovesick twenty-year-old who'd just had to visit sweet Lucille in Pittsburgh.

But the corporal was charged with some highly unusual offenses our board had never heard brought before: possession of two rounds of 7.62-mm rifle ammunition, possession of a weapon, to wit "a small caliber pistol," ten counts of "lending money for profit," "gambling aboard a troopship," and orally threatening to kill a fellow Marine. These charges might seem serious enough to a person unfamiliar with the Marine Corps environment of 1963, but to those of us on the board they were baffling.

The charge of possession of 7.62-mm ammunition (the standard Marine issue for the M-14 rifle) was truly bizarre. In Camp Lejeune, rifle ammunition was as common as pine straw. I doubt if there was a footlocker tray on the base that didn't contain a few rounds. Ammunition and shell casings were used as paperweights and doorstops.

"Possession of a weapon" was almost equally surreal. We all possessed weapons: M-14 rifles, M-60 machine guns, rocket launchers, mortars, pistols, flame throwers, grenades, knives, and bayonets, not to mention the nearby tanks, artillery, and fighter aircraft. A "small caliber pistol" was simply no big deal.

"Lending money for profit." Young enlisted Marines in 1963 and, I suspect, in any year since the Corps was founded in 1775, were chronically short of cash. Their pay was ridiculously low and, even though their food, housing, and uniforms were provided by a grateful nation, they did have incidental expenses such as weekly haircuts, shoe-shine gear, brass polish, civilian clothes and the like, and beer

and a pizza once in a while. Even the most naive among us knew that such Marines sometimes borrowed money from their fellows who, in turn, would be unlikely to lend if they couldn't profit from the transaction. Gambling aboard a troopship was, of course, unheard of.

Threatening to kill a person might sound daunting to a civilian, but in the course of the usual dialogue between 1963 Marine noncoms and the privates and PFCs under their command, it was probably a milder threat and was never taken literally.

The corporal pleaded guilty to all counts except the last, explaining to the court that all he had threatened to do to the party of the second part was "kick his teeth out." The court went into closed session and the members scratched their collective head and wondered aloud what we could never have asked in open court: What in the world was going on? We concluded that this heretofore picture perfect Marine had somehow managed to seriously alienate either his 1st sergeant or company commander, who had then decided to teach him a lesson.

We had no choice. We found him guilty of all counts except the last and sentenced him to be reduced to private and thirty days' restriction. This was as mild a sentence as our board ever handed down and was received stoically by the defendant.

Life resumed at Two-Two and very shortly thereafter, my two-year cycle with the battalion being over, I lost touch with it and never did learn the story behind the corporal's (now private's) court-martial. When I was released from active duty six months later, at the end of my three-year commitment, I learned that the former corporal had decided not to pursue a career in the Marines and was asking to be released early so he could enroll at the University of Texas. This request was later granted.

I should mention that except when addressing or

talking about one's peers, first names were rarely used by Marines of that time. So it was that in August of 1966 when a lone rifleman went to the twenty-seventh-floor observation tower at the University of Texas and shot dead thirteen passersby, wounding thirty-one others before being himself shot dead by a police team, despite the fact that it was reported sensationally in the news media (which revealed that he had also shot dead his young wife and mother before going to the tower), the name Charles Whitman didn't strike a responsive chord in me.

Then the following week's Time magazine was delivered and I glanced at the cover and saw a familiar, handsome face. My first reaction was, "What's Corporal Whitman doing on Time's cover?" Then I realized in a rush of horror that Corporal Whitman and Charles Whitman were the same person and that the mayhem in far-off Austin had been caused by a person I knew very well. I still get a shiver when I think of seeing that magazine cover for the first time.

The autopsy of the former Cpl. Charles Whitman, USMC, an architectural engineering student at the University of Texas, revealed a "pecan-size" brain tumor that had evidently caused his aberrant behavior. One doesn't know whether to feel worse about the young man who had once shown such brilliant promise and whose life had ended so tragically, or about his poor anonymous victims.

—John F. Grimm lives in Bethesda, Maryland.

Charles Whitman

IKE RATES HIMSELF

At times a brush with history can be a brush with the future—and even with historians. As an editor I've had the luck to know six Presidents, in casual conversations or working relationships. One pertinent conversation dates to 1965, when I went over the last pages of Dwight D. Eisenhower's presidential memoirs with him.

We were in his Gettysburg office. I asked what he thought of a recent poll of historians, ranking American Presidents, in which he had come out way below normal.

My guess was that he might dismiss the poll, or be angered by it, or ask whether any of the historians had ever commanded anything larger than a row-

President Lyndon B. Johnson meets with former President Dwight Eisenhower in 1965 for advice on how to handle the press and public.

boat. Instead, his answer was calm and considered and, as DDE could often be, surprising. He put the fingertips of his big hands together and said (I paraphrase): Well, it depends a good deal on what happens with the fellows who come after us. If they managed to turn things around and undo what he and his "associates" (a favorite word) had been trying to do, and if they succeeded and made their programs look good, than the eight Eisenhower years would not be much more than a small blip on the screen of history. But if those who came after him in succeeding administrations did not fulfill their objectives, or looked less good, for whatever reason, then his years, the 1950s, would be better regarded.

The response appears, characteristically muted and less colloquial, in Waging Peace (pages 653-55). His answer and the two volumes anticipate LBJ's difficulties (I once heard DDE say the words "Stay out of land wars in Asia"), the advent of the civil rights violence, inflation, conservatism, economics as a form of warfare, Ronald Reagan, communist threats, and glasnost.

Since that moment, especially considering the full-scale academic and historical revisionism about his Presidency we have witnessed, it seems to me that if he had once lost the skirmish with history, he had won the battle and, to the extent that there may be one between historians and their subjects, the war.

—Samuel S. Vaughan is editor-at-large at Random House.

THE EAGLE STILL ALOFT

Shortly after leaving the Navy in the summer of 1968 to become an airline pilot, I was at the third-crew-member's station in the darkened recesses of the cockpit of a Boeing 707 airliner on the long, lonely leg from Honolulu to Manilla.

Being a flight engineer offered little of the satis-faction of commanding a Navy aircraft, and it presented a formidable challenge in keeping alert during the long night over the featureless Pacific. By the time the purser entered the cockpit with a request from the cabin, I was weary of trying to identify stars and doing mental three-place multiplication problems.

Charles Lindbergh photographed during a trip to the Philippines in August 1970.

"Captain," she said, "one of the passengers has asked to visit the cockpit for a few minutes."

"Do you know who he is?" the captain asked.

"No, I don't know him."

But the captain took no chances. "Please talk to him. For all we know he may be some kind of bigwig in the aviation industry or something."

She returned in a few moments with a business card. A tiny high-intensity lamp used to read closely printed charts was switched on. In the small circle of light, the name Charles A. Lindbergh stood out.

It flashed in my mind: "Good heavens! The first man to fly across the Atlantic has just asked to spend a few minutes talking about flying."

With a tight little cough, the captain said, "I think your passenger can come up here for a few minutes."

My mind was doing back flips. "Can such a legend still be alive?" I recall thinking foolishly. "Does he still wear a leather flying jacket?" But Charles Lindbergh was in the door, filling it with a frame heavier than the one that earned him the nickname Slim.

He put us at ease immediately, introducing himself with an outstretched hand. "Good evening, fellows."

To me the effect was as profound as if the Lincoln Memorial had spoken.

"Thanks for letting me come up to talk for a few minutes," he said almost apologetically. "I don't fly these days, but I like to look inside a cockpit from time to time."

He drew us out, asking polite questions about our flying careers but never once mentioning anything more about his own. "I'm going to Manila on personal business," he said. "I'm working on a research project of my own in the Philippines."

More pleasantries, and he excused himself with polite thanks to us for sharing the time with him. The door closed, and the legend that became alive became a legend again.

Most pilots amass a collection of memorabilia: logbooks, photos, pieces of aircraft—that sort of thing. I'm no different, but my favorite memory doesn't require a piece of picturesque hardware. My right hand will do. It's the one that shook the hand of Charles Lindbergh...in flight.

—E. R. Kallus lives in Danville, California.

DEATH IN MEMPHIS

The closest I ever felt to the pulse of history was on the morning after Dr. King was shot. I had flown to Memphis the night before and went from the motel where he was shot to the police station, where I found out which funeral home was preparing his body. When I arrived there after midnight, there were only two other journalists in the home's reception area (both from out of town, a writer and a photographer for Life). No local people joined us as we waited for dawn, listening to the morticians on the other side of a thin partition complaining of the way they would have to build a jaw replacement of plaster for the lower part of Dr. King's face that had been blown away. On the black radio station that the morticians were playing, King's live voice was audible, giving speech after speech. When the body was brought out, we three had a close look at the face before the manager of the home pinned a gauze over the top of the coffin. It was the first time I had seen Dr. King except in pictures. I thought he was dead, but I was wrong.

—Garry Wills is Henry F. Luce Professor of American Culture and Public Policy, Northwestern University.

The balcony of the Lorraine Motel, Mulberry Street, Memphis, Tennessee, April 6, 1968, just after Dr. Martin Luther King, Jr's, assassination on April 4, 1968.

BREAKING THE CYCLE

About one week after the rebellion and looting that took place in South-Central Los Angeles as a result of the Rodney King verdict, I was watching the news when a young man was handcuffed and placed in a police car. The announcer said, "The son of slain Black Panther leader Fred Hampton has been arrested on charges of looting in last week's riots." For a quick moment my mind rocked. The son of Fred Hampton living and looting in South-Central L.A. How could this be? How is it that of all the people rebelling, the police were instantly able to pick out the son of Fred Hampton? I relived the past anger that seems constantly to be at the forefront of black people's lives. Will society ever wake up? Will racism and inequality ever be abandoned? In the brief moment the son of Fred Hampton appeared on my television screen, I saw him as a nice-looking, angry black man and I wondered was he like his charismatic father? Did he stand for revolution? Did he hope to help the people? What has he been doing all these years? Questions I might never have answers to, yet, I will always wonder . . .

On December 4, 1969, Fred Hampton and his associate Mark Clark were slain execution-style in Chicago in a police raid dispatched by Cook County State's Attorney Edward Hanrahan. I was a sophomore in a high school near there at the time. I recall entering their West Side apartment where the door, walls, windows, and mattresses were riddled with bullets and soaked with blood. I can remember my outrage and the outrage of my peers. In this case, as in the Rodney King trial, the policemen were tried by a jury with no black members and to this day no one has been held responsible for the deaths of two African-American men.

Twenty months before the Fred Hampton and Mark Clark raid, on April 4, 1968, in Memphis, Tennessee, Dr. Martin Luther King, Jr., was shot to death. At that time, because of all the same pressures and frustrations, reasons, and excuses involved in the rebellion in South-Central L.A., we too reacted. I recall a long line of my high school peers running, screaming, looting, damaging buildings down Eighty-seventh Street on Chicago's South Side. Many of those buildings stayed boarded up for years. I was among them and I too looted and destroyed and wanted badly to hurt anyone who dared to be white and in our path at that moment. Most of us from the 1968—69 era are now adults and parents. What legacy have we left for our children to follow? And what contribution could I make to end this perpetual cycle of negativity and destruction?

As I watched the rioting and looting from my safe home in Chicago, Illinois, during the week of April 29, I felt numb, almost unconnected to the events. I understood why it was happening, but I felt too helpless and ineffective to do anything about it. In the weeks since, I have continued to read about those who were there and were hurt financially or physically, those who watched and ran to help clean up, offer food, friendship, whatever. I wanted to try to understand and learn because something was missing. Had I grown to be a working, struggling, credit-card—carrying adult whose passion and compassion were left behind in the sixties and seventies? I too needed to know "What can I do?" Yes, even from my home far removed from the immediate moment. But what can I offer that will have a lasting impact? What gesture will make a difference to the future so that this cycle is not repeated and I don't have to turn on my television when I'm fifty or sixty and see my children looting, damaging property, being beaten? What small gesture?

The answer came as I talked with my two sons, ages thirteen and ten. We discussed the Rodney King verdict, the jurors, the rebellion in L.A. I was very proud of my sons' responses, their ability to articulate what they saw and heard and how it made them feel and think. My thirteen-year-old at first thought the people accused of beating the white taxi driver should be acquitted just as the four policemen in the Rodney King beating were acquitted. But as we discussed right and wrong, fair and unfair, cause and effect, he began to realize that was not necessarily the answer either. I shared with them the experience of my own rebellion after the death of Martin Luther King and tried to help them see the cycle, the con-

Buildings smolder after arsonists and looters riot in Chicago following the death of Martin Luther King Jr. in April 1968.

nection that must be broken. We discussed the responsibility of each human being to make the correct choices for his life. I told my sons that as human beings we are all responsible for what happens in our homes, our neighborhoods, our communities, our world until the day we die. And I asked them to think about ways they could have handled their anger and frustration at a society that always seems to look in the other direction when it comes to us—African-Americans. I recognized that I may not be able to fly to L.A. to help the cleanup crews, and I am unable to send cash. But I can educate my sons and my three-year-old daughter so they understand the necessity of making correct choices. So they are never left feeling hopeless or helpless. So they are capable people who contribute to our society and help others do the same through their example. Perhaps, in this way, I can correct my own past error and shape a more positive future.

—Penda Benson-Davis is a housewife, mother of three, and a freelance writer.

TRUMAN SCHOLAR

From the time I was a young boy, one of my heroes was President Harry S. Truman. To me, the former haberdasher and county judge epitomized the model public servant.

Truman even had a physical impact on me. When I was in elementary school I read that he walked at a rate of 120 steps per minute. For months I practiced his pace, walking long distances and timing myself with a stopwatch until it became second nature. To this day I walk with a "Trumanesque" gait. And though I never had the privilege of personally meeting Harry Truman, he did come to know me, albeit fleetingly.

In 1969 I was attending the seventh grade at Ben Franklin Junior High School in Colma, California. During that year my history teacher, Mr. Puhr, assigned the class our first long-term homework project. We were to research and type a five- to seven-page biography of the subject of our choice. Naturally I chose Truman. I dived into my task with zeal: Instead of taking the allotted three months, I finished my paper in three days.

After completing my project, I reflected on something I had read in Truman's book, Mr. Citizen. Truman said a former president was obliged to answer mail from young people. I decided to take him up on his claim.

I wrote to Truman, told him about my assignment, enclosed my report, and asked him to read it over, make any necessary corrections, and let me know what he thought of it. I mailed the letter and report to Truman's home at 219 North Delaware Street in Independence, Missouri.

I never thought to make a carbon copy of the report (I don't think I knew carbon paper existed),

and hard as it is to imagine now, copying machines were not commonplace in 1969. So I sent the only existing copy of my essay. It simply did not occur to me that I might never get it back.

Weeks passed, then months. On the day our papers were due I still had not heard from the former president. I went to class empty-handed and

President Harry Truman.

explained my dilemma to Mr. Puhr. He held me up to ridicule before the whole class, calling me a liar and accusing me of neglecting the assignment.

"Don't tell me you sent your paper to Harry Truman," said Mr. Puhr. "Truman's been dead for almost twenty years. I ought to know. I watched his funeral on television!"

His funeral on television? There was no arguing with the teacher. I was a liar, Truman was dead, and I got an F.

As the weeks rolled by, I forgot about the unhappy incident. Then one day after school I came home and found waiting for me a large white envelope bearing the postmark of Independence, Missouri. In the upper right corner was the free-frank signature of Harry S. Truman. My heart pounded as I tore open the envelope.

Slowly I withdrew the contents. Enclosed was my original report, along with the following note written on Truman's personal letterhead:

April 29, 1970
Dear Jim:
I was very pleased to have your letter and manuscript. I am sorry I cannot help you with it, as I have a rule against working on another author's paper. It is clear, however, that you did your homework well.
Best wishes for success in your life.
Sincerely yours,
Harry S Truman

Not only did President Truman read my report and write me a personal letter, but he recognized me as a fellow author! This was pretty heady stuff for a twelve-year-old boy.

Also inside the envelope was a photograph of Truman bearing the inscription "To James Rogan from Harry S Truman."

The next day I made a point of being a few minutes late for Mr. Puhr's class, knowing he would demand I produce a late slip from the attendance office. When I walked into the classroom, he interrupted his lecture.

"Rogan," he demanded, "show me your late slip."

I walked up to Mr. Puhr and handed him Truman's envelope and its contents. "Here's my late slip, Mr. Puhr," I said with an air of defiance.

Mr. Puhr's lips tightened as he reviewed the documents. His face reddened. "Take your seat," he said. Having unfairly humiliated me before my classmates, my teacher made no effort to rectify his error. I sat down, but when the recess bell rang, I ran to the door, blocking the exit, held aloft my letter, and announced to my departing classmates, "If anybody wants to see the letter and autographed picture I got yesterday from the late President Harry Truman, I'll show it to you on the playground."

The Truman saga did not end there.

Mr. Puhr still refused to accept my paper, because it was late. I petitioned the principal and explained the circumstances. She overruled Mr. Puhr and told him to receive my project.

The following week Mr. Puhr handed back my paper in front of the entire class, telling me it was only a "fair" effort. He added he was marking it down for "repeated punctuation errors," among them my recurring blunder of failing to put a period after the middle initial S in Truman's name.

I explained to Mr. Puhr that the punctuation omission was purposeful, because Truman's middle name was simply "S" and did not require a period. Mr. Puhr rolled his eyes and commanded my classmate Dan Kelleher to bring him the T volume of the Encyclopaedia Brittanica.

"Let's see what the encyclopedia shows." Mr. Puhr thumbed through the book and located

Truman's biography. The encyclopedia listed the entry as "Harry S. Truman, with a period after the initial. Mr. Puhr smiled. "What do you say to that, Rogan?"

Confident in my research, I told him, "The encyclopedia is wrong."

"So!" thundered Mr. Puhr. "The encyclopedia is wrong, and Mr. Rogan is right! My, aren't we lucky to have such a brilliant student in our midst!"

My classmates laughed, and he teased me for the rest of the session, repeatedly calling on me to "confirm" that Columbus discovered America and George Washington was our first president.

After school I went home and again wrote my author friend in Missouri. "Dear President Truman," I scrawled, "You won't believe this teacher of mine. . .," and I laid out the entire story.

The school year ended without any response, and again I forgot about the debate. During summer vacation another letter arrived from Independence:

August 19, 1970

Dear Jim:

I was glad to autographed [sic] your engraved picture of the White House and it is being returned to you herewith.

The "S" in my name stands for the first letter of the first name of each of my grandfathers. In order to be strictly impartial in naming me for one or the other, I was given the letter "S" as a middle name. It can be used with or without a period.

I appreciate your very kind comments and send you best wishes.

Sincerely yours,

Harry S Truman

I took a closer look at Truman's letterhead. Sure enough, it bore the name Harry S Truman with no period after the middle initial.

A month later, on the first day of school, I went looking for Mr. Puhr and found him seated alone in his classroom. I showed him the second Truman letter; again he refused to give me credit. Only after I threatened to go to the principal did he grudgingly agree to raise my grade.

As I walked out of the classroom, Mr. Puhr called out my name. I turned in the doorway and faced him.

"Rogan," he said, "I'm very glad you won't be in my class this year."

—James E. Rogan is a former two-term Congressman from California.

THE MENTOR

During the fall semester of 1970, I was a graduate student at the University of Pennsylvania. It had been just two years since the assassinations of Sen. Robert F. Kennedy and Rev. Martin Luther King, Jr., and since the violent confrontation between antiwar protesters and Chicago police at the Democratic National Convention. Appealing to his "silent majority," Richard Nixon had won the election against Hubert Humphrey.

In Philadelphia that September black radicals had organized the Revolutionary People's Constitutional Convention. Convinced that the document drawn up in 1787 had been designed to oppress African-Americans and other minorities, they planned to draft a new social contract proclaiming the rights of people of all races and classes. The highlight of the conference was an all-day meeting on Saturday, September 5, at Temple University's gymnasium. Like many other twenty-somethings at the gathering, I doubted the event would lead to anything meaningful, but I was reluctant to miss any excitement.

Timothy Leary (center) with Abbie Hoffman (left) and Jerry Rubin.

I arrived early at the gym but stood in line for hours waiting to be admitted. Thousands had turned out for the affair, and the crowd outside began to grow impatient. As we drew closer to the door, we discovered that Black Panthers wearing combat fatigues and berets were frisking everybody for weapons. No one really liked this idea, but most of us accepted the near-paranoia of the times among radical whites and African-Americans alike. Not only were organizers fearful of right-wingers, such as the American Nazi party and the Ku Klux Klan, but they were just as wary of assassination attempts by the CIA or the FBI. Doubtless the Panthers would have preferred to restrict the conference to a blacks-only crowd, but Temple's administration had granted permission to use its facility with the proviso that the conference be open to the public.

After searching us, the Black Panthers led us in groups to bleacher seats in the upper tiers of the gymnasium. Over the sound system came a steady stream of acid rock and Motown interspersed with recorded diatribes on political repression, the police state, Police Commissioner Frank Rizzo, fascism, and the like. As we waited for the first speaker to arrive, I noticed a lone figure leaning against one of the building's massive concrete columns. His arms were folded, his expression was detached, and his head was covered in a mane of electrostatic curls. To me and many other white students, he was instantly recognizable as Abbie Hoffman. But most of the African-Americans who filed past ignored him. He was, after all, not a particularly imposing figure, being of slender build and average height. Seeing him in person for the first time, I found it hard to believe that this was the same man who had stood trial in Judge Julius Hoffman's courtroom only a year earlier, one of the celebrated Chicago Seven.

At a similar gathering of antiwar firebrands, Hoffman would have been treated as a founding father. However, to most blacks in the audience that day, he was just another white boy. Although he had spoken out many times in support of groups such as the Panthers, his concerns and methods were foreign to most urban blacks.

Still, if he was not well known, he was not unknown either. After several minutes a young man sitting next to me got up from his seat and approached Hoffman, exclaiming, "Hey, my man, how ya doin'?"

Hoffman turned and squinted. He obviously didn't know this fellow. The young man held out his hands, palms upward, and Hoffman, quickly recovering, slapped them. The gesture, the universal greeting of African-American youths at the time, was reciprocated.

"Jerry, baby, you talkin' today too?" the young man asked. He had mistaken Hoffman for Jerry Rubin, Hoffman's kindred spirit in the antiwar movement.

The Yippie icon started to correct his inquisitor, but by then the young man had signaled to a friend nearby. Soon three or four blacks were crowded around Hoffman, and I saw him smile awkwardly as a pen was pressed into his hands. Hoffman, who was easily a dozen years older than his admirers, graciously autographed their conference programs. The young man returned triumphantly to his seat next to me.

Intrigued, I asked him if I could see his program. On it Hoffman had written: "Everything I ever needed to know I learned from Abbie Hoffman. Peace, Jerry Rubin."

—Dennis E. Gale is the director of the Joseph C. Cornwell Center for Metropolitan Studies at Rutgers-Newark.

SPARE CHANGE

One of the perks of power, wealth, and fame is that those so favored never have to carry anything. Their luggage, briefcases, purses, wallets, umbrellas, and groceries are carried for them.

In the early 1970s I was on the staff of one of these noncarriers, Nelson A. Rockefeller of New York. He had just finished his four terms as governor and was in the interregnum between that office and vice presidency, which he was to assume under Gerald Ford in 1974. During this time of relative inactivity he was acting as the chairman of a politically power-packed commission named by Congress to study the ramifications of the recently enacted Pure Waters Act. Soon after he was named to chair this prestigious body, I was assigned to it as one of his two personal staff members.

He had flown down to Washington one morning from New York for a regular monthly meeting of the commission, and we were awaiting his arrival at National Airport's commuter terminal. As his private plane taxied to a stop, he debarked and greeted us all with his engaging smile, shaking hands all around and murmuring, "Excellent! Excellent!" As we worked our way through the terminal toward the door and the waiting limousine, he stopped in front of the bank of pay phones.

Now I have been panhandled in nearly every state in the nation. I have been hit up by the halt and the blind in New York City, solicited by the Salvation Army's bell-ringing foot soldiers in small towns all over the country, importuned by the homeless and hungry in city streets everywhere. But this had never happened to me before.

"I must make a call," announced one of the richest men in America. Then he turned to me and said, "Can you spare a dime?"

—John C. Waugh, a former journalist, lives in Pantego, Texas, and writes history books.

Nelson A. Rockefeller.

THE WITNESS

In September of 1975 I was appointed minority counsel to the U.S. Senate Committee on Rules and Administration. I was thirty-four years old and had previously served as a legislative assistant to Senate Minority Leader Hugh Scott. Our committee consisted of five Democrats and three Republicans. The Republican members were Mark Hatfield from Oregon, Bob Griffin from Michigan, and Hugh Scott from Pennsylvania. The committee was chaired by the senior Democrat, Howard Cannon of Nevada.

Ted Kennedy, speaking in 1975.

Rules and Administration was a catchall committee having jurisdiction over such disparate areas as Senate office space, the Botanic Gardens, the Library of Congress, and, oddly enough, the federal-election law. It was the proposed 1976 amendment to this law that almost cost me my job.

The committee was holding hearings on this amendment in our hearing room in the Russell Office Building, then known simply as the Old Senate Office Building. An ornate, beautiful, and high-ceilinged room, once home to the Senate Commerce Committee, it could accommodate fifty to sixty people if the subject matter before the committee aroused any great interest.

That was not the case on the day of my near undoing. In addition to the five or six sitting committee members, there were approximately twenty staff members, a few journalists, and several curious tourists in attendance. Most of the staff members sat in front of the raised and curved committee table. Others sat immediately behind their senators, waiting patiently for a whispered directive, request, or instruction. I sat behind our ranking member, Mark Hatfield.

The only witness to testify that day was Senator Edward Kennedy of Massachusetts, a cosponsor of the bill. Since most, if not all, of the committee members supported the amendment, Senator Kennedy's remarks would be no more than icing on an already baked cake. Midway through his prepared text the bell on the legislative clock in the room rang, indicating that a vote was about to take place on the floor of the Senate. The Russell Office Building was located a long stone's throw from the Capitol. Senator Cannon apologetically interrupted Senator Kennedy and announced a twenty-minute recess, which would allow the committee members enough time to proceed to the Capitol to vote.

The room emptied quickly of all senators, including Kennedy. Moving from my assigned seat and lowering myself into Senator Cannon's chair, I gaveled, regained the staffers' attention, and launched into my Western Pennsylvanian imitation of Kennedy's Boston accent. After an initial confused silence my audience jumped right in, firing questions and insults as fast as I could drop my r's and widen my a's. I was enjoying myself immensely when suddenly my audience fell quiet. I continued chirping away. Finally I noticed our chief of staff making the international sign of impending doom: a finger drawn across the throat. A few seconds elapsed before I realized that the throat to which he alluded was my own.

Apparently Senator Kennedy had not voted but had been caught up in conversation outside the corridor and then had drifted back to the staff offices behind the committee room. He was at that moment behind me, observing my performance. Visions of my wife and two infant daughters, soon to be destitute, flashed through my mind. In those days the mere allegation that a staffer was "personally obnoxious" was sufficient grounds for dismissal, and I had no doubt that a "sincerely regret" letter from Mark Hatfield was only a day away.

As I rose, turned, and started to mumble a feeble and terror-inspired apology, the senator raised his hand, grinned, and said in a much better Kennedy accent than my own, "Actually, you sounded more like Bobby than me."

—Andrew Davis Gleason is an attorney in Johnstown, Pennsylvania.

WHAT SHE WORE

A handful of graduates from my college have gained notoriety, but none, certainly, was more notorious than Sally Rand. In the fall of 1976, early into my senior year at Columbia College in Columbia, Missouri, Sally came back for a visit—and then some.

I was a student of the music department, and all of us in the performing arts had been apprised of her forthcoming participation in an alumni (read that fund-raising) variety show. I was not as prepared for the knock on my dorm-room door by a breathless co-ed saying, "We're trying to furnish a room for Sally Rand. Can you contribute anything?" The college had made arrangements for Ms. Rand at the finest hotel in town. She had countered by stating emphatically that she wanted to stay in the same dorm she had stayed in as a girl, St. Clair, now the "Nancy-can-we-have-your-bedspread?" dorm. Reportedly, Sally had said, "I just want to be one of the girls."

I must say, building on the unfortunate circumstances of a girl who had only two days before vacated one of the private rooms on our floor, we did a respectable job of making her feel at home. In retrospect I suppose she accomplished most of that on her own.

Her door was open nearly all the week she lived among us, and she would smile and motion us in if we (understandably) looked her way. She had brought a huge trunk of pictures, some of which made us blush, and she told stories as only one who has lived them can. Early in her visit she looked up at my shadowy roots and said, "You're just the young woman I need to bleach my hair."

Two nights later she knocked on my door wrapped in a sheet, toga-style, and asked if I was ready. I wasn't sure. We went down the hall to the large communal bathroom. I sat her in a chair and started applying the solution she provided, trying not to notice the two rows of fine scars around her hairline and ears. After a while she said she was too warm, and threw off the sheet. I briefly tried embarrassedly to cover her, knowing that the boys on the floor below walked by this open door on their way to the ice machine. Then I remembered whom I was dealing with. This was the woman who was once arrested four times in one day at the 1933 Chicago World's Fair. It was only fair to play by her rules. So she sat there through the rest of the process gloriously nude from the waist up, wearing a ludicrous crown of purple foam.

The next night I walked into the kitchen for ice and, quite obviously, startled her ironing my bedspread. She mumbled something about having wrinkled it taking a nap.

She spoke to our Psychology of Human Sexuality class and was wonderfully candid, embarrassing, and charming us all.

No one talked of much else the week after her fan dance at the variety show. None of us had had any idea of the grace, the acrobatics, the fantasy, the sensuality involved in her heavily blue-lighted act. No one in the audience could tell quite what she did or didn't wear during her dance, and most of us backstage wouldn't talk at that time. But—since it's been fifteen years—I feel I can put to rest a question that tormented tens of thousands in its time: The seventy-two-year-old woman mesmerized us all while wearing a pair of flesh-colored fishnet pantyhose. Amen.

A week after she left our school, I was lying on my bed reading and noticed an odd place in my bedspread. Upon further examination I discov-

ered that a burned spot had been covered with an iron-on patch. Sally had, indeed, made herself one of the girls.

—Nancy Crocker is an actress and writer in Minneapolis, Minnesota.

Sally Rand during the height of her fame, left, and in a photo taken years later with her costume revealed.

AS THE SHAH FELL

I was eleven, and my family had been living in Iran for more than three years while my father was attached to the American Embassy in Tehran. In its Middle Eastern way, both lazy and exuberant, Tehran had been good to me. But that was about to change. In early November of 1978, after months of escalating tensions, my school became engulfed in an anti-shah demonstration that broke its bounds and turned into a riot. That afternoon on the soccer field, we dropped to the ground when a nearby building blew up; a fire set by rioters had ignited the big diesel fuel tank in the basement. Though shaken, our teachers tried to maintain a normal schedule for the rest of the day, even though we could hear the crowds growing outside the school compound. At day's end we were told via loudspeaker not to go to our buses but to return to our homerooms and await instructions. Our room was on the second floor, and my classmates and I rushed to the window to look over the compound wall to see what was happening.

As far as we could tell, it was chaos. Everyone was waving a sign and yelling angrily. A few people lay scattered on the street and sidewalks; we couldn't tell if they were hurt or dead. Finally we saw tanks approaching the crowd, apparently to contain the riot or cut off escape. At the age of eleven one doesn't think of danger, only adventure, and we crowded around the open window—an eager audience to the unfolding drama.

As the tanks moved closer, an Iranian friend of mine, Neda, started to pray. This scared me. Did she know something we didn't? We all knew her father had something to do with SAVAK, the Iranian secret police, and we waited nervously for something to happen. We heard the low-flying helicopters before

we saw them, and although we suspected that the yellowish gray smoke billowing in their wake was not a good thing, we had no idea it was tear gas until we were overcome. We could barely see or speak as we stumbled downstairs into the courtyard. Outside we managed to find a few adults, who hurried us back inside to wash out our eyes. That just made the stinging worse.

Finally my bus number was called. Our principal boarded after us and ordered all foreign-looking students to lie on the floor with our coats over our heads until we passed through the worst of the rioting. Ours was an international school, but there were enough Iranian students sitting up so as not to raise suspicion. With our bus driver yelling at each roadblock, we managed to make it to the northern suburbs where most of us lived.

Rather than snow days we began to have riot days, and we spent the next two weeks at home while unruly mobs surrounded our school. This was fine with us, and we arranged "curfew sleepovers" to alleviate the boredom. During one such sleepover I learned to belly dance (sort of). At another, in an apartment on the main north-south road through Tehran, we watched from a window at two in the morning as hundreds of the shah's troops rumbled ominously past.

It happened two more times; we would go to school only to be sent home to wait another two weeks. Each time we returned to class more friends had left. First the Iranian students fled, then the students from the Middle Eastern nations, finally the Western Europeans. The last to be pulled out of school were the American, British, and Norwegian students. Neda was one of the first to go, and she vanished without a trace. I walked over to her house one day during our enforced holiday to find it empty. The neighbors would tell me nothing.

Every evening I'd go up to the roof with my father to watch the riots, which grew bigger and bigger, defying the curfew. He would radio the embassy, letting them know what was going on in our neighborhood. Some nights the military shot up huge flares, like fireworks, to aid in their work; other nights the demonstrators set large buildings on fire. Every night was quite a show, and given that I was stuck at home, it was the most interesting thing I saw all day.

One day my mother sent me to the corner store for eggs. Anti-American rhetoric was getting worse and worse, but my mother thought that since we had lived here for almost four years, everyone knew us and we would be safe. She was wrong. I had my first lesson in mob psychology that day, when my neighborhood friends threw stones at me on my way home from the store. Although none of them hit me, the message was clear: We were no longer welcome in this country. I did not go out alone again.

Soon afterward an embassy official telephoned our house. Because of the increasing death threats against Americans, and in anticipation of a demonstration to mark Ashura, one of the most holy days of Shiite Islam, all nonessential personnel were being evacuated in forty-eight hours. We could pack two suitcases each. If the situation improved, we would be able to return, maybe before Christmas. My father would stay behind, but not in the house. My sister, then five, screamed that she did not want to go, this was home, she would stay. I—amazed and thrilled, truth be told, at the turn our previously peaceful life had taken—began packing.

I don't remember what I took with me; it was nothing special. Later, when we knew we would not

be able to return, I remembered vividly what I had left behind: my stuffed animal collection, jewelry box, photo albums, books, drawings, records—in short, my life.

The next afternoon, a crisp, clear winter's day, all the evacuees met at the embassy; the cars and vans in its motor pool had been bulletproofed four years earlier after a few terrorist attacks on Americans. We milled about nervously, waiting for word on what would happen next. One family had brought their myna bird, hoping to take it with them. Finally our convoy, with a Marine guard escort, set off for Mehrabad Airport.

The streets were absolutely still because everyone was already at the airport. I was not prepared for the crush of desperate humanity trying to get a seat on any of the planes out. Most of the commercial flights into Tehran had long since been canceled; Pan Am had been chartered to work the evacuation. Planes staffed by volunteer crews were landing, boarding, and taking off every hour. Sadly, while other nations were doing what they could for their citizens, there were not many choices. Iranians who wanted to leave had to persuade their countrymen to let them out and a foreign government to let them in. Desperation mounted, and I saw rolls of rials change hands a number of times. Some families had camped out at the airport for days, putting their names on every list for a flight out. Rumors were flying about Khomeini's imminent return. I found out later many of the evacuation flights did not have proper clearance, and everyone feared trouble.

On the plane I found three or four classmates, which was not surprising since the entire expatriate population was trying to leave. Everyone was quiet as we took off. Soon the magnitude of what had happened started to sink in, and the adults talked about whether they would ever be back and what they had

Demonstrators carry a photo of Ayatollah Khomeini during an anti-shah demonstration in December 1978.

left behind. In many cases whole households had been sacrificed for the chance to leave before the anti-American sentiment burst into violence. When we left Iranian airspace and began flying over Turkey, the adults cheered, after which everyone perked up. I left my seat to play cards with my friends. We all congratulated one another on being part of something so exciting and wondered if anyone outside Iran would believe us.

Barely aware of the commotion the revolution had caused in the rest of the world, we were surprised when a flight attendant asked us if the rumors were true, if the shah was on the plane. We laughed and said that if he were, everyone would know it. She explained that there had been talk that he would try to leave the country in disguise. Hearing that, we jumped up and set about looking for him. Since his picture had been everywhere in Tehran—in shops, in homes, even inside the cover of our school notebooks—we figured we had as good a chance as any to discover him.

We debarked in London expecting to stay with friends for only a few days. But following an initially peaceful demonstration, order in Iran swiftly and completely broke down. Although not politically sophisticated, I understood momentum, and on some level I knew that the momentum was not in our favor. We waited in London for two weeks with growing uneasiness and then, relinquishing all hope of returning to Iran, flew to my grandmother's house in Indiana.

Three weeks after we left, the shah fled and Khomeini returned triumphant. Iran became an Islamic republic. Diplomatic relations between the United States and Iran deteriorated, then disintegrated. My father stayed until June of 1979, avoiding being taken hostage by a few months.

Some days a slant of light, a languid camel at the zoo, or a mercantile transaction of exuberant proportions reminds me that politics can become very personal.

—Amy Rukea Stempel, a freelance writer, lives in
Arlington, Virginia.

A "TOUGH LITTLE CHURCHMAN"

During one of my early visits to Poland, long before I even dreamed of writing about that nation, a counselor said, "If you want to catch the real spirit of this land, you ought to visit that tough little churchman down in Cracow," and in this way I met the formidable Karol Cardinal Wojtyla. I had long talks with him and found him to be as promised, a clever, fighting clergyman, taller than I had been led to believe, and much better at English. I remember his sparkling eyes and the way he grew excited when those about him spoke of his long battle to protect Catholic Poland from the pressures of Communist Russia. I concluded from that first visit that here was an unusual man in a difficult position.

Years later, after several other visits, I was taken back to Cracow by an American television crew that wanted to film me in conversation with some high official of the Polish Catholic Church, and by a stroke of luck we were able to make an extensive film with my old friend Cardinal Wojtyla in the garden of his residence as he spoke on the problems of serving as a leader in a church surrounded on all sides by Communists. He was sagacious, witty, totally aware of his position, and eager to share his thoughts. I finished the interview thinking: "This fellow knows precisely what he's doing and what he hopes to achieve."

On an October day in 1978 American newscasts flashed the astonishing report that a Polish cardinal had been elected Pope, and after the name had been mispronounced hideously—it's voy-tee-ya—I realized that this miracle involved my old acquaintance. In the next three hours my phone rang incessantly, because the networks had discovered that the only television interview in English with the new Pope was the one I had made. On the evening news that night the film, a handsome one, flashed around the nation demonstrating that the new man was amiable, clever, and a master of English.

I had had a brush with history without knowing it. Had I in that first meeting with Wojtyla had an inkling that he might one day become Pope? Not a glimmer. Did I suspect it at the end of the television interview? Not a chance. On the other hand, when as Pope he proved to be the great man the world knows, was I surprised? Not at all.

—James A. Michener was the author of *Chesapeake* and *Alaska*, among many other titles.

The man who would be Pope—Karol Cardinal Wojtyla.

THE EMPEROR AND I

From 1965 to 1985 my wife and I and our two daughters lived in a modern house we had built in Bethesda, Maryland. Several years after ours went up, a house was constructed on the lot next door and put up for sale. It was a big Federal colonial that sat empty for some months and then was bought by the Japanese Embassy to house their finance minister.

These diplomats were good neighbors, though very formal. Each of them—there were three ministers in turn during the years we lived there—came to pay a courtesy call shortly after moving in, greeted us with warm formality whenever we saw one another outside, and had us over for at least one formal dinner party. I grew accustomed to seeing, while I was working on some chore at the head of my driveway, the ministers, members of their families, and various servants, men and women young and old, coming, going, or working about outside.

Emperor Hirohito inspects cherry blossoms in 1981.

The time came when Emperor Hirohito came to Washington on a state visit. This was a very big deal: The Emperor of Japan rarely made state visits, and never to the United States. There were fears that lingering animosities from World War II might induce demonstrations or even a rash act by some deranged person. Exceptional security precautions were taken for the emperor's safety, especially at Blair House, the residence across the street from the White House where our most important state visitors are put up.

During the week of Hirohito's visit, I saw unusual levels of activity across the driveway. Big black cars were coming and going, and there were always one or two parked in their drive. They seemed to have added some servants. Whenever I happened to be outside they had people about: maids going in and out of the kitchen, chauffeurs standing around, an elderly fellow wearing a cardigan working in the gardens, cutting flowers, and always burly young men in dark glasses muttering into their lapels. The servants, even the new ones, smiled and nodded as ever. The young men didn't. The activity is hardly surprising, I thought. The minister must be going to official functions day and night and maybe entertaining there in the house as well. Once the emperor's visit was over, things quickly got back to normal.

A few years later we were at a dinner party given by the most recent minister. After the meal the minister got expansive. "You know," he said, smiling at me, "I must tell you something. When our emperor visited Washington, our two governments were so concerned with his safety that although we made everyone believe he was staying at Blair House, he really stayed here in this house the whole time."

Well, of course. All that activity and all those people. The emperor was there. Every time I took out the garbage that week, I realized, or came out to do some chore or wash the car, what those guys with the black aviator glasses had been muttering into their lapels was "Relax. It's only the dentist next door."

And then I thought of the old man working in the garden. I never saw him before that week; I never saw him after. A personal equerry of the emperor, perhaps? Or a valet or a butler? Probably. Except, who knows? I've read that Hirohito was a putterer. Maybe while the governments of two great powers spent great efforts protecting him, he came out and cut flowers for the house. Maybe that old gentleman in the cardigan nodding politely to the dentist across the driveway was the Emperor of Japan.

—Jay L. Wolff is a dentist in Alexandria, Virginia.

NO FREE RIDES

I met Ronald Reagan in late October 1980, just a few days before the election that would put him in the White House. In fact, our encounter occurred under circumstances that might have caused me considerable embarrassment or more.

I was in Washington, D.C., on business and had scheduled lunch with a good friend before heading home to Texas. We had worked together in Washington several years earlier, before I moved to Houston, where I tried to ignore politics and politi-

cians. My friend had stayed active in politics and was then working in the Reagan campaign. We had agreed to meet at the campaign headquarters in Arlington, Virginia.

After lunch I noticed four buses filled with passengers waiting in front of the headquarters building. My friend told me these would take the campaign staff to Dulles Airport to bid farewell to the candidate. Mr. Reagan was flying to Cleveland for a debate with President Carter and then directly to Houston

Republican candidate Ronald Reagan shakes hands with supporters at a rally during his campaign for the 1976 Florida presidential primary.

and California, so this would be the last opportunity before the election for the staff to see him and for him to thank them.

That reminded me: I had to call a cab to take me to Dulles also. "Why not hitch a ride on one of these buses?" my friend asked. "At least it will save you cab fare."

Reluctantly I got on the last of the four buses and sat in one of the few remaining seats. It faced sideways. To my left was a well-dressed middle-aged man with an oversize Reagan button on his lapel. Across from me was a young mother with her son, whom I took to be about five. This, I thought, was to be his introduction to history.

I felt uneasy as the buses pulled out. My uneasiness developed into a subdued panic as we drove toward Dulles Airport. What if they find out that I am not on the Reagan campaign staff? That I have not even worked in the campaign in Houston? What if they were to suspect me of being a plant by the Democrats? Worse, what if the Secret Service were to suspect me of baser motives? What had my friend gotten me into?

And then the real questions began. Observing my luggage, the young mother across from me asked whether I was flying to Cleveland with Mr. Reagan.

"No," I responded, trying to say as little as possible.

"Where are you going?"

"Houston."

"Oh," she said, "you're going to Houston in advance of Mr. Reagan."

"You might say that."

The gentleman to my left took up the inquisition: "What are you doing in Houston?"

"I live there."

"No, no. I mean, what are you doing in the campaign there?"

I was trapped. Now what? Did I confess that I wasn't doing anything in the campaign, merely bumming a ride to the airport? That, in effect, I was crashing their farewell party?

"I do whatever I'm asked to do," I said.

"I see. You're a troubleshooter."

"You might say that." I was becoming more nervous by the moment.

Sensing my reluctance to talk, the gentleman to my left slid closer to me and, in a barely audible voice, whispered, "It's hush-hush, isn't it?"

"Yes," I said. "Yes, it is."

There were more questions, but they were easy: "How are we doing in Texas?" "What is the weather like in Houston at this time of the year?"

I could see the terminal in the distance as the buses approached Dulles Airport. But to my horror I realized that we were heading in the opposite direction. We were being taken to a special runway far from the terminal where the plane that would carry the candidate to Cleveland was parked.

While the others left the bus, I held back to talk with the driver. "Please let me know if you can't take me to the main terminal on time," I pleaded. "If not, I'll have to start walking now."

"No problem," he assured me. "There is plenty of time."

Reassured, I was the last person off the last bus. By the time I rejoined the group of well-wishers, the roped-off area where they had been assembled was full. I found a spot at the entrance to this area, closest, as it turned out, to where the candidate's helicopter would land.

Mr. Reagan's advisers began to arrive and board the plane. One was George Shultz, who had been my boss's boss when we both were at the Treasury Department. Then Mr. Reagan's helicopter approached and landed a short distance from his campaign workers. The future president and first lady stepped to the runway and walked straight toward the nearest worker—me! Perhaps because I was first, the candidate went through his entire thank-you speech in what appeared to be a dress rehearsal for what would follow.

"I want to thank you for all you've done in this campaign on our behalf. Because of your hard work and tireless efforts, we're going to win this coming Tuesday."

The next president shook my hand for no more than ten seconds. Yet it seemed more like ten minutes. Mrs. Reagan shook my hand too and also thanked me for my efforts—though her thank-you and handshake were much briefer.

The candidate and his wife worked their way down the line, squeezing hands, or sometimes merely touching them, and repeating parts of the thank-yous they had just given me in full. As I watched down the line, I caught the eye of the man who had been sitting next to me on the bus. He was looking directly at me, and I could tell from his expression what he was thinking: "Who is that very important troubleshooter from Houston whom Mr. Reagan sought out first and with whom he talked so long?"

The campaign workers returned to the buses once Mr. and Mrs. Reagan were on board the plane. Our little party of four resumed the same seats at the front of the last bus. The caravan pulled out and headed back to campaign headquarters, but when it reached the main drive to the terminal, our bus peeled off and headed straight to the terminal. The driver opened the door and, in a voice that all could hear, boomed, "Here you are, Dr. Johnson. Have a safe trip to Houston."

As I rose to leave the bus, the gentleman to my left stood up. He looked me in the eye, clasped my right hand in both of his, and said earnestly, "It's been a privilege to have met you and to know that such capable and dedicated people are working on Mr. Reagan's behalf. We're winning because of people like you. Thank you and good luck in Texas."

I stumbled off the bus, my brush with history—and with politics—at an end.

—Dr. William A. Johnson is a professional economist, now retired and living in Palmyra, Virginia.

THE TALL JAPANESE

The occasion was the Japan Society's annual dinner at the Waldorf-Astoria Hotel a few years ago, and the guest of honor was the prime minister of Japan. Titans of industry attend this dinner; the ballroom was filled with CEOs from Fortune 500 companies and their wives. In the half-dark, as the spotlight swept the three-tier dais, diamonds and gold studs twinkled in candlelight.

The place was full of Secret Service agents from Washington and security men from Tokyo, all in dinner jackets. The guards from Tokyo are tall; if Nippon ever decides to challenge the Boston Celtics, these lean, rangy Japanese could try out for the team.

I was standing at one side of the room, waiting to be called to a seat on the dais, and I began talking with one of the Japanese guards.

I said, "You don't often see this many powerful people in one room in America." He asked me, in accented English, to explain. I spoke of the importance of our relations with Japan and said an invitation to dine with its prime minister, even in a crowded ballroom, was a social distinction. We stood in the shadows talking until my name was called, and I left him to walk up onstage and be introduced.

The next event was the introduction of the prime minister. I turned to watch, and there in the spotlight was my Japanese acquaintance, who wasn't a security guard at all. He was Prime Minister Yasuhiro Nakasone.

He paused and, with a smile, gave me a nod of recognition, a little bow.

The man next to me said, "I didn't know you knew him."

I said, "You meet all kinds of people in my line of work."

—John Chancellor was a longtime anchor and commentator for NBC News.

Japanese Minister Yasuhiro Nakasone speaks at a convention in November 1982.

PHOTO CREDITS